IF IGNORANCE IS BLISS,
WE SHOULD ALL BE ECSTATIC

Fred Leavitt

Published by Open Books

Copyright © 2021 by Fred Leavitt

No part of this book may be reproduced, scanned, or distributed in any printed or electronic form without permission except in the case of brief quotations embodied in critical articles and reviews.

Interior design by Siva Ram Maganti

Cover image © fran_kie shutterstock.com/g/frankies

ISBN-13: 978-1948598446

I dedicate this book to Diane, Jess, Mel, Ian, Jeff, Tia, and Eli.
You've all enriched my life enormously. I love all of you.

Fred

CONTENTS

Chapter 1

INTRODUCTION

"An idea that is not dangerous is unworthy of being called an idea at all."—Elbert Hubbard

Radical skepticism: the philosophical position that knowledge is impossible. Radical skeptics hold that doubt exists as to the veracity of almost every belief.

Around 430 BC, the Oracle at Delphi said that Socrates was the wisest man in Athens. Socrates was not convinced and set out to prove the Oracle wrong. But after questioning many supposedly learned Athenians, he eventually concluded that he indeed was the wisest. In Plato's *Apology*, Socrates says "I neither know nor think that I know;" and "True knowledge exists in knowing you know nothing." He contrasted his position with that of everyone else. Although they also did not know, they thought or pretended that they did. My goal for this book is to make readers as wise as Socrates. Even wiser, because Socrates thought he knew many things, including knowledge of the gods, the art of love, how to ask questions, and the result of drinking poison hemlock.

I trained as a scientist (PhD in psychopharmacology) but soon became disillusioned by drug research. Too many articles in even top-notch journals were either methodologically unsound or fraudulent. So I studied research methodology and, to my dismay, learned that conclusions from other areas of science were also often untrustworthy. Of course, untrustworthy information is not restricted to scientific material. Long before Donald Trump began ranting about

1

"fake news," I had realized that the media and government spokespeople could not be trusted. Eventually, I came to the depressing conclusion that the amount of information stored in my little brain was probably exceeded by the amount of stored misinformation.

It's a long way from poor data collection or even outright fraud to the bizarre subject matter of this book. Readers may agree that many alleged facts are inaccurate while questioning the sanity of anyone who jumps from there to the conclusion that nothing can be known. Yet that's where the trail ineluctably dragged me. For a preview of what follows, consider the following hypothetical experiment. You have developed a new lie detector test. Convinced that it is infallible, you recruit 1,000 people to try to beat it. You give them a series of questions and ask them to tell one or more lies among their answers. Your device detects every lie and never calls a truthful response a lie.

But then comes subject 1,001. Asked a question, he answers "yes" and your device indicates that he's telling the truth. He's asked a second question immediately afterwards and says "yes" again. To your great surprise the device again registers truthfulness. The man swears that he really believes what he said. He submits to a psychiatric evaluation and is found free of any major disorder. He is not delusional. You test him again. Same results. Here are the two questions:

Do you anticipate with near certainty the occurrence of thousands of events: the sun will rise, the alarm will ring, food will have a certain taste, and friends and enemies will behave in predictable ways?

Do you agree with the philosophical position called radical skepticism that you can never know anything about the past, present, or future with even the slightest probability that it's true?

Albert Camus wrote that human beings spend their lives trying to convince themselves that their existence is not absurd. What could be more absurd than belief in radical skepticism? Maybe being certain of two important beliefs that contradict each other.

I am a real-life model for subject 1,001, and my strange and contradictory beliefs make me lonely. I long for company and for resolution. That's my motivation for writing this book. Read on and you too will join me in facing absurdity.

Many books cite testimonials on the back cover: "I read X's book and, within six days:

- lost forty pounds."
- earned $200,000."
- became fluent in Mandarin Chinese."

My approach is different. I present no case histories or descriptions of private bull sessions with God. I cite many scientific studies but only as non-crucial supplements. In fact, in Chapter 12 I argue that scientific studies cannot be trusted. Readers who wish to prove me wrong will have no basis for accusing me of lying or making up data. My arguments stand or fall on their merits, fortunately not on my character or intelligence.

> *"Only one thing is certain—that is, nothing is certain. If this statement is true, it is also false."*—Ancient paradox.

Most readers would probably agree that we live in an uncertain world. They'll yawn at the material in the next few chapters that illustrates uncertainty in every direction. They knew it all along. But their skepticism doesn't go far enough. Radical skeptics believe that Socrates' protestation of ignorance should be taken literally. They argue that he and everybody else really know nothing. They go even further. They claim that no justification can be found for saying that any form of knowledge is even probably true or any event even probably likely to happen. Radical skeptics are not sure that Socrates ever said what he's been accused of saying, or even that he ever existed.

Many famous philosophers have grappled with the problem and then advised others to ignore it. For example:

- David Hume: Tis evident, that so extravagant a Doubt as that which Skepticism may seem to recommend, by destroying every Thing, really affects nothing, and was never intended to be understood seriously, but was meant as a mere Philosophical Amusement.

- Bertrand Russell: Skepticism, while logically impeccable, is psychologically impossible, and there is an element of frivolous insincerity in any philosophy which pretends to accept it.

I find their responses unacceptable. If they claim that knowledge is possible, let them prove it. The burden of proof is on the person asserting a claim, not on skeptics to disprove it. Nobody has disproved the existence of ghosts or a twin planet to earth on the opposite side of the sun, but that's not evidence for their existence. Even if arguments for skepticism were deficient, knowledge claims would be unjustified without positive evidence. Of course, it might seem obvious that evidence is all around you, coming through all your senses. Keep reading and you'll see that the obvious is wrong.

"We can know only that we know nothing. And that is the highest degree of human wisdom."—Leo Tolstoy

An infinite number of alternatives always exist to virtually all claims to knowledge. The butler did not always do it, even when all the evidence points in his direction. Given the meagerness of our data bases amidst the vastness of time and space, the explanations we accept may represent nothing more than failure of the imagination. The attitude in rejecting radical skepticism is captured in a short poem by Stephen Crane.

THE WAYFARER

The wayfarer,
Perceiving the pathway to truth,
Was struck with astonishment.
It was thickly grown with weeds.
"Ha," he said,
"I see that none has passed here
In a long time."
Later he saw that each weed
Was a singular knife.
"Well," he mumbled at last,
"Doubtless there are other roads."

Chapter 2

EPISTEMOLOGY

Epistemology: the philosophical study of the nature, origin, and limits of human knowledge.

Fallibilism: the epistemological thesis that no belief can ever be conclusively justified, i.e., there will always remain doubt as to the truth of any belief.

Almost all contemporary epistemologists and almost every contemporary theory of knowledge argue for some version of fallibilism. Fallibilists try to cope with radical skepticism by denying that knowledge requires absolute certainty. They often add that many beliefs are certain beyond reasonable doubt.[1] In chapter 17 I take the absurd position that the fallibists are wrong. But please don't skip right to chapter 17 (or toss the book). The chapters that precede it lay necessary groundwork.

> *"Whoever wishes to become a philosopher must learn not to be frightened by absurdities."*—Bertrand Russell

I wear two hats. When my normal hat is on, I go about day-to-day living. I fully accept that there is an external reality and things are pretty much the way they seem. I plant seeds in my garden

---

1. Hetherington, Stephen. Fallibilism, *Internet Encyclopedia of Philosophy*, http://www.iep.utm.edu/fallibil/ (The many hyperlinks throughout the book were all accessed on 6/12/20.)

and expect them to turn into corn or zucchini or snap peas. I visit my doctor when sick and take whatever medicine she prescribes. I turn on the TV and settle back to watch.

But when I wear my philosophy hat, radical skepticism takes over. I realize that my day-to-day beliefs cannot be justified. That's a huge problem, because my two hats are completely incompatible with each other and something's got to give.[2] I lie to myself—although probably less than the vast majority of people lie to themselves. They never even challenge their basic beliefs.

So, radical skepticism is an absurd and pointless philosophical position. Maybe, but denying it on the grounds that it causes discomfort is akin to denying there is such a thing as cancer because it causes discomfort. Continued reading will prove that there are only three possible conclusions.

1. The reasoning that leads to radical skepticism is flawed. One or more errors invalidate it.

Philosopher G.E. Moore argued that the radical skeptical position should be quashed at birth. He wrote that, if a seemingly sound argument leads to a bizarre and implausible conclusion, the argument may not be sound after all. He considered the argument that his hands and body don't really exist, and his refutation takes the following form: It's intuitively obvious that my hands exist. The fact that they exist is much more obvious than the truth of

---

2. In the interest of full (and hardly surprising) disclosure, I admit to assuming some knowledge even when wearing my philosophy hat. I expect that hitting certain keys on my computer will lead to certain letters showing up on the screen, and I assume that there are other sentient beings in this world, some of whom may read what I write. I expect a great many events to occur predictably. Starting on page 76, I use logical arguments to show that *all* logical arguments suffer at least one fatal flaw. I cite many scientific studies despite showing that scientific studies cannot be trusted—even further, that studies and studiers might not exist except in my own mind. But the fact that I don't live the consequences in no way invalidates radical skepticism.

any of the premises used in the argument for radical skepticism, therefore it makes more sense to believe that my hands exist than to accept the lines of reasoning in the skeptical argument.[3]

Moore encouraged readers to search for errors in either the premises or the argument form. His point is a good one, so every step leading to my outrageous conclusions should be carefully evaluated. I followed his advice, read and reread, diligently and deliberately, and am convinced—there are no serious flaws. But if someone should find one, please email me at fredlvtt@gmail.com. I'd be delighted to know.

Either of the other two candidates requires a profound change in how we see the world.

2. Radical skepticism is correct, which implies that reality is much different from what it seems, and everything we think we know is likely to be incorrect. I do mean everything.

3. Reasoning, which we humans pride ourselves on, is not a reliable path to truth.

Yes, those really are the choices. They give me cognitive dissonance of the highest order.

To provide inspiration for myself while writing this enormously strange and unsettling material, I posted the story *The Emperor's New Clothes* by Hans Christian Andersen over my work desk. Andersen's emperor paraded before his subjects in what they were told were new clothes. They all remarked on the splendor of his apparel until a little boy said what was indisputable but had been unspeakable: the emperor was naked. Andersen's message was that wishful thinking distorts reality and should be resisted. Like the little boy I wonder why others are silent. Like him, I do nothing more than state the obvious.

---

3. An observation that weakens Moore's position is that sixty to ninety percent of individuals who have a limb amputated experience phantom sensations in the amputated limb. They have the sensation that it is still attached. Phantom sensations may also occur to other body parts. See https://www.sciencedirect.com/topics/neuroscience/phantom-limb.

Several Assumptions Underlie Almost All Claims to Knowledge

Several assumptions underlie almost all claims to knowledge:

(a) We can generally trust our senses.
(b) We can generally trust our reasoning abilities.
(c) There are laws of nature, i.e., certain unwavering regularities.
(d) We can learn those laws.
(e) The future will resemble the past.

The assumptions should be recognized as such—'assumption'—a statement accepted as true without proof. Chapters 10 and 8 show that the first two assumptions are unwarranted. A little reflection shows that assumption (c) is probably satisfied. Life is full of regularities, and regularities—patterns—indicate that something lawful is going on. Trillions of my past predictions have been confirmed. I've eaten every day of my life and never been seriously poisoned. My car usually starts, and when my phone rings there's usually someone on the other end. When I press a button, interact with a friend, breathe, or move in any way, in the vast majority of cases the expected outcome occurs. Night reliably follows day, the seasons change on schedule, and children mature into adults. Even if my memories are all wrong, the faulty memories themselves show regularities; and whatever their origin, regularities imply laws.

But assumption (d) cannot be justified. Although deep, eternal, unchanging laws may exist, we don't now, and never will, know any of them. The claim is sometimes made that great writers such as Shakespeare reveal universal truths. Okay, name one.

Assumption (e) is also without merit. Lacking any proof that the future will resemble the past, there is no basis for using past observations to justify future expectations. And proof is beyond reach. David Hume wrote, "All inferences from experience suppose, as their foundation, that the future will resemble the past... If there be any suspicion that the course of nature may change, and

8

that the past may be no rule for the future, all experience becomes useless and can give rise to no inference or conclusion."

Chapter 3

THE ILLUSION OF KNOWLEDGE

Stephen Gould wrote that "...the human mind operates primarily as a machine for recognizing patterns."[4] Deducing a pattern, a possible relationship between variables that had seemed unrelated, is hailed as discovery of THE relationship between them. The discovery of a possible cause for events of previously unknown origin is hailed as discovery of THE cause. We seek and find patterns even when there are none. We see a man in the moon, faces on Mars, and an entire nativity scene on a piece of toast.

Certain traits are perceived as going together even when the data do not show any association between them. They are called illusory correlations. For example, a tennis player may wear a new outfit for a match, and if she does exceptionally well she may continue wearing that outfit for matches because she believes there's a connection between clothing choice and performance. The Draw-a-Person test is widely used by psychotherapists but based on illusory correlations, for example, that people who draw human faces with large eyes tend to be paranoid. Chapman and Chapman showed subjects a series of drawings that were randomly paired with a description of the personality characteristics of the individual who supposedly had produced them. The subjects then estimated the correlations, in actuality zero, between various physical

---

4. Gould, S. ((1999) *Questioning the Millenium.* NY: Harmony Books.

features and personality characteristics. Most subjects reported that people who drew large eyes are paranoid, and people who drew large genitals are concerned about their sexuality. Clinicians tend to believe in the same illusory correlations despite research showing otherwise.[5]

Consider a hypothetical example. You're captured by terrorists who require you to play a game. They display twenty cards from an ordinary deck and indicate whether each card is good or bad. Then they turn over two more cards and ask you to classify them. If you misclassify either card, they'll pull all your teeth. If you guess correctly, they'll set you free along with a voucher good for a twenty percent discount at any Denny's restaurant. Table 1 classifies the first twenty cards, with AS = ace of spades, KD = king of diamonds, and so forth. The next two cards are the 9C and 7⒑C. You are asked where to put them. Would your future include edentation or a bargain meal?

Table 1: Are the cards good or bad?

Good	Bad
AS	KH
AC	8H
2S	AD
3C	2D
2C	6H
4S	4D
10C	5H
7C	10D
JS	JD
QC	QD

If the above results had occurred naturally, without a smirking, no-account author behind the scene, the pattern would have

---

5. Chapman, L. & Chapman. J. (1969) Illusory correlation as an obstacle to the use of valid psychodiagnostic signs. *J Abnormal Psych*, 74: 271-80.

seemed obvious. Black cards are good, red cards are bad. You would put both additional cards in the left column. But there are other possibilities—to be precise, an infinite number of them. For example, cards spelled with an "i" (any five, six, eight, nine, or king plus any diamond) are bad and all others are good. (So, 6C is bad and 7C is good.) Or, cards spelled with fewer letters than every card in the bad column are good and all others are bad. So, 6C is good, 7C bad.

If you think the above contrived, that's probably because our intellects can comprehend only the simplest of patterns. Addition and subtraction seem hopelessly complex to two-year-olds, and even the smartest dog can't learn to parse a sentence.

> "Nothing is so alien to the human mind as the idea of randomness."—John Cohen

Three Types of Legitimate Beliefs

I wrote above that doubt exists as to the veracity of *almost* every belief. There are three types of legitimate beliefs, but they're not enough to get a person an offer to compete on the TV show *Jeopardy*.

I know:
- that I know nothing.
- that I exist. This is Descartes' famous Cogito ergo sum.[6]
- when I experience certain body sensations or feelings. I know when I have a headache.

> "Our knowledge is a receding mirage in an expanding desert of ignorance."—Will Durant

---

6. René Descartes is sitting in a bar, having a drink. The bartender asks him if he would like another. "I think not," he says and vanishes in a puff of logic.

Chapter 4

THE FOUR PILLARS OF KNOWLEDGE

Four separate pillars help us to (seemingly) understand the world. That is, everything we (think we) know comes from one of only four sources. None can be trusted.[7] Philosopher Immanuel Kant proposed one source. He argued that we are born with certain innate knowledge. Instinct theorists and people who believe that psychiatric disorders such as schizophrenia are inherited diseases are, at least to some extent, Kantians. Studies within the past two decades seem to show that newborn babies know and can do a great deal. Kant would have been pleased.

Religious faith is a second pillar. People of faith are told who created the world, when He did it (in some religions, to the day and almost always by a He), and what happens when we die. They are taught when and how to pray, how to dress, what not to eat and drink, which books to read, movies to watch, music to listen to, and the appropriate circumstances and positions for having sex.

Reason is a third pillar. We use our reasoning abilities to figure things out. Whereas mindless animals experience only an endless succession of random stimuli, humans discern patterns. We use

---

7. It is interesting to note that Jesus, who has inspired faith in so many, was crucified. Another pillar is reason. Socrates, the epitome of a man of reason, was condemned to drink poison hemlock. And Galileo, the great empiricist, was forced under threat of torture to recant his conclusions.

mathematics and logic to advance from simple observations to complex deductions.

The fourth and largest pillar is empiricism (sensory data). We interact with the world through the five classical senses (vision, hearing, taste, smell, and touch). In fact, biomedical researchers have shown that we have more than just those five. The naïve view is that we observe, and then we know. Seeing is believing. Ha!

Chapter 5

KANT'S PILLAR: A PRIORI KNOWLEDGE

The pendulum has swung back and forth among philosophers on the issue of innate knowledge. Descartes, writing in the mid-seventeenth century, proposed that we are born with knowledge of geometric truths. Leibniz, a few years later, agreed. He said that we don't need empirical evidence to know that $1 + 1 = 2$. Empiricist John Locke demurred, maintaining that the minds of newborns are like clean white paper, with nothing written on them. In his view, everything we know comes from our interactions with the world. Immanuel Kant, born twenty years after Locke's death in 1704, claimed that certain beliefs, such as "God exists" and "Every event has a cause," precede experience. Empiricists, including Thomas Hobbes and David Hume, were on Locke's side and disagreed with Kant. But the pendulum now leans heavily toward Kant and other nativists.

Recent sophisticated experiments show that even six-month-old babies act as though they understand connections between causes and effects. They show awareness that objects still exist when they are hidden. When their expectations are not met, they spend more time looking.

Noam Chomsky[8] argued that some language-specific genetic

---

8. Chomsky, N. (1986) *Knowledge of Language, Its Nature, Origin and Use.* NY: Praeger.

factor enables human babies to rapidly learn complex languages. Despite substantial structural differences between Germanic, Romance, Oriental, and Arabic languages, and extremely variable environments, children adapt. Chomsky concluded that we must be born with a universal innate grammar.

Biologist Edward Wilson argued that religious beliefs are innate. He wrote, "The predisposition to religious belief is ... in all probability an ineradicable part of human nature."[9]

Neuropsychologist Michael Persinger might consider himself a Kantian.[10] Persinger patented a helmet consisting of a bunch of solenoids that, when placed on the head, deliver pulses of electromagnetic radiation to the brain's temporal lobes. He claimed that subjects sitting in a sound-proofed chamber and stimulated in these areas experience powerful mystical visions; and he inferred that mystical knowledge is stored in the temporal lobes. Many of the approximately 1,000 people he has stimulated reported being in contact with and directly perceiving individuals such as Elijah, Jesus, the Virgin Mary, Mohammed, UFOs, and the Sky Spirit. Journalists dubbed his device "The God Machine."

The animal kingdom offers many examples of innate knowledge. In Don Marquis's *Tales of Archy and Mehitabel*, Archy the cockroach pities humans because they are born ignorant and must struggle to learn the ways of the world. Archy says that insects are born knowing all they need to know. Archy would have approved of Kant. Jack London's short story *To Build a Fire* is another fictionalized account that emphasizes the value of innate knowledge. The protagonist, accompanied by his dog, sets out in freezing weather to visit his friends. Trusting in his ability to protect himself from the cold with fire, he tries three times to build one. But all are soon extinguished and he freezes to death. The dog eventually trots off

9. Wilson, E. (1979) *On Human Nature*, Cambridge: Harvard U. Press.

10. Persinger, M. et al. (2010) The electromagnetic induction of mystical and altered states within the laboratory. *J Consciousness Exploration & Research*, 1: 808-30.

to shelter. The dog's innate knowledge saved it whereas the man's unwarranted confidence in information gained from others, along with his logic and reason, doomed him.

Many bird species migrate thousands of miles each year and then reverse the journey a few months later. Large birds such as swans learn migration routes from their parents, but in most small bird species migration routes are genetically programmed. Young birds can innately navigate to and from their wintering area.

If our minds at birth were clean slates, every neuron in a network would have the same probability of connecting to every other neuron, depending on specific individual experiences. But Markram and Perin, working with rats, found that clusters of neurons in the neocortex connected in highly predictable and constrained ways. Their data suggest that the basic features are similar for all animals belonging to the same species; and that they are building blocks that contain a kind of innate knowledge.[11]

But whether or not the nativists are right is irrelevant to the issue of radical skepticism. Skeptics question the correctness of beliefs, not their origins. As will be discussed later, the belief that God exists is probably incorrect; and many quantum physicists disagree that every event has a cause.

Newly hatched ducklings seem to support the nativist position. They "know" that the first moving object they see will be their mother, so they follow it. They imprint. But when nasty biologists came along and substituted objects like shiny balls or shoes, the ducklings followed those too. Their a priori "knowledge" was incorrect. Go to https://www.youtube.com/watch?v=cgCTPBU69Sw to see a short video of imprinted ducklings.

Biologists have also tricked birds that migrate. A stimulus for migration in many birds is shortening length of day. When caged birds were exposed to artificial light and then released, they flew in the wrong direction.

---

11. Perin, R. et al. (2011) A commentary on a synaptic organizing principle for cortical neuronal groups. *Proc National Acad Sciences*, 108: 5419-24.

As for Persinger's God machine, the variety of envisioned "Gods" strongly suggests that the experience is a product of the subjects' cultures and prior beliefs, not a glimpse of ultimate reality.

Other seemingly direct means to achieve higher states and gain immediate knowledge include powerful drugs, chanting, and meditation. They may be intense, but trustworthy they are not. Hold hands with someone you love while listening to soft music and gazing into a misty moonlit night. Let your mind float dreamily. You may experience the overpowering feeling that all God's creatures are part of a cosmic whole. You may laugh at the sterile rationalism that pales before your newfound wisdom. Then read about Auschwitz or Hiroshima or Bosnia or Darfur. Step onto the killing fields of Cambodia, see the street children in Brazil, take a trip to Baghdad, or visit the site where New York's twin towers once stood.

Chapter 6

PILLAR 2: RELIGIOUS FAITH

Faith in one's abilities or another's good intentions requires evidence from prior observations. That is, such faith depends on reason and sensory data, two of the other pillars of knowledge. But some beliefs are formed and maintained despite the flimsiest of evidence. People watch a televised trial and become certain which party is lying. They hear an interview and assume they have direct access to the respondent's inner thoughts. They buy a lottery ticket and make vacation plans. He sees her breasts jutting out underneath a flimsy top and becomes convinced he's found a lifetime soul mate.

Religious faith does not seem to require supporting evidence. (But see below.) Ambrose Bierce defined faith as "belief without evidence in what is told by one who speaks, without knowledge, of things without parallel." Bertrand Russell wrote, "When there is evidence, no one speaks of faith. We do not speak of faith that two and two are four or that the earth is round. We only speak of faith when we wish to substitute emotion for evidence." He also said that the difference between faith and reason is like the difference between theft and honest toil. Faith is belief by decree. In the beginning was THE WORD. Belief in a supreme being who can do anything and can be invoked to explain anything is a—shall I say it—godsend.

The faithful know the truth. Their bible, pastor, rabbi, imam, or personal mystical experience tells them so. Faith is not merely belief in the absence of evidence—it's belief despite evidence, as when creationists discount overwhelming evidence for the theory of evolution.

I attended college in the Bible Belt of the southwestern United States and took an ethics course taught by a Methodist minister. Many of his lectures were devoted to praise of the New Testament. I objected and became, in the strongest sense, the devil's advocate. One day I related a famous incident wherein a theologian had said to Thomas Huxley that a philosopher is like a blind man in a dark room looking for a black cat that isn't there. Huxley admired the metaphor, then added that the theologian would have found the cat. A perfect riposte. I laughed, but nobody joined in. My classmates and the teacher all agreed that it would have been better to find the cat, nonexistent though it was.

I've told that story to friends and enjoyed their looks of astonishment. We felt superior to those unenlightened folks. We were mistaken. Everybody clings to irrational, unjustified beliefs. They make the world comprehensible, so they are rarely challenged. Reevaluation might lead to the realization that they are false. Prior actions based on false beliefs might be seen retroactively to have harmed loved ones. Apostasy is difficult, tantamount to acknowledging having blundered or been duped into accepting crucial elements of our existence that are not so. Nevertheless, Russell and Bierce were wrong—religious faith is based on powerful evidence.

The Origins of Religious Faith

Humans are born with active brains. Within days after birth, helpless infants recognize the caretakers who provide food, warmth, and shelter. Just a few hours after birth, infants imitate adults' smiles, frowns, and other expressions. Given a choice, babies gaze longer at a picture of their mother's face than at the face of a female stranger. They turn their heads toward a pad containing their own mother's milk but not toward pads containing milk from other mothers. Even fetuses recognize their mother's voice. In one study, sixty fetuses were played a two-minute audiotape of either their own mother or another woman reading a poem. The fetuses' heart rates accelerated to their mothers' voices and decelerated to that of the stranger.[12] Given their total dependence on caretakers, infants are primed to trust them. It isn't surprising that when parents and other relatives, peers, community leaders, and church dignitaries claim to know the truth, infants and young children accede.

Richard Dawkins wrote, "Natural selection builds child brains with a tendency to believe whatever their parents and tribal elders tell them. Such trusting obedience is valuable for survival… But the flip side of trusting obedience is slavish gullibility."[13] The gullibility continues throughout life and makes us susceptible to the assertions of people in positions of authority. So, parents learn THE TRUTH from their parents and pass it on to their children. After instilling the initial beliefs, they encourage the children to maintain them.

The best evidence available to young children is the words of their parents or other caretakers, and even adults should generally trust authorities. I believe that the earth is round and smaller than the twinkly things that light up the night sky—not because I was clever enough to deduce those facts on my own, but because others told me so. Authorities have also convinced me that enormous reptiles once roamed the earth and Saudi Arabia gets hot.

But the public and private beliefs of many authority figures do not always correspond, as when prominent athletes and movie stars hawk products or politicians open their mouths. Even sincere educated guesses may be far off the mark. See Appendix 1 for a few predictions and proclamations by experts.

One result of blind trust in authorities is that people, especially

---

12. Kisilevsky, B. et al. (2003) Effects of experience on fetal voice recognition. *Psychol Sci*, 14: 220-4.

13. Dawkins, R. (2006) *The God Delusion*. Boston: Houghton Mifflin.

children, develop many false beliefs. Children hear about a fairy who exchanges money for teeth and a fat man laden with presents who slides down chimneys, and they believe. Many, probably most, also incorporate their parents' religious and philosophical convictions. As they grow older—often within a few years of being toilet trained and disabused of the reality of Santa Claus but before learning the multiplication table—they become certain about what happens after we die and which one particular bible, of more than 1,000 available around the world, speaks the literal truth. From then on, they expend little more cerebral energy on developing and evaluating the religious and philosophical convictions that are at the core of their being than on whether they should have eggs or cereal for breakfast.

The problem with blind submission to authority is that parents, teachers, and everybody else, are fallible. Theologians, although they may be experts in interpreting a bible, don't know any more than laypeople whether any particular bible tells the truth. Even if bibles were inspired by miracles, they were transcribed by fallible humans.

Why there are so many Religions

There are more than 730 established religions in today's world and as many as 100,000 different faiths since the dawn of humankind. More than two billion Christians accept Jesus as their savior, but the various Christian denominations disagree on key points. More than one billion Muslims follow the teachings of Muhammad, and almost one billion Hindus pray to many gods. Buddhists, Confucians, Baha'is, Jains, Shintoists, and Sikhs together total about 500,000,000 and have widely divergent beliefs. So do about 100,000,000 Mormons, Jews, Scientologists, Christian Scientists, and the spunky Jehovah's Witnesses who ring your doorbell with free copies of *Watchtower* and *Awake*.

Eric Dietrich posited that religiosity is an evolutionary adaptation that helps keep groups and tribes together. Natural selection produces lots of variation within a given type of adaptation, for example, a huge variety of feather types. Specific details don't matter. The same is true of language. All peoples speak a language. The constraints are loose, so languages vary widely in their sounds and structures. What matters is that the sounds have meanings. Religiosity is also an evolutionary adaptation that can be accomplished in many ways, and that, in all likelihood, is why there are so many religions.[14]

People from different backgrounds differ in preferences for food, mates, music, literature, and football teams. Even perceptions depend heavily on personal history. How else can we explain why people with normal vision may view the same drawing and report different images, as in the famous young woman/old woman image in Figure 1. If the evidence for religious beliefs were trustworthy, preferences would be independent of time and place of upbringing. They are, of course, not. More atheists live in Azerbaijan than Atlanta, more Baptists in Biloxi than Bombay, more Catholics in Cincinnati than Calcutta, more Jews in Jerusalem than Jakarta, and more Muslims in Malaysia than Mississippi. The boring demographic details reflect the obvious fact that people living within a broad general region are exposed to the same newspapers, TV shows, songs, films, games, and books. For the same reason, football fans from Cincinnati are more likely than Chicagoans to root for the Bengals whereas Chicago residents prefer the Bears. A noteworthy difference between religious and football beliefs is that Bengal fans do not claim that their team's playbook is the only true one or that Chicago fans worship false idols.

---

14. Dietrich, E. (2015) Why are there so many religions? https://www.psychologytoday.com/blog/excellent-beauty/201504/why-are-there-so-many-religions.

Figure 1: Old Lady/Young Lady.

"Eskimo: 'If I did not know about God and sin, would I go to hell?' Priest: 'No, not if you did not know.' Eskimo: 'Then why did you tell me?'"—Annie Dillard

"Scriptures. The sacred books of our holy religion, as distinguished from the false and profane writings on which all other faiths are based."—Ambrose Bierce

"If triangles had a God, he would have three sides."—Montesquieu

"I am waiting/for them to prove that God is really American."—Lawrence Ferlinghetti

"I'm still an atheist, thank God."—Luis Buñuel

A Few Strange Religious Beliefs

All of the following bits of "knowledge" are found in respected mainstream American religions. All at one time or another have had the sanction of the highest church authorities. Many still do.[15]

- A race of giants once roamed the earth, the result of women and demi-gods interbreeding. (Evangelical Christianity.)

- Evil spirits can take control of pigs. (Evangelical Christianity.)

- A talking donkey scolded a prophet. (Evangelical Christianity, Judaism.)

- A righteous man can control his wife's access to eternal paradise. (Mormonism.)

- Brown skin is a punishment for disobeying God. (Mormonism.)

- A prophet once traveled between two cities on a miniature flying horse with the face of a woman and the tail of a peacock. (Islam.)

- Neither cats nor dogs should receive blood transfusions. Blood meal must not be used as garden fertilizer. (Christian Science.)

- Sacred underwear protects believers from spiritual contamination and, according to some adherents, from fire and speeding bullets. (Mormonism.)

- When certain rites are performed beforehand, bread turns into human flesh after it is swallowed. (Catholicism.)

- Invisible supernatural beings reveal themselves in mundane objects like oozing paint or cooking food. (Catholicism.)

- Believers can drink poison or be bitten by snakes without being harmed. (Evangelical Christianity.)

---

15. Tarico, V. (2-12) The 20 weirdest religious beliefs. https://www.alternet.org/2019/01/20-weirdest-religious-beliefs/

- Sprinkling water on a newborn, if done correctly, can keep the baby from eons of suffering should he or she die prematurely. (Catholicism.)

- Waving a chicken over your head can take away your sins. (Judaism.)

- Putting a dirty milk glass and a plate from a roast beef sandwich in the same dishwasher can contaminate your soul. (Judaism.)

- There will be an afterlife in which exactly 144,000 people get to live eternally in Paradise. (Jehovah's Witness.)

- Each human being contains many alien spirits that were trapped in volcanoes by hydrogen bombs. (Scientology.)

- A supernatural being cares what you do with your penis. (Evangelical Christianity, Catholicism Judaism, Islam, Mormonism, Christian Science, Jehovah's Witness.)

Religious Faith is Beneficial

Church attendance is a social occasion. People meet future friends, spouses, and business associates at church socials. By accepting the traditional beliefs of their community, they become part of a team. Congregations form powerful voting blocs. It's unlikely that, in the foreseeable future in the U.S., an avowed atheist will be elected to an important national office.

Faith enables people to achieve feats that would otherwise be beyond their capabilities. Imagine having to walk across a long, foot-wide plank suspended between the rooftops of two tall buildings, with no net down below. The terrifying task would likely end in death. Yet walking would be effortless if the plank lay on the ground. A hypnotist or evangelist who convinced you that a high plank was on the ground might save your life. Your unjustified faith might save your life.

Philosopher Blaise Pascal argued that faith makes practical sense. He wrote that, if God exists, believers will be rewarded while disbelievers suffer eternal damnation. If He doesn't exist, belief and disbelief won't matter. In other words, faith separates children of God from benighted fools whose loving creator, if He exists, damns them to burn eternally in Hell. But Pascal didn't consider all the alternatives. God may not be all-loving. She may be indifferent to humans or no longer capable of interfering with their lives. She may be malevolent. He may like spunky people who defy Him, may detest yespeople. That is all beside the point: whether or not Pascal's wager is wise, having a reward for believing does not make the belief true. Beneficial illusions are still illusions. Furthermore, given the thousands of different religions that have been practiced since antiquity, a small minority at most could possibly hold accurate beliefs. Many Americans accept that the Red Sea parted for Moses and angels sing in heaven, but they scoff at the idea of Zeus hurling thunderbolts or dances bringing rain. Would Pascal advise them to bet across the board?

Pascal didn't play fairly. Under his conditions, there is no penalty for incorrect beliefs. But consider a modification in which, if a loving God rules the universe, believers and nonbelievers fare equally well. But if Satan is top dog, nonbelievers are unaffected while believers suffer an excruciatingly painful death. Would you believe? The question is not just irrelevant, it's silly. If beliefs could be shaped that easily, the human condition would be one of delirious happiness. We'd have no concerns about war, pestilence, famine, or global warming, and we could eliminate the concept of God. He is, after all, only a middleman who rewards loyal subjects with eternal happiness. Why not just believe that eternal happiness is our birthright.

Anthropologist Marvin Harris also claimed that religious faith makes practical sense, though for reasons different from Pascal's.[16] Harris asserted that, despite appearances to the contrary, no world religions decrease the potential for the nutritional wellbeing of their followers. People often require a manufactured "divine intervention" to get them to act in their best interests. For example, the

---

16. Harris, M. (1998) *Good to Eat*. Long Grove, IL: Waveland Press.

Hindu religion bans killing cows, which is the only reason why cows are not routinely killed for their meat. The ban benefits Hindus, because cows are much more valuable to them for plowing fields and providing milk. Harris wrote, "Westerners think that Indians would rather starve than eat their cows. What they don't understand is that they will starve if they do eat their cows." For similar reasons, Jews and Muslims don't eat pork. Although a common explanation is that pigs are dirty—impure, unclean, and therefore not to be eaten—a more realistic one is that pigs are not adapted for arid habitats. Lacking sweat glands, they need external sources of moisture to control their body temperature, which is why they wallow in mud. They would be prohibitively expensive to maintain in the hot Middle East. Wealthy people might have been tempted to raise a few pigs as luxury food. In the long run, that would have endangered precious resources. So it was better to have people believe that God decreed, "Thou shalt, under no circumstance, eat pigs."

Faith benefits at both ends of the happiness spectrum. It gives hope to people in foxholes, or starving, or enslaved—if not for this world, then for the next. Bishop George Berkeley wrote, "I can easily overlook any present momentary sorrow when I reflect that it is in my power to be happy a thousand years hence." At the other end, successful people, cognizant of the fact that fame, power, wealth, and health are subject to fortune's whims, may believe that God will be touched by their thankful prayers and shield them from any downturns.

> "Religion is what keeps the poor from murdering the rich.
> Religion is excellent stuff for keeping common people quiet."
> —Napoleon Bonaparte

> "One man's theology is another man's belly laugh."
> —Robert Heinlein

> "This human world of ours would be inconceivable without the
> practical existence of a religious belief."—Adolf Hitler

"Who says I am not under the special protection of God?"
—Adolph Hitler

Extreme realists—people who assess their skills and the state of the world with relative accuracy—are depression-prone. Many psychotherapists encourage such people to construct illusions, i.e., to find faith in something. They rationalize that illusions foster optimism and happiness. Unquestioning faith comforts and consoles. Faith in an omniscient, omnipotent creator and benevolent universe, or in any illusion that softens our harsh world, imparts courage and the strength to persevere.

Digression—Maybe not so Beneficial

Benjamin Franklin stated that "religion will be a powerful regulator of our actions, give us peace and tranquility within our minds, and render us benevolent, useful and beneficial to others." Dostoyevsky wrote, "If God does not exist, then everything is permissible."

Many devout people agree with Franklin and Dostoyevsky and believe that the world would be plunged into chaos without some version of the Ten Commandments to provide a moral compass. For example, after the horrific 2012 school shooting in Newtown, Connecticut, Arkansas Governor Mike Huckabee blamed it on the fact that "we have systematically removed God from our schools." After another shooting, *Fox News* host Bill O'Reilly declared, "As the world becomes more secular, civilized restraints to bad behavior drop." (O'Reilly was fired from Fox TV after multiple allegations of sexual harassment against him were revealed.)

Obedience to the commandments depends much more on criminal law than religious faith. I have posed the following question to thousands of students, many of them regular churchgoers, in dozens of classes: "If you could be invisible for a day and commit any crime you wanted with no danger of being caught, would you commit a crime?" Virtually every student raised her or his hand.

"To give a man full knowledge of true morality, I would send him to no other book than the New Testament."—John Locke

And why should people follow the dictates of the New Testament? To help with an answer, I constructed Table 2. On the left are several well-known biblical injunctions about morality. On the right are my translations.

Table 2

Whatsoever a man soweth, that shall he also reap.	Virtuous people shall be rewarded; wicked people shall be punished.
Woe unto them that call evil good and good evil.	Ditto
We walk by faith, not by sight.	"
He that believeth not shall be damned.	"
Cast thy bread upon the waters; for thou shalt find it after many days.	"
The eye that mocketh at his father, and despiseth to obey his mother, the ravens of the valley shall pick it out, and the young eagles shall eat it.	"
He that loveth pleasure shall be a poor man.	"
Eye for eye, tooth for tooth, hand for hand, foot for foot.	"
Whoso sheddeth man's blood, by a man shall his blood be shed.	"
The way of transgressors is hard.	"
The wages of sin is death.	"
What is a man profited, if he shall gain the whole, and lose his own soul?	"
The sufferings of the present time are not worthy to be compared with the glory which shall be revealed in us.	"

It is easier for a camel to go through the eye of the needle, than for a rich man to enter into the kingdom of God.	"
The meek shall inherit the earth.	"

Taken along with the stories of Job, Abraham, and other biblical VIPs, the table shows that virtue is most emphatically NOT preached as its own reward. Given the payoffs—eternal paradise or damnation in exchange for a brief lifetime of goodness or evil, respectively—nothing besides disbelief in the bible or extreme stupidity can account for immorality. Satan himself would join the Salvation Army.

He who donateth half his fortune to charity shalst be called generous. But if he receiveth one hundred gold pieces for each he donateth, then he is nothing more than a cunning businessman.

Rather than providing the moral foundations for a healthy society, religion may contribute to social problems. A very small percentage of people convicted of violent crimes identified themselves as atheists. Gregory Paul used interview data collected by the International Social Survey Program on religious belief and practice of 23,000 people in thirty-eight nations. Paul correlated the findings with data from the UN Development Programme on societal health, homicide rates, youth suicide, sexually transmitted disease, teen pregnancy, and rates of abortion. He concluded that populations of the more secular democracies, in which the theory of evolution is widely accepted, feature relatively low rates of lethal crime, juvenile-adult mortality, sex related dysfunction, and abortion. Rates are much higher in nations in which most citizens believe in and worship a creator. The most theistic prosperous democracy, the U.S., is by almost all measures the most dysfunctional of the developed democracies.[17]

Within the U.S., strong religious beliefs and denial of evolution

---

17. Paul, G. (2005) Cross-national correlations of quantifiable societal health with popular religiosity and secularism in the prosperous democracies. *J Religion & Society*, 7: 1–17.

are similarly positively correlated with rates of societal dysfunction. The strongly theistic, anti-evolution south and Midwest have markedly worse homicide, mortality, STD, youth pregnancy, marital, and related problems than the northeast where societal conditions, secularization, and acceptance of evolution approach European norms.

Paul cited several sources to show that Christianity had the capacity to stop Nazism before it came to power, and to reduce or moderate its practices afterwards, but repeatedly failed to do so because the principal churches were in the pay of the Nazis. According to standard biographies, the principal Nazi leaders were all born, baptized, and raised Christian. Most grew up in strict, pious households where tolerance and democratic values were disparaged. Nazi leaders of Catholic background included Adolf Hitler, Joseph Goebbels, and Heinrich Himmler. The Holocaust Museum in Washington, D.C. has several photographs of Nazi leaders including Hitler fraternizing with leaders of the Catholic Church. See https://encyclopedia.ushmm.org/content/en/photo/adolf-hitler-greets-reich-bishop-ludwig-mueller.

> *"Say what you will about the sweet miracle of unquestioning faith,*
> *I consider a capacity for it terrifying and absolutely vile!"*
> —Kurt Vonnegut

In recent years, many U.S. senators and representatives have received high approval ratings from influential Christian right advocacy groups. One reason is that leaders of the Christian right, and millions of their followers, believe the words of a history text that has sold more than 100,000 copies since its first printing in 1989. The book, *America's Providential History*, is used in home schooling, private and public schools, religious schools, political seminars, discussion groups, colleges, and seminaries.

A short description of the book posted on Amazon reads "The secular or socialist has a limited resource mentality and views the world as a pie (there is only so much) that needs to be cut up so that everyone can get a piece. In contrast, the Christian knows that the potential in God is unlimited and that there is no shortage of resources in God's earth. The resources are waiting to be tapped."

Many in the Christian right believe that the return of the son of God is imminent. Upon His return, the righteous will enter heaven and sinners will be condemned to eternal hellfire. So, there is no reason for concern about global warming, pollution, or other destruction of the environment; they are welcome, because they signal the coming Apocalypse.

Figure 2: Does he know something
that we don't know?

"With or without religion, you would have good people doing good things and evil people doing evil things. But for good people to do evil things, that takes religion."—Steven Weinberg

Faith (of Others) is Very Beneficial to Some

The founder of Scientology, L. Ron Hubbard, once said "Writing for a penny a word is ridiculous. If a man really wanted to make a million dollars, the best way would be to start his own religion." Most religious leaders are charismatic figures whose opulent life-styles depend on encouraging others to keep the faith. So, how much is sharing the word of God worth? Below are some estimates of net worths:[18]

- Joyce Meyer: $8 million
- Franklin Graham: $10 million
- T.D. Jakes: $18 million
- Rick Warren: $25 million
- Creflo Dollar: $27 million
- Joel Osteen: $40 million
- Benny Hinn: $60 million
- Pat Robertson: $100 million
- Kenneth Copeland: $500 million.

> *"If God existed as an all-powerful being, He would not need the money that faithful believers donate to their churches."*
> —Donald Morgan

Televangelists, rabbis, priests, and mullahs are not the only ones who benefit from the faith of others. Karl Marx called religion the opiate of the masses. Opium reduces both physical and emotional pain and induces pleasant dreams. The rich and powerful can rest more comfortably when the downtrodden dream that acceptance of their harsh existence is a small price to pay for eternal salvation.

Religious Leaders Have God's Cell Phone Number

In the 1980s, Pat Robertson claimed that God told him, "I want you to run for president of the United States." In 2004, God told

---

18. https://www.google.com/search?q=televangelists+net+worth&o-q=televangelists&aqs=chrome.4.69i57j0l7.104613j0j4&sourceid=-chrome&ie=UTF-8

him that President Bush would easily win reelection against John Kerry. In Robertson's words, "I really believe I'm hearing from the Lord it's going to be like a blowout election in 2004." God didn't restrict his messages to presidential politics. God told Robertson to buy a television station for his ministry. Robertson considered buying the cheapest transmitter available, but God said, "Pat, I want you to have an RCA transmitter." Robertson also explained that God inflicted a massive stroke on Israeli prime minister Ariel Sharon because He disliked Sharon's foreign and domestic policies. He called the 9/11 terror attacks that killed about 3,000 people divine retribution against America for its tolerance of gays, feminists, and the American Civil Liberties Union.

In 1987, evangelist Oral Roberts announced to his television audience that God had told him that he must raise $8 million within the next twelve months or he would die. (His flock—flock, a term used to refer to both a church congregation and a group of sheep—raised the money.)

Two days after the 9/11 attacks, Jerry Falwell defended God's honor and excused Him for what others might have considered a rash action: "The abortionists have got to bear some burden for this because God will not be mocked. And when we destroy 40 million little innocent babies, we make God mad. I really believe that the pagans, and the abortionists, and the feminists, and the gays and the lesbians who are actively trying to make that an alternative lifestyle, the ACLU, People for the American Way, all of them who have tried to secularize America, I point the finger in their face and say: you helped this happen." He added, "AIDS is not just God's punishment for homosexuals; it is God's punishment for the society that tolerates homosexuals."

In October, 2003 on the television show *Crossfire*, Falwell explained that, when pushed, God is a shrewd strategist. Falwell said He arranged for President Clinton to be elected and reelected so that Americans would beg for somebody else.

But, strange as it may seem, God miscalculated. He underestimated America's depth of perversity and had to administer additional dollops of tough love. So, in the words of wealthy televangelist John Hagee (NPR interview in 2006): "All hurricanes are acts of God, because God controls the heavens. I believe that New Orleans had a level of sin that was offensive to God, and they were recipients of the judgment of God for that." And, "Hurricane Katrina was, in fact, the judgment of God against the city of New Orleans."

And we still haven't learned. Evangelical Christian and former Republican presidential candidate Michele Bachmann informed us that the deadly coronavirus was punishment for sexual immorality.[19] Bachmann, interviewed on *CBN News*, said "You know we've strayed so far from God into sexual immoralities such as the homosexual lifestyle, masturbation and porn, is it any wonder God is mad? The coronavirus is God's way of bringing us back to the light. If we give up these sins, God will take the virus away." She was echoed by Reverend Ralph Drollinger, who taught a bible class to members of President Donald Trump's cabinet. Drollinger blamed the virus on God's disgust with "depraved minds," i.e., gay people and environmentalists.

Bachmann, Drollinger, and similar types seem to fully understand God's reasoning, so He must not always work in mysterious ways. Still, it's curious to think that His powers are so limited that he can make his will known only through others—even more curious that he picks people like Robertson, Roberts, and Falwell. Couldn't he write the Ten Commandments in the sky for everyone to see? Or whisper in everybody's ear? Maybe we just haven't appreciated his great sense of irony.

Maybe They Had a Bad Connection

Every profession has its share of hypocrites and criminals, but religious leaders—the ones who instill moral codes in their

---

19. https://thebiznews.org/2020/03/26/bachmann-god-will-end-coronavirus-if-we-give-up-porn-masturbation/

followers—should not compete with pornographers and snake oil salesmen for the moral vacuum award.

The eighth commandment says "You shall not steal." According to a *Forbes Magazine* website, financial fraud in churches is rampant. A 2013 study projected ecclesiastical crime to be $37 billion worldwide (nearly six percent of the total $594 billion given to churches). Losses due to mismanagement of funds totaled $8 billion. In contrast, the total spent on mission work to introduce Christianity to more people throughout the world is $32 billion. There are pressures to keep findings of fraud private. The article cited a report that estimated that as much as ninety-five percent of fraud within churches goes undetected or unreported. The website https://signposts02.wordpress.com/2013/01/21/an-overview-of-religious-financial-fraud/ has written about extensive fraud in religious institutions.

The sixth commandment says "You shall not murder." Jerry Falwell must have thought he was exempt. He said, "You've got to kill the terrorists. And I'm for the president to chase them all over the world. If it takes ten years, blow them all away in the name of the Lord." Another exemptee, Pat Robertson, told TV viewers that Venezuelan President Hugo Chavez was turning his country into a launching pad for communist infiltration. So, Robertson said, "If he thinks we're trying to assassinate him, I think we really ought to go ahead and do it."

The sixth commandment obviously doesn't apply to God himself. See the website http://dwindlinginunbelief.blogspot.com/2010/04/drunkwith-blood-gods-killings-in-bible.html#sthash.ohSOJDcU.dpuf. It tallies biblical events such as the flood of Noah, Sodom and Gomorrah, and the slaughter of heathens by the Machabees to estimate 25 million people killed by God.

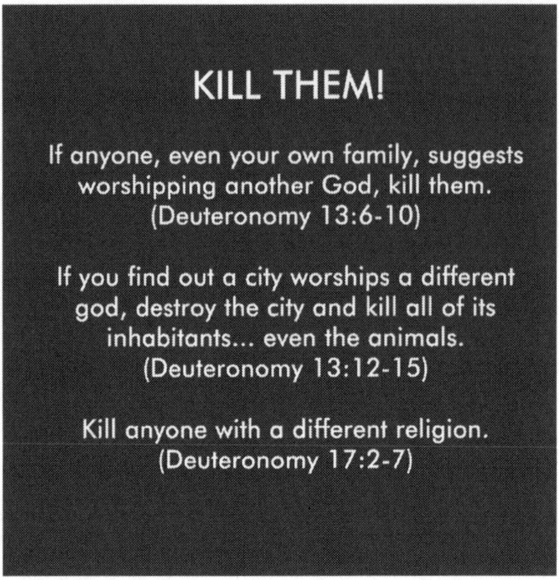

KILL THEM!

If anyone, even your own family, suggests
worshipping another God, kill them.
(Deuteronomy 13:6-10)

If you find out a city worships a different
god, destroy the city and kill all of its
inhabitants... even the animals.
(Deuteronomy 13:12-15)

Kill anyone with a different religion.
(Deuteronomy 17:2-7)

Figure 3: Bible Instructions.

The website ClergyGoneWild.com tracks crimes committed by members of the clergy. It lists the following categories: Sex Abuse, Thefts, Violence, Drug Abuse, Cults & Religiholics, and Bigotry. It listed the following under sex abuse:

- Child Abuse. (Eight hundred forty-three articles.)
- Internet Solicitation. (Thirty-five articles.)
- Other. (One hundred ninety articles.)
- Public Sex. (Twenty-one articles.)
- Solicitation. (Thirty-four articles.)

The website listed 127 cases of murder, nineteen of spousal abuse, and 146 under "other acts of violence."

In 2014, the Vatican released statistics on how it has disciplined priests accused of raping and molesting children: 848 priests were defrocked and another 2,572 given lesser sanctions over the previous decade. The number is probably not substantially different from that of clergy from other religious traditions.

Alabama evangelist Paul Acton Bowen was a youth minister

for teenage boys, a best-selling author, and chaplain for the 2012 Olympics. In June, 2020, he was sentenced to 1,008 years in prison for his guilty pleas to sexually abusing a half dozen teenagers.

"If kids got raped by clowns as often as kids get raped by preachers it would be against the law to take your kid to the circus."
—Dan Savage

"Whenever we read the obscene stories, the voluptuous debaucheries, the cruel and tortuous executions, the unrelenting vindictiveness with which more than half the bible is filled, it would be more consistent that we call it the work of a demon than the word of God. It is a history of wickedness that has served to corrupt and brutalize mankind."—Thomas Paine

The Pope nominated Mother Teresa for sainthood a year after her death in 1997. A miracle had to be attested. A Bengali woman named Monica Besra claimed that a beam of light emerged from a picture of MT, which she happened to have in her home, and relieved her of a cancerous tumor. Christopher Hitchens wrote, "Surely any respectable Catholic cringes with shame at the obviousness of the fakery."[20] Her physician, Dr. Ranjan Mustafi, says that she didn't have a cancerous tumor in the first place and that the tubercular cyst she did have was cured by a course of prescription medicine. He was not interviewed by the Vatican's investigators.

Hitchens wrote that MT was a friend of *poverty*, not of the poor. She said that suffering was a gift from God. "She was a friend to the worst of the rich, taking misappropriated money from the atrocious Duvalier family in Haiti (whose rule she praised in return) and from Charles Keating." Keating received a ten-year prison sentence for his part in a savings and loan scandal. During the course of his trial, she pleaded to the judge for clemency. Hitchens, noting that her global income was more than enough to outfit

---

20. Hitchens, C. (1995) *The Missionary Position: Mother Teresa in Theory and Practice.* London: Verso

several first class clinics, and that she never published an audit, asked what happened to the money. He wrote, "The primitive hospice in Calcutta was as run down when she died as it always had been." He added that "The decision not to do so [upgrade]... is a deliberate one. The point is not the honest relief of suffering, but the promulgation of a cult based on death and suffering and subjection." One of her volunteers described her "Home for the Dying" as resembling photos of concentration camps. No chairs, just stretcher beds. Virtually no medical care or painkillers beyond aspirin. Hitchens noted that Mother Teresa "checked into some of the finest and costliest clinics and hospitals in the West during her bouts with heart trouble and old age." He concluded, "Many more people are poor and sick because of the life of MT: Even more will be poor and sick if her example is followed. She was a fanatic, a fundamentalist, and a fraud."

> "If a man would follow, today, the teachings of the Old Testament, he would be a criminal. If he would follow strictly the teachings of the New, he would be insane."—Robert Green Ingersoll

> "I like your Christ, I do not like your Christians. Your Christians are so unlike your Christ."—Mahatma Gandhi

Other People also Get Messages from God

- Deanna Laney believed that God ordered her to kill her children on Mother's Day. Laney said that on the day of the killings she saw Aaron with a spear, then throwing a rock, then squeezing a frog. She believed God was suggesting she should either stab, stone, or strangle her children. In a videotaped interview with the prosecution psychiatrist, Mrs. Laney tearfully recounted the savage attacks and the torture that followed. "I didn't want to kill my kids at all....I felt like I had no choice. Because God told me to do that, and I was taught you obey God."

- Jennifer Cisowski maintained that voices in her head told

her to test her faith in God. The young mother repeatedly slammed her eight-month-old infant son to the ground and down a flight of stairs in his grandmother's home. She said she believed he would rise from the dead if her faith were strong enough.

- Teresa Ann Archie chased her daughter through their home, shooting her twice in the back after becoming convinced her sixteen-year-old was possessed by Satan. She told police Shavon's last words were, "Mama, don't shoot me, I love you." She replied, "I know, baby, but I have to do the Lord's will."

- On the morning of June 20, 2001, Andrea Yates, a Houston housewife, made breakfast for her five children and then methodically drowned each one in the family's guest bathroom. Shortly before the murders, her doctor had taken her off her medication. She soon began receiving communications from God telling her to kill the children to protect them.

- On October 19, 2005, young mother Lashuan Harris stripped the clothing from her three young boys and dropped them one by one over the railing on Pier 7 to drown in San Francisco Bay. Her psychiatrist testified that Harris believed God had told her to put her boys into the Bay; she thought she was sending them to heaven.

- Paul Durant, forty-seven, admitted in court that he beat Karen Durrell, forty-one, to death with a mallet at her home in 2004. Following his arrest, Durant wrote to a newspaper from his prison cell, saying that he had been driven to kill and eat Durrell by messages delivered to him by God via his television.

Points to Ponder

The first humans roamed the earth about 100,000 years ago. Why did God wait about 98,000 years before sending his messenger (Jesus, Muhammad, Buddha)?

The ancient Egyptians worshiped over 2,000 gods. The ancient

Greeks believed that the heavens teemed with gods, and many of them were malicious. Has new evidence emerged to justify the notion of one exclusively benevolent being?

Historian Lord Acton wrote that "Power corrupts, and absolute power corrupts absolutely." He referred to politicians, but wouldn't his warning apply to an omniscient, omnipotent being? The Old Testament paints a decidedly unflattering picture of God's character. He commanded people to keep slaves and execute blasphemers. He took everything away from his faithful servant Job—family, health, and possessions—just to test whether Job would stay devoted. What insecurity! In the Hebrew bible, God asks Abraham to sacrifice his son Isaac on Mount Moriah and doesn't even deign to give a reason. What a sadist!

The biblical god is superior to us in both strength and ability to create special effects, so if he existed and we knew what he wanted (directly, not via some power-seeking evangelist claiming a pipeline), it would behoove us to obey. Slaves do not fare well who displease their masters. But he's not a good role model. Willie Nelson sang, "Mama Don't Let Your Babies Grow Up to Be Cowboys." Humanitarian mamas won't let them grow up to be God either.

People of deep faith are called god-fearing. "The fear of the Lord is the beginning of wisdom" (Prov. 1:7). Ponder that. Fear of an all-loving being seems misplaced, even ungrateful. Loving children of loving parents aren't called parent-fearing. Yet many true believers worship a god whose level of tolerance is far below the standards of most mothers.

Even a supreme being may have occasional lapses of attention. He must get excruciatingly bored from watching day after uneventful day as televangelists eke out their ascetic lives and priests instruct altar boys. Oops, bad examples. The point is that he may not know what his creations will do at every moment throughout eternity, and his small gaps in knowledge may become chasms of ignorance. He might miss a trivial insult that triggers a murderous rampage or a bacterium that initiates a deadly plague. On the other hand, if he is always aware, always having us perform precisely as choreographed, it's hard to see how we can be faulted for bad behavior. Who deserves the blame, he or Attila? He or Torquemada, Hitler, and Saddam? If an engineer built an automaton that tortured and killed people, we would consider the engineer to be either incompetent or evil. Should worshippers hold God to a lower standard?

There are no sensory data supporting the existence of an omniscient, omnipotent, beneficent god. If there were, faith would be superfluous. In fact, there never will nor can be unambiguous data. Even if a Being appears someday with powers beyond human comprehension, the existence of others with still greater powers would remain a possibility. Even if you could be transported by a time machine to December of the year 1 BC, and personally witness the crucifixion of Christ, and hang around until Easter and be first to greet the resurrected Jesus, that would not prove the existence of an all-powerful, loving God.

Nobody, not even Pat, Jerry, or Bill, could know the Being's reasons for creating humans and intervening in our affairs. The gulf between us and the creator of the universe would certainly be greater than that between us and pigs. A pig with deep faith might attribute omniscience, omnipotence, and beneficence to the farmer who feeds it—right up until Christmas morning.

Imagine a science fiction scenario in which extraterrestrial beings land on earth and assemble the leaders of all the world's religions. Eager to know which is correct, they let each leader make his or her case. What evidence would they give? "God told me so." "It says so in the bible." "On Easter Sunday I bought a bushel of potatoes, and one of them was the spitting image of the Virgin Mary." Would a Christian's tale of the son of God rising from the dead play better than the Hindu story that each soul undergoes many reincarnations until it is united with the Universal soul? Or a Mormon representative's account of how the angel Moroni visited Joseph Smith and told him where a book inscribed on gold plates was buried? Would Jehovah's witnesses be most persuasive—they believe that death is the end for all nonbelievers, but post-death

Witnesses will live on a new, improved earth with an elite ruling class of 144,000? Or the Jewish fable that God told Abraham (seventy years old and childless) that his descendants, like the stars, would be too many to count?

God's promise to Abraham raises the issue of sex. Many religious leaders argue that sex (at least for others) should be indulged in only for the purpose of procreation.[21] Masturbation, abortion, homosexuality, condoms, and premarital, oral, and anal sex, are all sins. But if procreation is the sole purpose—if God wanted to produce 7,000,000,000 of us—why didn't he do it all at once? With no birth canal to navigate through, human heads and therefore brain sizes could have been much larger. Oh well, that might have reduced the number of worshippers.

Maybe Christians and Muslims would expect the large numbers of devotees to count in their favor, but large numbers do not constitute proof. After all, millions of people (although enough only by Supreme Court decree) thought that George Bush would make a good president. Furthermore, no religion attracts a majority of the world's people. ET would end up shaking her three heads in dismay.

> *"One of the proofs of the immortality of the soul is that myriads have believed it – they also believed the world was flat."*
> —Mark Twain

> *"I cannot believe in a God who wants to be praised all the time."*—Friedrich Nietzsche

> *"When you understand why you dismiss all the other possible gods, you will understand why I dismiss yours."*
> —Stephen Roberts

> *"There have been nearly 3,000 Gods so far but only yours actually exists. The others are silly made up nonsense. But not yours. Yours is real."*—Ricky Gervais

---

21. Does this mean that post-menopausal women who engage in sex are sinful?

One more question: If creatures as wise as ET would not be convinced, why let the likes of Pat Robertson convince you?

The Persistence of Religious Faith

Religious beliefs are highly resistant to challenge. The baffling problem is not how they originate but why so many persist in the face of powerful evidence that they are wrong. One reason is that people frequently ignore or even actively avoid information that would challenge any of their long-held and cherished beliefs. Francis Bacon wrote, "The human understanding, when it has once adopted an opinion ... draws all things else to support and agree with it. Though there may be (more) instances to be found on the other side, yet these it either neglects or despises, or else by some distinction sets aside and rejects." In the same vein, he wrote, "The first conclusion colors and brings into conformity with itself all that come after."

Some beliefs imply many others. For example, belief in infallibility of the Pope implies that abortion is wrong, assisted suicide is wrong, and sex outside marriage is wrong. Giving up on a central belief—one related to religion, country of birth, race, gender, occupation, life partner, and so forth—involves a much greater cognitive overhaul than changing a peripheral one. It may require an entire reevaluation of life, which at least partially explains why so many people are hostile to the theory of evolution; acceptance would require renunciation of years of Sunday school lessons.

> "Ideas that require people to reorganize their picture of the world provoke hostility."—James Gleick

Being disabused of the belief that Venice is the capitol of Italy might embarrass but probably not cause serious discomfort; being disillusioned about deeply held religious beliefs might devastate. Most religious people are saved from devastation by bible stories, catechisms, and other lobotomizing techniques. So, although children eventually outgrow their beliefs in Santa and the tooth fairy, maturity is, as often as not, associated with increased religious fervor. The Old Testament recounts an argument between God and Satan. The devil claimed that Job was a good man only because God had blessed him with a loving family and material wealth. So God, ever the Fair Minded Sportsman, granted Satan permission to torment Job. Satan took away his livestock and servants and caused the deaths of his ten children, then afflicted him with horrible skin sores. Yet Job continued to bless Him in his prayers. Eventually the cumulative misfortunes wore Job down, and he cursed the day he was born. But his friend Elihu cheered him up by explaining that God inflicts pain so that the sufferer can fully appreciate His love and forgiveness when he has recovered. God appeared to Job in the form of a whirlwind, and Job acknowledged His unlimited power. God, notoriously susceptible to flattery, gave back Job's health and property and blessed him with new children. In syllogistic form:

> God often tests people's faith.
>
> <u>People who pass the test will be rewarded in the end.</u>
>
> Therefore, no matter how bleak things may seem, it pays to keep the faith.

Individuals may have occasional crises of doubt, as did the apostle who became known as "Doubting Thomas." The death of a loved one may cause people to question how God could be so cruel. Their spiritual advisors, that is, the ones who divvy up the proceeds from collection plates, recount the warm, fuzzy story of Job. What a deterrent to disbelief. The inhabitants of Sodom and Gomorrah were wicked, so God destroyed their cities. But first He sent two angels to Lot, commanding him and his family to flee. The angels said to Lot, "Escape for thy life; look not behind thee." Lot and his wife and daughters hastened away, but Lot's wife disobeyed the angels and looked back. God, pissed off at such a horrible betrayal, turned her into a pillar of salt. The clear message: "Never question authority."

Most present-day religions are based on an alleged powerful

and unique event that occurred many generations ago. No current adherents experienced the event directly. Why then, Paul Connelly asked, do some religions last for centuries based on essentially hearsay evidence?[22] He wrote that the original event can be reenacted or new experiences created. Examples are rituals with psychoactive drugs, rigorous ascetic disciplines, meditation, penitence, exposure to the majesty of a Gothic cathedral, and mass prayers. Dramatically interesting experiences can be retold in memorable ways. Most religions encourage believers to show their fealty by displays of public prayer, painful rites of passage, or even martyrdom. These further ratchet up belief.

Believers are occasionally exposed to the thoughts of doubt-provoking heathens. They are reassured by the Creation story, a particularly insidious neuron destroyer. According to Jewish, Islamic, and Christian religions, Adam and Eve were the first humans and lived a blissful existence in the Garden of Eden. But one day Satan, in the form of a serpent, approached Eve and convinced her to eat from the forbidden tree of knowledge (forbidden, because God wanted to keep them ignorant). Eve gave some of the fruit to Adam, and he ate too. God found out, though not immediately—further evidence that even the omniscient are occasionally caught napping—and His blood pressure soared. He banished the miscreants from the garden and told Eve that she would be punished by having to endure painful childbirths. Also, she would be second to Adam instead of being his equal. As for Adam, he would have to toil and sweat just to survive. The moral is clear: The more sensible-seeming the heathen, the stronger must be the resistance. Knowledge is the devil's work. Rationality is evil. Apostasy is treason. Believers dare not resolve the crisis by seeking meaningful evidence. They must dismiss enigmas and anomalies by recognizing that the Lord works in mysterious ways (although every preacher in every tiny church all over the world seems to know precisely what He wants).

---

22. Connelly, P. (2002) Why do religions persist? http://www.darc.org/connelly/religion3.html

Faith is Antithetical to Truth

Jerry Coyne asserted that religion and science are incompatible.[23] They operate in ways that are intrinsically opposed. Science "has an exquisitely refined series of methods honed over 500 years to find out what's real and what's false; religion doesn't have a method to weed out falsehoods." Coyne's book begins with an anecdote. He gave a lecture on evolution and afterwards was approached by an attendee. The person agreed that the scientific evidence was very convincing—"but I still don't believe it."

> *"The religion of one age is the literary entertainment of the next."*—Ralph Waldo Emerson

Any deeply religious people who have read this far are probably angry, confused, and already working on refutations. Agnostics and atheists might be applauding. They are in for a surprise. The remaining two pillars, no less than faith, are constructed with substandard materials that cannot support their own weight.

---

23. Coyne, J. (2015) *Faith vs. Fact: Why Science and Religion are Incompatible*. NY: Viking Press.

Chapter 7

LEAVITT LIED

I never posted the Hans Christian Andersen story "The Emperor's New Clothes" over my desk. You can't believe everything you read.

Chapter 8

PILLAR 3, PART 1:
EVERYDAY REASONING

Most theologians value reason and observation as well as faith. By contrast, many tough minded scientists, philosophers, and other intellectuals have narrow visions. Philosophers give preeminence to logical analysis and scientists to sensory data, but both groups presume that we can generally trust both our reasoning abilities and our eyes and ears. They belittle faith—yet at the same time they show unquestioning faith in reason and empiricism. Two quotes are appropriate:

> *"The superstition of science scoffs at the superstition of faith."*
> —James Froude

> *"Reason is itself a matter of faith. It is an act of faith to assert that our thoughts have any relation to reality at all."*
> —G.K. Chesterton

What sets humans apart from other animals, our specialty and humanity's crowning glory, is ability to reason. Many philosophers believe that only through reason can certain knowledge ever be attained. But, as shown below, reasoning abilities are greatly over-rated (which presents a paradox, since this entire book attempts to persuade through reasoning).[24]

Evolution and Reasoning

As is true of all animals, humans compete with each other for limited resources. Human competition is often subtle, with outcomes decided more by brainpower than brute strength. Two tempting conclusions are that (a) natural selection exerted intense pressure on our reasoning abilities until, today, they have reached near perfection; and (b) our current reasoning strategies generally lead to correct beliefs. The conclusions would be a good example of the fallibility of reasoning. Decisions based on careful reasoning often result in *poorer* outcomes than those guided by intuition. Wilson and Schooler asked subjects to choose between art posters, brands of jam, and university courses.[25] Some subjects were asked to think carefully about their choices and others to make snap decisions. The results were unambiguous—the "thinking" subjects were more likely to either change their minds later on or be dissatisfied with their choices.

Stich explained why our reasoning abilities are usually considerably less than optimal.[26] An abbreviated version of his comments, most of which also apply to the trustworthiness of sensory systems, is given below. He also pointed out that inferential strategies differ from culture to culture, and no strategy is inherently superior. So, if two modes of reasoning lead to different conclusions,

---

24. The paradox is not particularly deep. Expert logicians have shown that even careful reasoning does not ensure correct conclusions. So, either: even careful reasoning does not ensure correct conclusions; or the conclusions from expert logicians can't be trusted. In either case, "knowledge" gained through reasoning cannot be trusted.

25. Wilson, T. & Schooler, J. (1991) Thinking too much: Introspection can reduce the quality of preferences and decisions. *J Personality Social Pych*, 60: 181-92.

26. Stich, S. (1990) *The Fragmentation of Reasoning*. Cambridge, MA: MIT Press.

we can't use reasoning to decide which if either is correct.

1. Genes that generate truths and avoid falsehoods may be physiologically expensive. Genes that do a poorer but still acceptable job may be selected because they are cheaper. Stich gave an analogy: the more money paid to a private detective, the more information the detective will discover; but a point of diminishing returns is reached, so most clients settle for less than maximum information.

2. Belief in something false may have different import from disbelief in something true. Avoiding a healthy food in the mistaken belief that it is poisonous is less serious than eating a poisonous food in the mistaken belief that it is edible. As a rule, believing on weak evidence that danger is present has survival value and is favored by natural selection. But such a belief system produces more errors than a strategy of always demanding good evidence.

3. Natural selection has limited options. The bodies of animals might be improved if constructed out of space age alloys, but they are not. The raw materials for improving our brains may not be available.

4. A single gene often affects two or more distinct traits. The overall effects of a gene may be positive, but it may have some negative effects. For example, the same genes that make a person of reproductive age attractive to potential mates may make the person more susceptible to diseases of old age. The genes that influence reasoning ability may be less than optimal because they have other, more important, functions.

5. Even if natural selection had optimized reasoning abilities, truth would not be the inevitable outcome. Natural selection acts on characteristics that affect reproductive potential, which does not always require having an accurate view of the world. Recall the example from p. 26 about having to walk across a long, narrow plank suspended between two

tall buildings. It would be a hazardous feat except to people who believed that the plank lay on the ground. Reasoning that led to the truth would be fatal. The natural selection of plank-walkers would not favor great thinkers. Self-deception often enhances reproductive potential. Biologist Robert Trivers wrote:

> If deceit is fundamental to animal communication, then there must be strong selection to spot deception and this ought, in turn, to select for a degree of self-deception, rendering some facts and motives unconscious so as not to betray—by the subtle signs of self-knowledge—the deception being practiced. The best way to convince people of what you are saying is to believe it yourself. The conventional view that natural selection favors nervous systems which produce ever more accurate images of the world must be a very naive view of mental evolution.[27]

Self-deception is common. Eighty percent of respondents rated themselves in the top thirty percent of all drivers. Most college students judged themselves to be more popular than average. When 829,000 high school seniors rated their ability to get along with others, less than one percent rated themselves as below average. Sixty percent rated themselves in the top ten percent and twenty-five percent rated themselves in the top one percent. Similar results have been reported for other traits including fairness, virtuosity, luck, and investing ability.[28]

"Lying to ourselves is more deeply ingrained than lying to others."—Fyodor Dostoyevsky

"The worst of all deceptions is self-deception."—Plato

---

27. Trivers, R. (in preface to Dawkins, R. (1976) The Selfish Gene. London: Oxford U Press).

28. Mele, A. (2000) *Self-Deception Unmasked.* Princeton University Press.

Donald Hoffman extended Stich's argument. He wrote that our perceptual world is nothing like the world of reality. Evolution is about fitness, how well a given strategy achieves the goals of survival and reproduction. Evolution by natural selection ensures that an organism that sees reality as it is will *never* be more fit than an organism of equal complexity that sees none of reality but is just tuned to fitness. He gave an example: An organism tuned to fitness might see both small and large quantities of some resource as red, to indicate low fitness, and intermediate quantities as green, to indicate high fitness. It sees no distinction between small and large reds—only red or green. Hoffman wrote, "If I see something that I think of as a snake, I don't pick it up. If I see a train, I don't step in front of it. I've evolved these symbols to keep me alive, so I take them seriously. But it's a logical flaw to think that if I take it seriously, I also have to take it literally."[29]

Mercier and Sperber, also writing from an evolutionary perspective, agreed with Stich that reasoning does not necessarily lead to more accurate conclusions about the world. Instead, they see it as a tool to help win arguments and persuade others to see facts in a particular way. It "helps us justify our beliefs and actions to others, convince them through argumentation, and evaluate the justifications and arguments that others address to us."[30]

As our ancestors tried to figure out uses for a newly discovered plant or a new hunting strategy, various ideas were offered. The most effective reasoning typically won the day. Mercier and Sperber wrote, "Reasoning is generally seen as a means to improve knowledge and make better decisions. However, much evidence shows that reasoning often leads to epistemic distortions and poor decisions." In their view, poor performance in standard reasoning tasks is explained by the lack of context. When the same problems

---

29. Hoffman, D. (2019) *The Case Against Reality: Why Evolution Hid the Truth from Our Eyes.* NY: W. W. Norton & Company.

30. Mercier, H. & Sperber, D. (2018) *The Enigma of Reason: A New Theory of Human Understanding. Cambridge, MA:* Harvard Press

are placed in a proper argumentative setting, people do much better. But not because they seek the truth; their goal is to find arguments supporting their views.

> *"Reason doesn't work like a judge or teacher, impartially weighing evidence or guiding us to wisdom. It works more like a lawyer or press secretary, justifying our acts and judgments to others."*
> —New York Times book reviewer William Saletan

Human Reasoning is Far from Perfect

Hayek pointed out that for any apparatus to fully understand something, it must be more complex than the thing explained. So, to fully understand human reasoning, a human mind would have to be more complex than itself. That sounds tricky.[31]

If reason were so powerful, people would more often be persuaded to change their views. Yet throughout recorded history, illustrious philosophers wrote lengthy, eloquent arguments about what people can know, and illustrious others rebutted them. All used reason and probably believed they were right. But they disagreed, so most or all were wrong. Did they fail to understand the laws of reason? Did Plato screw up? Descartes? Wittgenstein? Then the laws must be extremely difficult to follow.

Every year, brilliant lawyers present arguments to the United States Supreme Court. Every year the nine justices, chosen in large part because of their exceptional powers of reasoning, listen attentively and render decisions. But whenever the dust settled on arguments concerning gun control, abortion, first amendment rights, affirmative action, and so forth, the votes of most judges were highly predictable. Brilliant Samuel Alito drew one conclusion, brilliant Ruth Bader Ginsburg the opposite, and brilliant Clarence Thomas was mute.

Andrew Martin and colleagues developed an equation based

---

31. Hayek, F. (1955) *The Counter Revolution of Science*. NY: Free Press of Glencoe

on six factors to predict how each of the justices would vote in every case argued before them in 2002. The equation predicted seventy-five percent of the decisions correctly, strongly suggesting that the carefully reasoned arguments carried less weight than the justices' preexisting biases.[32]

Decisions, even those that have major consequences, are often influenced by irrelevant factors. Danziger and colleagues collected data on 1,112 judicial rulings over a ten-month period by eight judges who presided over parole boards in Israel. The judges took two daily food breaks that broke up the day's work into three distinct decision sessions. The percentage of favorable rulings dropped from about sixty-five percent to nearly zero within each decision session and returned abruptly to about sixty-five percent after each break.[33]

Much of everyday reasoning leads to incorrect conclusions, and normal people often behave irrationally and unwisely. Business people know that advertisements with attractive actors and actresses in the foreground may override reason in persuading potential customers. If black turns up several times in a row on a Las Vegas roulette wheel, unsophisticated bettors often place their chips on red on the grounds that red is overdue. The behavior, based on faulty reasoning, is common enough to have been given a name: the gambler's fallacy.

Examples of Irrationality

Psychologist Jean Piaget showed that young children invariably think illogically in some situations. In one of several similar demonstrations, he placed two short, fat glasses with equal amounts of liquid in them in front of a child. Then, while the child watched,

32. Martin, A. et al. (2004) Competing approaches to predicting Supreme Court decision making. *Perspective on Politics*, 2: 761-7.

33. Danziger, S. et al. (2011) Extraneous factors in judicial decisions. *Proc Natl Academy Sciences*, 108: 6889-6892.

he poured from one short, fat glass into a tall, thin one. The child stated that the tall thin glass held more water than the remaining short, fat one.[34] Gruber and Voneche gave examples of several other types of illogical thinking in young children.[35] To see some examples, go to https://www.youtube.com/watch?v=gnArvcWa-H6I. Piaget believed that most people eventually outgrow such thinking. Maybe, but confidence in our logical abilities does not rest on a stronger foundation than the child's. How can we be so arrogant as to assume that twenty-first century adult *Homo sapiens* has reached the pinnacle of logical thinking!

In fact, we clearly haven't reached a pinnacle. Aristotle organized and defined thirteen common logical fallacies. The list has expanded so that, today, about 300 fallacies are recognized. They occur frequently enough that they've received names. Because of space considerations, I list only five below.

1. Red Herring Fallacies: An irrelevant statement is used to distract the reader. The term originated with the occasional use of smelly fish to throw hunting dogs off the track of the fox in English fox hunts.

Example: Tree huggers constantly try to save the environment, but we can't make this world an Eden. Adam and Eve got bored in Eden.

Comment: The idea of Adam and Eve getting bored in Eden throws a listener off the goal of saving the environment.

2. Cause and Effect Fallacies: A reasoner assumes that something directly causes something else, but the result is actually a matter of coincidence.

Example: Nations that add fluoride to their water have higher cancer rates than those that don't. Therefore, fluoride causes cancer. (Nations that add fluoride are generally wealthier, with

34. Piaget, J. (1965) *The Child's Conception of Number.* NY: W.W. Norton
35. Gruber, H. & Voneche, J. (1977) *The Essential Piaget.* NY: Basic Books.

better health care for their citizens. So people live longer, and older people are more likely to get cancer.)

3. Unsupported Generalization Fallacies: These occur when broad generalizations are made from specific facts.

Example: Bobby and Amanda are twins, and both excel at sports. All twins excel at sports.

Comment: Just because some twins are good athletes does not justify the broad generalization that "All twins excel at sports."

4. The tu quoque fallacy occurs when a person deflects criticism by turning the critique back against the accuser.

Example: A psychiatrist shows a patient a Rorschach ink blot. The patient says he sees a naked woman. The psychiatrist holds up a second blot: "What do you see in this one?" "Two naked women," the patient answers. "Fine, what about this one?" "A couple having sex." The psychiatrist says, "Your problem is that you're obsessed with sex." "I'm obsessed with sex?" the patient replies, "you're the one with the pornography collection!"

5. The fallacy of amphiboly occurs when a grammatical ambiguity creates misunderstanding.

Example: A doctor examines a patient with an unknown ailment. "I can't figure out what's wrong with you," the doctor says, "but I think it's due to drinking." "Okay," the patient replies, "I'll come back when you've sobered up."

Heuristics

When people reason, they often use rules of thumb, educated guesses, or mental shortcuts. Called heuristics, these strategies allow people to solve problems and make judgments quickly and efficiently. But, as shown by the extensive research of Tversky and Kahneman, heuristics often lead to error.[36] Below are three of the

36. Tversky, A. & Kahneman, D. (1981) The framing of decisions and the

many heuristics they discussed:

- **The availability heuristic** involves making decisions based upon how easy it is to bring something to mind. When an infrequent event can be brought easily and vividly to mind, this heuristic overestimates its likelihood. For example, people overestimate their likelihood of dying in a dramatic event such as a tornado or terrorism. People are more easily swayed by a single, vivid story than by a large body of statistical evidence.

- **The representativeness heuristic** involves making a decision by comparing the present situation to the most representative mental prototype. For example, some people believe that eating fatty foods makes a person fat. A physician may succumb to the representative heuristic by diagnosing a patient by judging how similar the patient is to the stereotypical patient with that disorder.

- Anchoring and adjustment is a heuristic that people often use when they estimate a number. They start from a readily available number—the anchor—and shift either up or down to reach an answer. This often leads to error, because they do not shift far enough away from even clearly irrelevant anchors. In one experiment, Dan Ariely had subjects write down the last two digits of their social security number, then asked how much they would pay for a fancy bottle of wine. People with higher numbers were willing to pay more.[37] Tversky and Kahneman had subjects estimate the number of African countries in the United Nations after they watched a researcher spin a roulette-type wheel. The wheel was rigged to stop on only ten or sixty-five. Subjects who saw the number ten estimated, on average, twenty-five countries; subjects who saw the number sixty-five estimated forty-five.

---

psychology of choice. *Science*, 211: 453-8.

37. Ariely, D. (2008) *Predictably Irrational: The Hidden Forces that Shape Our Decisions*. NY: Harper Collins.

Many other types of irrationality have been identified.

- People reason differently about two pieces of logically equivalent information that differ only in wording. Two examples of this framing effect:

  Beef described as seventy-five percent lean received higher ratings than beef described as twenty-five percent fat.[38]

  More people support an economic policy if the employment rate is emphasized rather than the associated unemployment rate.[39]

- Experimental subjects rated a disease that kills 1,286 people out of every 10,000 (which comes to 12.86%) as more dangerous than one that kills 24.14% of the population. (Subjects judged one or the other.)[40]

- If a person prefers X if A is true and also prefers X if A is false, then the person prefers X whether A is true or false. So it shouldn't matter whether she knows if A is true. That seems rational, but this section shows that people are not always rational. Shafir and Tversky asked students whether they would buy a ticket for a Hawaii vacation in three different situations: They had passed a big test, they had failed the test, or they didn't yet know whether they had passed or failed. Most said they would buy the ticket if they had passed and even more said they would buy it if they had failed. But a substantial percentage said they wouldn't buy a ticket until

---

38. Levin, I. & Gaeth, G. (1988) How consumers are affected by the framing of attribute information before and after consuming the product. *J Consumer Research*, 15: 374-8.

39. Gachter, S. et al. (2009) Are experimental economists prone to framing effects? A natural field experiment. *J Economic Behavior & Organization*, 70: 443-6.

40. Yamagishi, K. (1997) When a 12.86% mortality is more dangerous than 24.14%: Implications for risk communication. *Applied Cognitive Psych*, 11: 495-506.

they found out whether they had passed or failed.[41]

The examples above show that people are often irrational. West and colleagues rubbed it in.[42] They showed that superior intelligence does not protect against cognitive errors and, in fact, often makes people *more* vulnerable to them. West and colleagues asked undergraduates to solve a variety of well-known problems. They also collected students' scores on the SAT, the Need for Cognition Scale (which measures "the tendency for an individual to engage in and enjoy thinking"), and two other measures of "cognitive sophistication." Students who scored well on the measures of cognitive sophistication were slightly *more* vulnerable to common mental mistakes.

Motivated Reasoning

People frequently ignore or even actively avoid information that would challenge any of their long-held and cherished beliefs. Comedian Henny Youngman wrote, "When I read about the evils of drinking, I gave up reading." Albert Einstein, told that certain facts refuted his theory of relativity, said, "The facts are wrong." The facts were wrong, but it's generally poor policy to ignore disconfirming evidence.

People look for evidence that supports their beliefs and remember it better than disconfirming evidence—which they fail to seek, devalue, forget, or ignore. Others, less facetiously than Henny Youngman, say when confronted with unpleasant information, "I refuse to believe that..." In his book *Miracles*, C.S. Lewis wrote that he knows only one person who has seen a ghost, and that person doesn't believe in ghosts. Lewis's point was that if a person's worldview does not allow for the existence of ghosts, then even seeing a ghost won't convince the person of their existence.

Washburn and Skitka had subjects read about a study with

---

41. Shafir, E. & Tversky, A. (1992) Thinking through uncertainty: nonconsequential reasoning and choice. *Cognitive Psych*, 24: 449-74.

42. West, R. et al. Cognitive sophistication does not attenuate the bias blind spot. *J Personality Social Psych*, 103: 506-13.

results that were either consistent or inconsistent with their attitudes about issues such as carbon emissions. The subjects interpreted numerical results and decided what the study concluded. After being informed of the correct interpretation, they rated how much they agreed with and trusted the researchers' interpretation. Both liberals and conservatives denied the interpretation when it conflicted with their attitudes.[43]

For most important issues, both sides can produce supportive reasons. Truth seekers should consider the counterarguments. Yet people tend to restrict their media coverage of issues to newspapers, magazines, and television shows that support their viewpoints; and they choose likeminded friends. So, although they can call forth good reasons in defense of their positions, they fail to realize that the other side may also have good—and maybe even better—ones. At a later time, if the belief is questioned, the justifications are readily remembered but the counterarguments are not.

> *"What the human being is best at doing is interpreting all new information so that their prior conclusions remain intact."*
> —Warren Buffett

During the 2008 U.S. presidential election season, Valdis Krebs analyzed purchasing trends on Amazon.com.[44] He considered that two books were linked if they were often bought together or by the same buyer. He also looked at bought pairs—people who bought this book also bought that book. His findings reflected the deep divide in the country between conservative and liberal voters. There were neither connections nor intermediaries between conservative and liberal books—each cluster was completely closed off to the other. People ignored books of non-conforming opinions. Krebs

---

43. Washburn, A. & Skitka, L. (2017) Liberals and conservatives are similarly motivated to deny attitude-inconsistent science. https://doi.org/10.1177/1948550617731500

44. http://www.thenetworkthinkers.com/2012/10/2012-political-book-network.html

did a similar mapping in 2012 and found a few connections between the two book networks, but the voter base remained polarized. There were two tightly defined clusters.

The *Atlantic Monthly* cited a study in which volunteers listened to very staticky speeches. Some were about smoking—either linking it to cancer or disputing the link—and some were attacks on Christianity. The subjects could press a button that reduced the static for a few seconds. Most smokers tuned into the speech that suggested cigarettes might not cause cancer, whereas nonsmokers were more likely to press the button for the antismoking speech. Frequent churchgoers let the anti-Christian speech dissolve into static whereas the less religious typically gave the button a few presses.[45]

Taylor and Brown (1988) posited that motivated reasoning is beneficial; it leads to an unrealistically positive but often adaptive self-image and views of the world.[46] Ziva Kunda reviewed a large and burgeoning scientific literature on motivated reasoning. Kunda wrote, "People motivated to arrive at a particular conclusion attempt to construct a justification of their desired conclusion that would persuade a dispassionate observer." Following are a few examples from Kunda:[47]

- Subjects led to believe that toothbrushing or caffeine consumption was bad for their health reported having performed those behaviors in the recent past less frequently than did subjects led to believe that the same behaviors were good for their health.

- Subjects induced to theorize that a given trait (extraversion or introversion) was conducive to academic success came to view

45. https://www.theatlantic.com/science/archive/2017/03/ this-article-wont-change-your-mind/519093/

46. Taylor, S. & Brown, J. (1988). Illusion and well-being: A social psychological perspective on mental health. *Psychological Bulletin*, 103: 193—210.

47. Kunda, Z. (1990) The case for motivated reasoning. *Psych Bull*, 108: 480-98.

themselves as characterized by higher levels of that trait than did other subjects, presumably because they were motivated to view themselves as possessing success-promoting attributes.

- Subjects were exposed to a training session that extolled the virtues of either social skills or task skills for success in business; afterwards, the subjects enhanced their self-ratings on whichever was associated with success and deflated their self-ratings on the other.

- Subjects were given a laboratory test said to diagnose the presence of a potentially risky (fictitious) enzyme deficiency. Subjects diagnosed as having the deficiency rated it as less serious and health threatening and the diagnostic test as less accurate than did subjects diagnosed as not having it.

- Smokers were less persuaded than nonsmokers by the Surgeon General's report about the health risks of smoking, which suggests that people threatened by scientific evidence are motivated to disbelieve it.

- Subjects read an article claiming that caffeine was risky for women. Women who were heavy caffeine consumers were less convinced by the article than were women who were low caffeine consumers. No such effects were found for men. Only subjects who stood to suffer serious personal implications if the article were true doubted its truth.

- Subjects who were for or against capital punishment were exposed to two studies with different methodologies, one supporting and one opposing the conclusion that capital punishment deters crime. Subjects were more critical of the research methods used in the study that disconfirmed their initial beliefs than they were of methods used in the study that confirmed their initial beliefs.

"The reasoning process is more like a lawyer defending a client
than a judge or scientist seeking the truth."
—Social psychologist Jonathan Haidt

"So convenient a thing is it to be a rational creature, since it enables us to find or make a reason for everything one has a mind to."—Ben Franklin

Test your reasoning skills. The answers are on page 262.

Problem Set I

1. A bat and a ball cost one dollar, ten cents in total. The bat costs one dollar more than the ball. How much does the ball cost?

2. A lake has a patch of lily pads. Every day, the patch doubles in size. If it takes forty-eight days for the patch to cover the entire lake, how long would it take for the patch to cover half the lake?

3. There are two train stations, A and B. Trains leave both stations every hour on the hour, and the trip in each direction takes six hours. The tracks are next to each other, so passengers can see the trains coming from the opposite direction. If they watch, how many trains will they see during their journey?

4. A famous mathematical problem is called the Monty Hall dilemma. Game show contestants are shown three doors. Behind one is a new car and behind the others are far less attractive prizes. The host knows what's behind the doors. Say the contestant chooses door one. The host then opens one of the other two doors, say door three, which inevitably reveals an unattractive prize. The host then asks if the contestant wants to stick with her original pick or swap to door two. What should she do?

5. Jack is looking at Anne, but Anne is looking at George. Jack is married, but George is not. Is a married person looking at an unmarried person?

   Yes   No   Cannot be determined

6. As I was going to St Ives
   I met a man with seven wives
   Every wife had seven sacks
   Every sack had seven cats
   Every cat had seven kits
   Kits, cats, sacks, wives
   How many were going to St Ives?

Chapter 9

PILLAR 3, PART 2: FORMAL AND INFORMAL LOGIC

"Reason itself is fallible, and this fallibility must find a place in our logic."—Nicola Abbagnano

"Logic: The art of thinking and reasoning in strict accordance with the limitations and incapacities of the human misunderstanding."—Ambrose Bierce

Inductive Arguments

Inductive arguments are those in which a conclusion is inferred from two or more premises. The strengths of inductive arguments vary, but even the strongest never lead to certain conclusions. The conclusions become more or less probable, based upon the evidence given. There are no guarantees. A sound inductive argument with true premises may still lead to a false conclusion. Here is an inductive argument that, I hope, is true for now, but almost surely won't be true in a trillion years:

For every day of my life, the sun has risen in the east.

Therefore, tomorrow the sun will rise in the east.

Mathematicians often search for patterns in numerical relationships and then assume that the pattern holds for all numbers. They are reasoning inductively. Their challenge is to prove the assumption, which requires deductive reasoning. Inductive reasoning is excluded from mathematical proofs.

Following are three examples of inductive reasoning in mathematics. The first leads to a true conclusion, the next two to false ones.

- Consider the numbers 5, 15, 35, 45, 65, 95. Every number ends in 5 and is divisible by 5. An inductive inference is that every number that ends in 5 is divisible by 5. The inference is correct.

- Consider the expression $n^2 - n + 41$. For every value of n shown below, and all the values in between, the result is a prime number.

  $1^2 - 1 + 41 = 41$, a prime number
  $2^2 - 2 + 41 = 43$, a prime number
  $3^2 - 3 + 41 = 47$, a prime number
  $10^2 - 10 + 41 = 131$, a prime number
  $12^2 - 12 + 41 = 173$, a prime number
  $40^2 - 40 + 41 = 1,601$, a prime number

  But an inductive inference that the pattern holds for all values of n would be incorrect: $41^2 - 41 + 41$ is not a prime.

- Circles can be divided into regions. The first circle below, with 2 dots, has 2 regions. The second, with 3 dots, has 4. Four dots divide the circle into 8 regions and 5 dots divide it into 16. There's a clear pattern here, and using induction we confidently predict that 6 dots divide the circle into 32 regions. Nope.

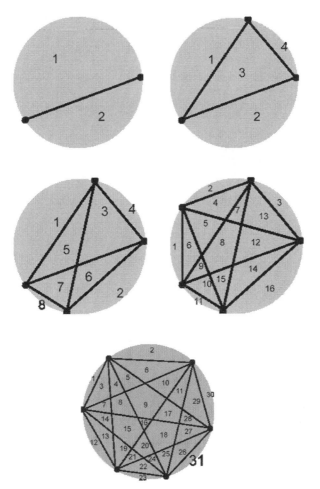

Figure 4: Dividing a circle into different regions.

Following are three nonmathematical examples in which an inductive inference may be incorrect:

- He is fifty. He is articulate and healthy-looking. He drives a nice car. Therefore, at some point in his life he probably worked for a living.

  o It's quite possible that somewhere on earth lives a bright middle-aged Kuwaiti emir, or Rockefeller or Rothschild, who drives a different luxury car every day, with hands never soiled by work.

- Imagine a courtroom in which jurors hear that: (a) the defendant hated the murder victim; (b) the defendant was seen with the victim shortly before the murder occurred; (c) the defendant's fingerprints were on the murder weapon; and (d) the defendant confessed to the murder. The obvious and irresistible inference is that the defendant murdered the victim.

  o Mystery writers routinely contrive scenarios in which a brilliant detective analyzes equally compelling evidence and derives an unforeseen and startling conclusion. The conclusion that the defendant was guilty might have been reasonably inferred from evidence, but the evidence might have been wrong. The defendant, for reasons known only to him, may have only pretended to hate the victim; the person seen with the victim may have been disguised to look like the defendant; the fingerprints expert may have erred or lied; the weapon found at the scene may have been a clever replica of the murder weapon; the defendant may have confessed to protect another; or creatures from a distant galaxy may have taken over his mind and forced a confession. The possibilities, both straightforward and fanciful, are limitless.

- You see a small furry creature and hear it meow. You conclude that it's a cat.

  o Maybe, but you might be viewing a remarkably life-like cat robot. Maybe somebody slipped a powerful hallucinogenic drug into your orange juice. Or maybe those mischievous creatures from a distant galaxy are having fun with you.

If you refuse to concede the possibility of such scenarios, your reasons for doing so will require other premises. As noted below, to prove premises true requires additional premises. All inferences rest on premises that are assumed true only because they suit the disposition of the inferrer. The process of proving premises can never end.

> "Since proofs need premises, it is impossible to prove anything unless some things are accepted without proof."—Bertrand Russell

Most scientific and everyday reasoning is inductive. Our senses reveal the immediate present and we use inductive logic to generalize. But even if our senses were infallible, generalizations require the assumptions that what has not yet been observed resembles what has been observed; that what is true here is also true there; and that future events and laws of nature will resemble past ones. Believers might try to justify their faith in induction by saying that the future has always resembled the past, so it will continue to do so in the future. That's a good example of circular (and thus invalid) reasoning: it assumes what it set out to prove—namely, that the future will resemble the past. As philosopher David Hume noted, that assumption cannot come from experience. It's just a wish. Bertrand Russell made Hume's concern vivid by invoking a chicken, fed by a man every day of its life and eventually learning to expect the daily feedings, yet in the end having its neck wrung by the very man who had been feeding it. Russell added that, although instincts cause us to believe that the sun will rise tomorrow, we are in no better position to judge than was the chicken. Russell concluded that there is no rational basis for induction:

> "The general principles of science, such as the belief in the reign of law, and the belief that every event must have a cause, are as completely dependent upon the inductive principle as are the beliefs of daily life. All such general principles are believed because humankind has found innumerable instances of their truth and no instances of their falsehood. But this affords no evidence for their truth in the future, unless the inductive principle is assumed."[48]

---

48. Russell, B. (1948) *Human Knowledge: Its Scope and Limits*. London: George Allen and Unwin.

The claim that a statement is true needs evidence to support it. Call the support reason X. But X must also be supported. Call that reason Y. Y must also be supported, and on and on, ad infinitum. The process always ends at an arbitrary stopping point. Wherever it is, the endpoint locates an act of faith, no more justified than believing in leprechauns. You may have a rationale for your particular stopping point, but a rationale is not a proof. This only somewhat irrelevant sentence illustrates the point that todo conocimiento es incierto.

Despite Hume and Russell, many political and sports pundits have fashioned lucrative careers out of foretelling. Their television and newspaper audiences believe that these "experts" are tremendously insightful. Philip Tetlock showed otherwise. Over a period of twenty years, Tetlock asked 284 of them—people who appear on television, get quoted in newspaper articles, advise governments and businesses, and participate in punditry roundtables—to assess the probabilities that certain events would occur within the following few years.[49] For such issues as political freedom, economic growth, repression, and recession, he asked them to rate the probabilities of three alternative outcomes: would there be more of it, less of it, or no change. He asked them about areas of the world in which they specialized and also about areas in which they had no special expertise. Would there be a nonviolent end to apartheid in South Africa? Would Gorbachev be ousted in a coup? Would the United States go to war in the Persian Gulf? Would Canada disintegrate?

By the end of the study in 2003, the experts had made 82,361 forecasts. And performed worse than if they had simply assigned an equal probability to all three outcomes—if they had given each possible future a thirty-three percent chance of occurring. Forecasters with the biggest news media profiles were especially bad.

After analyzing the accuracy of economic forecasters, Prakash

---

49. Tetlock, P. (2005) *Expert Political Opinion: How Good is it? How Can We Know?* NJ: Princeton U. Press.

Loungani concluded that "The record of failure to predict recessions is virtually unblemished." His analysis revealed that economists had failed to predict 148 of the past 150 recessions.[50] Hall of Fame baseball player Yogi Berra was less arrogant than the pundits. He said, "It is hard to make predictions, especially about the future."

Inductive Inferences are Ambiguous

If Hume destroyed the illusion that induction can be rationally justified, philosopher Nelson Goodman put a stake through the dead.[51] For Hume, inductive inferences were straightforward. "The sun will rise in the east tomorrow because that's what it's always done." But Goodman showed that an infinite number of inductive inferences can be drawn from any body of data. For example, in a world in which all emeralds ever observed have been green, the obvious inductive inference is that all are green and will be so in the future. So Goodman coined a word, 'grue.' Grue refers to objects that are green before a certain specified date but change color and are blue from that date on. Then, prior to that date, all evidence supporting the induction "All emeralds are green" equally supports "All emeralds are grue." Nobody has formulated an acceptable reason for inferring to the first rather than the second. Or to "All emeralds are grack, grellow, or gravender."

If grue emeralds seem silly, how about butterpillars? Someone with no knowledge of caterpillars or butterflies might have a difficult time accepting that those creatures that have spent their entire lives crawling will after a certain date have metamorphosed into beautiful fliers.

---

50. Loungani, P. (2000) How accurate are private sector forecasts? Cross-country evidence from consensus forecasts of output growth. *IMF Working Paper No. 00/77*: 26 June

51. Goodman, N. (1973) *Fact, Fiction and Forecast*. IN: Bobbs Merrill.

Attempts to Rebut Hume and Save Induction

C.D. Broad wrote that "Induction is the glory of science and the scandal of philosophy."[52] Not surprisingly, much of philosophy since Hume has been an attempt to deal with the scandal. Donald Williams and David Stove used similar strategies in their attempts.[53] They proceeded roughly like this: Start with a simple inductive argument:

All observed Xs have been Ys. Therefore the next observed X will be a Y.

That's an example of an argument that, Hume showed, cannot be rationally justified. But suppose the two statements are changed to:

There are far more Xs than Ys. Therefore the next randomly chosen X will probably be a Y.

Then, say Williams and Stove, if the premise is true, the conclusion is probably true. Therefore they have justified inductions of that general form.

Their argument rests on the notion that, if a large sample is drawn randomly from a population, the probability is high that the proportions in the sample approximately match the proportions in the population. For example, suppose an urn contains an unknown proportion of black and white balls. Suppose you pull out 100 balls and each one is white. Although not certain, wouldn't you be justified in inferring that the next one you pull out will be white? Wouldn't it be rational to have confidence in your inference, given the evidence of your prior picks?

---

52. Philosophers are easily scandalized. Kant thought it a scandal that we accept the existence of things outside ourselves with no proof. Martin Heidegger responded, "The scandal of philosophy is not that the proof is yet to be given, but that such proofs are expected and attempted again and again." John Searle was scandalized that philosophers have made so little progress on the problem of free will.

53. Williams, D. (1947) *The Ground of Induction*, Harvard: Harvard University Press; Stove, D. (1986) *The Rationality of Induction*, Oxford: Clarendon Press

Hume says, "No." He claims that all such arguments presuppose that the future resembles the past—an assertion that cannot be rationally justified. See above. Also, their argument doesn't deal with problems like grue emeralds.

Formal Logic—Deductive Arguments

The above paragraphs show that both informal reasoning and inductive reasoning are imperfect. Whereas laypersons often construct apparently logical arguments to justify whatever conclusions they have previously reached, logicians try to do better. They specify clear rules for proper arguments. According to the popular view, correct reasoning follows certain universal principles based on rules of logic, probability theory, decision theory, and so forth. Conclusions from such reasoning must be correct—with iron-clad certainty.

Or maybe not. Many logicians disagree with the popular view. Formal logic was invented in classical Greece and integrated into a system of thought by Aristotle. For him, logic was a system for advancing knowledge. Yet, as Donald Simanek noted, nearly every argument and conclusion he made about physical science was wrong.[54] Susan Haack pointed out that all arguments that justify deductive reasoning appeal to the very principles of inference that are in question.[55] William Alston made a similar observation: "... anything that would count as showing that deduction is reliable would have to involve deductive inference and so would assume the reliability of deduction."[56] As far back as 1895, Lewis Carroll of *Alice in Wonderland* fame argued that every valid deductive inference presupposes that deductive inferences are truth-preserving.

---

54. Simanek, D. (2008) Uses and misuses of logic. https://lockhaven. edu/~dsimanek/logic.htm

55. Haack, S. http://www-personal.umich.edu/~jdmitrig/26%20-%20 Haack%20and%20Carroll.pdf

56. Alston, W. (1993) *The Reliability of Sense Perception*. NY: Cornell U. Press

Complicating matters even more, logicians and decision theorists have proposed many principles of reasoning, and several are incompatible with each other. Gottlob Frege "...made brilliant use of his logical insights when developing his philosophical programmes concerning mathematics and language... Unfortunately, the system Frege eventually developed was shown to be inconsistent."[57]

There is tension between teachers of Aristotelian (traditional) logic and modern symbolic logic. Edward Simmons wrote that they are radically distinct disciplines.[58] Bertrand Russell called traditional logic "as definitely antiquated as Ptolemaic astronomy." And "...the Aristotelian doctrines with which we have been concerned in this chapter are wholly false, with the exception of the formal theory of the syllogism, which is unimportant. Any person in the present day who wishes to learn logic will be wasting his time if he reads Aristotle or any of his disciples."[59] In contrast, Jacques Maritain wrote that traditional logicians reject much of modern logic as mistaken and not logic at all.[60]

Skeptic philosopher Agrippa, who probably lived a few hundred years after Socrates, is credited with what has come to be known as Agrippa's Trilemma. The Trilemma contends that reasoning never leads to sound conclusions, because all reasoning must commit at least one of three fallacies:

- Infinite regress: The claim that a statement is true needs evidence to support it. But the evidence must also be supported, and on and on, ad infinitum.

- An uncertain assumption: Foundationalists claim that some

57. King, P. & Shapiro, S. (195) The history of logic. In *The Oxford Companion to Philosophy* (pp. 496-500) Oxford U. Press.

58. Simmons, E. (1961) *The Scientific Art of Logic: An Introduction to the Principles of Formal and Informal Logic*. Milwaukee: Bruce Publishing.

59. Russell, B. (1945) *A History of Western Philosophy*. NY: Simon & Schuster.

60. Maritain, J. (2014) *A Preface to Metaphysics*. Charleston, SC: Nabu Press.

beliefs are self-evident and can be used as starting points for complex arguments. For some foundationalists, mathematics and logic provide basic beliefs: "2+2=4;" "If X is true, then X cannot be false." Other foundationalists insist that basic beliefs come from direct sensory experience: "That cat is black." But sensory data are suspect. See p. 88-101. Internal feeling is another candidate: A person who claims to have a headache may be lying, but it is hard to see how he or she could be mistaken. Nevertheless, neither that nor any of the other candidates leads to the enormous number of complex, detailed beliefs that are part of everyone's worldview. Furthermore, if everyone gets to choose their own basic beliefs, many mutually incompatible ones will emerge. The foundationalist approach essentially abandons attempts to justify reasoning.

- Circular reasoning: Coherentists assert that statements can be valid if they fit into a coherent system of other known facts or beliefs. They don't all have to be supported by more fundamental statements; they are considered provisionally true if part of a coherent whole. But coherentism is circular: A explains B, B explains C, and C explains A. Circular arguments are invalid. Furthermore, many statements cohere with many others, so it is possible to develop a belief system that is both coherent and entirely untrue.

"Several logicians have in the last fifty years been trying to find some simpler and better mode of ascertaining when arguments are good, but they have not yet agreed upon the subject."
—W. S. Jevons

Aristotle described three fundamental laws of thought that play an important role even today with writers about logic:

The *law of identity*: A thing is identical with itself.

The *law of noncontradiction*: No statement is both true and false.

The *law of excluded middle*: For any proposition, either that proposition is true or its negation is true.

The laws may seem obvious. If the law of the excluded middle is violated—if we allow something to be both X and not X—then anything at all can be proved. For example, start with the sentence (A) "Today is Tuesday and today is not Tuesday," and prove that (B) "Every conclusion in this book must be accepted without question."

1. If (A) is true, then "Today is Tuesday" is true; and so is the following sentence: (C) Either "Today is Tuesday" or "Every conclusion in this book must be accepted without question."

2. But, according to (A), "Today is not Tuesday." It follows that "Today is Tuesday" must be false.

3. If "Today is Tuesday" is false, then (C) is true only if "Every conclusion in this book must be accepted without question." Oh well, we knew that anyway.

Nicolai Vasiliev rejected the *laws of noncontradiction* and *excluded middle*.[61] Robert Anton Wilson developed a classification system in which propositions can be assigned one of seven values: true, false, indeterminate, meaningless, self-referential, game rule, or strange loop. J. Lukasiewicz founded 3-value logic.[62] He argued against the law of the excluded middle, and many quantum physicists follow his lead. Lukasiewicz pointed out that insisting that things be either tall or not tall, blue or not blue, and old or not old divides the world too simply.

Nicholas Gisin has made many important contributions to quantum mechanics. He recently published four papers that he believes will enable physicists to better understand the nature of time. His approach requires using intuitionistic mathematics, a philosophy of mathematics that was introduced by mathematician L.E.J. Brouwer in 1907. In intuitionistic mathematics, the law of excluded middle doesn't hold. Propositions are either true, false, or

61. Stelzner, W. (2014) Nicolai Vasiliev's *Imaginary logic* and semantic foundations for the logic of assent. https://doi.org/10.4000/philosophiascientiae.972

62. Lukasiewicz, J. (1970) On three-valued logic. In Borkowski, L. (Ed) *Selected Works by Jan Lukasiewicz.* Amsterdam: North-Holland.

indeterminate. Gisin argues that indeterminacy is much closer to our everyday experience than the absolute determinism advocated by classical physics.[63]

The next section deals with syllogisms. A syllogism is a logical argument in which a conclusion is inferred from two or more premises. A syllogism is valid if the conclusion follows from the premises. One or both premises may be false in a valid syllogism, in which case the conclusion may be true or false. But if all the premises are true, then a valid syllogism must lead to a true conclusion. (At least, so goes the party line. But see p. 84-85 for dissenting opinions.) Evans and colleagues presented subjects with syllogisms of the form:

No cigarettes are inexpensive.
<u>Some addictive things are inexpensive.</u>
Therefore, some addictive things are not cigarettes.

and:

No addictive things are inexpensive.
<u>Some cigarettes are inexpensive.</u>
Therefore, some cigarettes are not addictive.

Both syllogisms are valid, but the first conclusion is plausible and the second is not. Subjects nearly always judged syllogisms with a plausible conclusion as valid; they judged most syllogisms with false conclusions invalid.[64]

Consider a famous example:

All men are mortal.
<u>Socrates is a man.</u>
Therefore, Socrates is mortal.

"All men are mortal" and "Socrates is a man" are premises. As

63. Gisin, N. (2020) Mathematical languages shape our understanding of time in physics. *Nature Physics*, DOI: 10.1038/s41567-019-0748-5

64. Evans, J. et al. (1983) On the conflict between logic and belief in syllogistic reasoning. *Memory and Cognition*, 11: 295-306.

long as they are true, that particular argument form always leads to true conclusions—at least, according to instructors of introductory philosophy classes. So, we must accept Socrates' mortality. But if either premise is false or the argument form invalid, the conclusion should be rejected as unproven. Consider:

All men are mortal.
<u>Socrates is mortal.</u>
Therefore, Socrates is a man.

That argument has true premises and a true conclusion but is nonetheless invalid. To see that that is so, substitute "women" for "men" in the first premise. Although both premises would still be true, the conclusion, "Socrates is a woman," would of course be false. Other arguments of the same form may or may not lead to true conclusions. For example:

All people who read this book are brilliant.
<u>Socrates was brilliant.</u>
Therefore, Socrates read this book.

Logicians call an argument deductively valid if its conclusion cannot possibly be false when the premises are true. A deductively valid argument that also has true premises is called sound. Argument (a) below is valid and (b) is invalid. Neither one is sound.

a. I am holding one live elephant in my left hand and one live elephant in my right hand. Therefore, I am holding a total of two live elephants in my hands.

b. I have one penny in my left hand and one penny in my right hand. Therefore, I have a total of three pennies in both hands. (The argument is invalid even if I do have a total of three pennies in both hands.)

So, invalid arguments may lead to true conclusions and valid arguments to false ones. The next argument is valid. Is it sound?

The thesis of this book is that certain or even probable knowledge is unattainable.

<u>Careful reasoning will detect no flaws in the arguments given.</u> Therefore, either the thesis is sound or reasoning cannot be trusted.

Please take a short quiz. Determine which of arguments 1-6 are valid.

Quiz

1. No sophisticated logicians make errors of reasoning. Some humans make errors of reasoning. Therefore, some sophisticated logicians are not human.

2. Some intellectually precocious children are sickly. Some intellectually precocious children can solve complex logic problems. Therefore, some sickly children can solve complex logic problems.

3. No sophisticated logicians are fools. No fools are professional violinists. Therefore, no sophisticated logicians are professional violinists.

4. My theory predicts that the liquid will turn brown when heated. I heated the liquid and it turned brown. Therefore, my theory is true.

5. We cannot know anything except through experience. Nobody has ever experienced the future. Therefore, nobody can know anything about the future.

6. Naive realism (the belief that the theories of science give a literally true account of the way the world is) leads to physics. Physics, if true, shows that naive realism is false. Therefore naive realism, if true, is false. Therefore it is false. (Bertrand Russell wrote this syllogism.)

According to traditional logic, arguments 1-4 are invalid and 5 and 6 are both valid and sound. Over the years, virtually none of my college students who tried the quiz got all of them right. Very few got only one wrong. The arguments' difficulty despite their brevity shows how limited are our abilities. Lengthier chains of reasoning may be impossible to evaluate even by people who know the rules—like trying to multiply two 5-digit numbers in one's head. Consider a well-known "proof" that 2=1.

$$\text{Let } a = x$$
$$\text{Then } a+a = a+x$$
$$\text{and } 2a = a+x$$
$$\text{and } 2a\text{-}2x = a+x\text{-}2x$$
$$\text{and } 2(a\text{-}x) = a+x\text{-}2x$$
$$\text{and } 2(a\text{-}x) = a\text{-}x$$

Divide both sides by a-x. The result is that 2 = 1.

People "know" that 2 does not equal 1, so they might be motivated to look for a flaw in the argument. They'd be sure there is one. If they are mathematically sophisticated, they'll note that the first step says that a = x. So, a-x=0. Then the last step is not permissible, because it requires dividing by zero.

Professional mathematicians often disagree on whether a proof is valid. Inglis and colleagues asked 109 mathematicians to judge a purported proof in undergraduate calculus.[65] There was substantial disagreement among them. Most participants who judged the proof valid did not change their minds when told why other mathematicians had judged it invalid.

Clearly, the rules of logic and good reasoning are difficult to apply. Yet a far more serious problem looms. My students assumed that anyone who applies the rules properly will get the correct answers. They may have been mistaken.

> "The principles of logic and metaphysics are true simply because we never allow them to be anything else."—A.J. Ayer

Conclusions Often Come First

Even if two disputants each reason flawlessly, they might never come

---

65. Inglis, M. et al. (2013) On mathematicians' different standards when evaluating elementary proofs. *Topics in Cognitive Science*, 5: 270-82.

to agreement if they start from different premises. But premises come from observations, perceptions, and values, all of which are subjective and subject to distortion. All the arguments below are valid.

Adam: My preacher conveys the word of (infallible) God. My preacher says abortion is wrong. Therefore, abortion is wrong.

Beth: Women have the right to control what happens inside their bodies. A developing fetus affects a woman's body. Therefore, a woman has a right to abort a developing fetus.

Clint: The second amendment to the U.S. Constitution gives citizens the right to bear arms. I am a U.S. citizen. Therefore, I have the right to bear arms.

Derek: The availability of guns to private citizens causes thousands of injuries and deaths each year to innocent victims. The government has a duty to protect its citizens. Therefore, the government has a duty to enforce gun control.

Ellen: No behavior between consenting adults is immoral. Homosexual sex typically involves behavior between consenting adults. Therefore, typical homosexual sex is not immoral.

Falwell: Sex is immoral unless the goal of the participants is procreation. Homosexual sex does not lead to procreation. Therefore, homosexual sex is immoral.[66]

God's helpers: The bible speaks the literal truth. Scientists claim that they have evidence showing that the bible does not speak the literal truth. Therefore, the scientists are wrong.

Heathen: Our senses and reasoning abilities are the most reliable sources of information. Our senses and reasoning abilities show that the bible does not speak the literal truth. Therefore, the bible does not speak the literal truth.

> "Logic: an instrument used for bolstering a prejudice."
> —Elbert Hubbard

To summarize, all arguments depend on premises assumed true only because they make a convenient stopping point. Can you

---

66. Does that imply that postmenopausal women who have sex are immoral?

think of a single premise that everybody would accept? Me neither. The stopping point is always arbitrary and always a matter of faith. Scientists, devil worshippers, and people who claim to have been abducted by aliens are on a par.

We'll Never Know if Our Tools of Reasoning Lead to Valid Conclusions

Although students occasionally disputed my answers to exam questions about facts and concepts, logic questions were exempt from criticism. I'd show where they had incorrectly applied a rule for evaluating syllogisms, and that would end the matter. No student ever asked "Who made up the rules?" Philosopher Peter Winch asked.[67] He concluded, "The criteria of logic are not a direct gift from God but arise out of and are only intelligible in the context of ways of living and modes of social life."

Take problem syllogism 1 above. It has the form, "No A is B. Some C is B. Therefore, some A is not C." No syllogism of that form, even if it has true premises, guarantees a true conclusion. For example: No mice weigh more than 100 pounds. Some mammals weigh more than 100 pounds. Therefore, some mice are not mammals. A form that even occasionally gives incorrect answers can't be trusted. It is invalid.

Problem syllogism 5, and all syllogisms of the same form, are valid. If they have true premises, their conclusions must follow. There are, according to teachers of introductory logic, no exceptions. But it would be more accurate to say that no exceptions are known. Some people would probably be unable to think of a faulty conclusion derived from a syllogism like 1. Maybe the rest of us just aren't smart enough to think of exceptions to 5. At some deep level of abstract reasoning, maybe 1 is valid and 5 invalid. What we call validity is nothing more than inability to think of counter examples.

---

67. Winch, P. (1958) *The Idea of a Social Science and Its Relation to Philosophy.* London: Routledge & Kegan Paul.

The rules are trusted because they match experience. In all my prior experiences, one apple plus one apple has equaled two apples. It follows that new experiences may lead to revision of the rules. Philosopher W.V. Quine wrote, ". . . no statement is immune from revision. Revision of even the logical law of the excluded middle has been proposed as a means of simplifying quantum mechanics; and what is the difference in principle between such a shift and the shift whereby Kepler superseded Ptolemy, or Einstein Newton, or Darwin Aristotle?"[68]

Some statements are true by definition. (Bald men have no hair. Roses are flowers.) Quine argued that such statements are not sharply different from statements like "There are no purple roses," whose truth value can be determined only by relying upon observation and experience. He wrote that all propositions that express any form of knowledge are ultimately judged by sense experience. In mathematics, no less than in physics, the notion of truth is pragmatic. Rules are accepted if they help us cope with the world.

Nelson Goodman also argued that empirical evidence can affect the acceptability of logical and mathematical proofs. He wrote that we modify either our principles of reasoning or our acceptance of given instances of reasoning or both until they are in mutual agreement.[69]

Quantum physicists successfully describe and explain a wide range of phenomena (see p. 195-204), both within and outside of laboratories. Yet ordinary logic fails when applied to quantum phenomena. Does this mean that the physicists' relevant inferences are illogical? Almost certainly not. It may indicate the need for a new logic better suited to quantum mechanics. Mathematician John von Neumann argued that ordinary logic cannot be applied to quantum phenomena.

Hilary Putnam argued that empirical facts about quantum

---

68. Quine, W. (1953) *From a Logical Point of View.* Cambridge, MA: Harvard U Press.

69. Goodman, N. (1965) *Fact, Fiction and Forecast.* Indianapolis: Bobbs-Merrill.

phenomena provide grounds for revising classical logic.[70] For example, in quantum logic, unlike classical logic, the validation of one proposition can destroy the validity of another proposition. In classical logic, if p is true, and either q or r is true, then either p and q is true or p and r is true. In symbols: p and $(q$ or $r) = (p$ and $q)$ or $(p$ and $r)$. This obvious principle is valid in classical logic but not in quantum logic.

Quantum physicist David Finkelstein (quoted in Herbert, p. 21) concluded: Einstein threw out the classical concept of time; Bohr throws out the classic concept of truth...Our classical ideas of logic are simply wrong in a basic practical way.[71]

In ordinary logic, a train either is or is not moving northward out of the Oakland station at five miles per hour. But quantum physicists do not accept that a given electron must either have or not have a certain momentum at a particular place. In an often repeated experiment, a beam of light is shined through a filter that absorbs all but horizontally polarized light. A second filter, placed behind the first, absorbs all but vertically polarized light. Any pair of crossed polarizers blocks all light from passing through, so the pair of filters is opaque. But a third filter can be placed between the other two, and light shines through. Herbert[72], discussing the experiment, illustrated the situation with an analogy: Suppose we pass animals through a gate which lets through only horses and rejects cows. Next we pass these horses through a second gate which lets through only black animals and rejects white ones. Only animals which are both horses and black can pass both gates. To our surprise, approximately half of such animals turn out to be cows!

---

70. Putnam, H. (1968) Is logic empirical? In Cohen, R. & Wartofsky, M. (eds.), *Boston Studies in the Philosophy of Science*, vol. 5 (Dordrecht: Reidel), pp. 216–241.

71. Herbert, N. (1985) *Quantum Reality: Beyond the New Physics*. NY: Anchor Press.

72. Herbert, N. (1985) *Quantum Reality: Beyond the New Physics*. NY: Anchor Press.

Reason Doesn't Tell about the World

Consider yet another syllogism: All A is B. Some C is not B. Therefore, some C is not A. Whether or not you judge the reasoning valid, unless you know what A, B, and C represent, you have not increased your knowledge of the world. Some mathematicians deliberately explore premises with no apparent real world connections, and their work often turns out to have practical implications. But in one important respect, logical conclusions from syllogistic reasoning are always uninformative. The conclusions rearrange information but present nothing that wasn't already available in the original premises. All reasoning either manipulates abstractions without connecting them to the real world or assumes prior knowledge. In either case, reasoning cannot be the foundation of real world knowledge. In short, any reasoned argument must have premises that had to come from somewhere. So, knowledge of the world can't begin with reasoning.

"Pure logical thinking cannot yield us any knowledge of the empirical world; all knowledge of reality starts from experience and ends in it. Propositions arrived at by purely logical means are completely empty as regards reality."—Albert Einstein

"The supreme triumph of reason is to cast doubt upon its own validity."—Miguel de Unamuno

"Reason's last step is the recognition that there are an infinite number of things which are beyond it."—Blaise Pascal

Chapter 10

Pillar 4: Empiricism Except for Science

Empiricism: the belief that all knowledge is derived from sense-experience.

Consider another syllogism: Tia is older than Eli. Eli is older than Rosie. Therefore, Tia is older than Rosie. If Tia, Eli, and Rosie are fictional individuals, the syllogism tells nothing about the world. If they are real, then the two premises—Tia is older than Eli and Eli is older than Rosie—are based on some sort of observation. All reasoning starts with premises that are either abstract and lead to abstract conclusions; or concrete and based on observation.

> *"All our knowledge has its origins in our perceptions."*
> —Leonardo da Vinci

Human sensory apparatus is nothing special. Bats hear sounds far beyond the human range, eagles have better eyesight than the most eagle-eyed human, moths smell pheromones in incredibly minute concentrations, and the taste receptors of supposedly non-discriminating pigs put human palates to shame. Other animals sense stimuli of which we are unaware. Some bird species respond to magnetic fluctuations, sawfish detect electrical voltages, and some fish detect tiny vibrations in water. Electromagnetic waves exist with an enormous range of frequencies, and humans see only a tiny portion of the spectrum. Honeybees and various other animals might consider even normally sighted humans blind, or at least seriously visually impaired. See Figure 5.

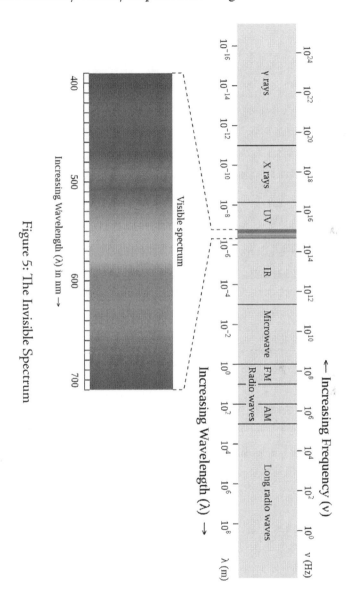

Figure 5: The Invisible Spectrum

Despite the limitations of our sensory systems, they are the portals through which (apparent) knowledge enters. Hardnosed empiricists believe that all knowledge comes through observations and inferences deduced from them. They assume that long-term survival would be impossible without accurate mechanisms for representing the world. The discussion on p. 52 on evolution of reasoning abilities shows that their view is incorrect.

Yet empiricism seems hard to dispute. Denial is an affront to common sense. In the 17th century, George Berkeley issued a denial. He said that only thoughts are real and matter does not exist. Samuel Johnson answered by kicking a large stone and saying, "I refute him thus." Johnson's response is often cited as an effective rebuttal. Not hardly.

Almost all important observations are second—or third—or tenth—hand. Few people have walked on the moon or seen the chromosomes of a fruit fly, and nobody I know attended the signing of the Magna Carta. Furthermore, observations don't help distinguish truth from illusion or tell about underlying reality. Mental institutions are crammed with people who hear voices, speak with long-dead relatives, and commune with God. Psychiatrists say they hallucinate. The visions of "normal" people are in the majority but not necessarily more soundly based.

Knowledge that Comes from Direct Sensory Experiences

An ancient Indian parable tells the story of six blind men who describe an elephant. The first man touches the elephant's side and says that an elephant is like a wall. The second touches a tusk and says that an elephant is like a spear. The third touches a trunk and says that an elephant is like a snake. For the fourth it's a knee and "like a tree." For the fifth, an ear and "like a fan," and for the sixth, the tail and "like a rope." The point is that each of the blind men apprehend only a tiny portion of reality. The parable hints at the problem but doesn't go far enough. The smug narrator, despite being sighted, observed incompletely. He could not have described the elephant with details obvious to its family, or to lions, fleas, or eagles.

"The human being is a blind man who dreams that he can see."
—Friedrich Hebbel

In his fascinating book *The Man Who Mistook His Wife for a Hat*, neurologist Oliver Sacks devoted a chapter to an intelligent man with healthy eyes whose behavior justified the title. The man also greeted fire hydrants and parking meters as though they were children.

Research on Perception

Our visual systems are constructed so that the images focused on our retinas are upside down. Our brains turn the images right side up. In 1897, George Stratten experimented on inverted vision.[73] He wore goggles that inverted everything he saw. His retinal images were right-side up and his world appeared upside down. At first he found it difficult, but within a few days his brain adapted to the inverted world and he was even able to ride a bicycle.

Visual stimuli are typically routed to the thalamus and from there to the visual cortex for processing. The cortex interprets the information and sends impulses to the next structure in the chain, the amygdala. The amygdala releases the appropriate neurotransmitters and hormones. But if the visual stimulus indicates imminent danger, the thalamus bypasses the cortex and sends the signal straight to the amygdala. The individual may then experience a powerful emotion without knowing why.

Please read the words in Figure 6.

Why did the chicken cross the the road?

Figure 6: Did you catch the second "the?"
Many people don't.

People with injuries to neural pathways connecting portions of the retina to certain parts of the brain become functionally blind.

---

73. Stratten, G. (1897) https://www.cns.nyu.edu/~nava/courses/psych_and_brain/pdfs/Stratton_1896.pdf

They deny being able to see, and all conventional measures of visual functioning support their claim. If a pear is held in front of them, they will claim to see nothing and the pupils of their eyes won't move or change in size. But if asked to guess which type of fruit has just been presented, they will say (while insisting that it's only a wild guess) "pear." The phenomenon has been reported often enough that it has been given a name, blindsight.[74] There have also been cases of deafhearing—people who lose the conscious experience of sound but remain capable of making responses based on noises.

Even completely sane people experience occasional sensory distortions. Did you ever think you heard the phone ring or your baby cry and then realize you were mistaken? It happens. Psychologists study illusions to which we're all susceptible. A book can show only visual examples, but illusions have been identified for every known sensory modality. For more visual illusions than the ones shown below, go to https://www.pcmag.com/news/21-optical-illusions-that-prove-your-brain-sucks.

For an example of an auditory illusion, go to: https://video.search.yahoo.com/yhs/search;_ylt=AwrVq7F6nkReZ-FUAzhwPxQt.;_ylu=X3oDMTByZDNzZTI1BGNvbG-8DZ3ExBHBvcwMyBHZ0aWQDBHNlYwNzYw—?p=mc-gurk+effect&fr=yhs-avast-securebrowser&hspart=avast&hsimp=yhs-securebrowser#id=7&vid=49ae8269dff-85c5e6b28383feca39f76&action=view. (If unavailable, type "Mc-Gurk effect.")

---

74. Celesia, G. (2010) Visual perception and awareness: a modular system. *J Psychophysiology.* 24: 62–67. doi:10.1027/0269-8803/a000014.

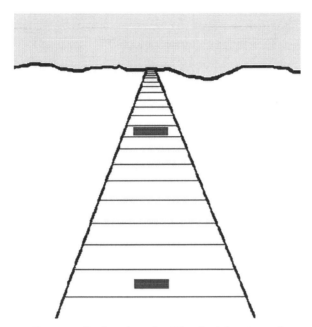

Figure 7: Railroad tracks: The thick horizontal
bars are the same length.

Figure 8: Building with parallel lines: The horizontal
lines are parallel to each other.

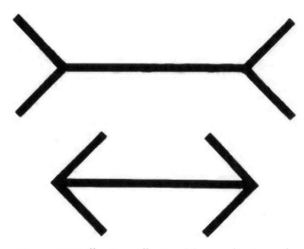

Figure 9: Muller-Lyer illusion: The two horizontal lines are the same length.

Researchers asked students from two colleges to watch a film that featured questionable officiating calls made during a football game between teams from the two colleges. The students were more likely to see the referees' calls as correct when it favored their school than when it favored their rival.[75]

"Some things have to be believed to be seen."—Ralph Hodgson

Empiricists Fight Back—Unsuccessfully

Empiricists don't insist that we see the world with total accuracy. They acknowledge the occurrence of errors such as hallucinations and sensory illusions, but they say that hallucinations are rare even among demented and intoxicated people; and illusions play a trivial role in daily life. Their conclusion is that sensory data are generally accurate. Rene Descartes claimed that God is good so he wouldn't let us be deceived on such a large scale as skeptical doubts suggest. Philosophers Gilbert Ryle and John Austin were encouraged by the evidence that sensory systems make occasional

---

75. Hastorf, A. & Cantril, H. (1954) They saw a game; a case study. *J Abnormal Social Psych*, 49: 129–134. https://doi.org/10.1037/h0057880

errors. They argued that our ability to detect illusions is evidence for the general trustworthiness of the senses. That is, from the fact that imperfections are occasionally but infrequently detected, they made the unwarranted inferences that imperfections are rare and perceptions are typically accurate. Adultery is also occasionally but infrequently detected—should we use that as evidence that adultery is rare?

Ryle and Austin asserted that inaccurate perceptual mechanisms are constantly eliminated by natural selection. But the view that long-term survival would be impossible without accurate mechanisms for representing the world is incorrect. See the discussion on p. 52 on evolution of reasoning abilities. Ryle and Austin were brilliant philosophers. Their argument supports the conclusion that human reasoning is fraught with pitfalls.

When Broad and Wade wrote about several cases of fraud in science,[76] empiricist Daniel Koshland, editor of the prestigious journal *Science*, wrote: "We must recognize that 99.9999 per cent of reports are accurate and true."[77] As shown in the next chapter, he seriously underestimated the incidence.

Reliable estimation of the frequency of illusions, delusions, and hallucinations is impossible. You may be experiencing one this very moment and not know it. Abraham Lincoln (if he existed) may have been wrong—It may well be possible to fool all of the people all of the time. Furthermore, even if our sensory apparatus rivaled Superman's, complete with X-ray vision, we'd still face two insurmountable obstacles to certain knowledge. First, the fidelity of human memory is, to put it charitably, considerably less than high. Nietzsche summed up the second obstacle in an epigram, "There are no facts, only interpretations." That is, an infinite number of conflicting interpretations are compatible with any given perception. Maybe it's churlish to point out yet another problem with

76. Broad, W. & Wade, N. (1982) *Betrayers of the Truth.* NY: Simon & Schuster.

77. Koshland, D. (1987) Fraud in science. *Science*, 235:141.

empiricism but, strictly speaking, it's self-refuting—empiricism is the claim that all knowledge is gained through the senses—a claim about knowledge that is not gained through the senses.

"We don't see things as they are, we see them as we are."
—Anais Nin

Our Low Fidelity Memories

"Memory says, 'I did that.' Pride replies, 'I could not have done that.' Eventually, memory yields."—Nietzsche

Nazi propagandist Joseph Goebbels said: "Repeat a lie often enough and it becomes the truth." Experimental evidence supports his assertion. Hasher and colleagues asked college students to look at a list of sixty plausible statements concerning matters about which they were unlikely to know anything. Some statements were true and some false. Two weeks later the students received a second list, and two weeks after that a third. Twenty statements appeared on all three lists, and the other forty were unique to each list. The students indicated their belief in each statement. During each session they showed about the same level of confidence in the truth of the one-time only statements, but they became increasingly confident from the first session to the second to the third in the truth of the repeated statements, whether they were true or false.[78]

Psychologist Elizabeth Loftus showed subjects a videotape of an automobile accident. Then she asked some subjects, "How fast were the cars going when they hit each other?" She asked others, "How fast were the cars going when they smashed into each other?" Afterwards, the subjects estimated the speeds of the cars. The ones who had heard "smashed into" estimated higher speeds than the "hit" subjects. In a second study, she assigned participants to one of three groups. They all viewed the accident film and were

---

78. Hasher, L. et al. (1977) Frequency and the conference of referential validity. *J Verbal Learning and Verbal Behavior*, 16: 107 – 112.

then asked either, "How fast were the cars going when they hit each other?" or "How fast were the cars going when they smashed into each other?" or nothing at all about the speed. They returned one week later and, without watching the film again, answered a series of questions. The critical question was, "Did you see any broken glass?" (The film did not show any broken glass.) More than twice as many subjects in the "smashed" group as in either of the other groups reported that they had seen broken glass. Her classic studies are relevant to discussions about the trustworthiness of both perception and memory.[79]

We can't trust that any of our memories are accurate. They are not perfect replicas of events we've experienced, and they are not played back like tape players play back recordings. Each recalled memory is actually an elaboration, with new details often included. Long-term memories are very susceptible to change.

False memories can easily be implanted. Loftus asked volunteers who had visited Disneyland as children, "Remember that wonderful day when Bugs Bunny hugged you at Disneyland?" Many remembered and gave many details. But the event never happened—Bugs Bunny is not a Disney character. In another study she had volunteers carry out or only imagine doing several tasks: common ones like flipping a coin and unusual ones like crushing a Hershey's kiss with a dental floss container. Later, fifteen percent insisted they had performed some of the actions. Loftus and colleagues have conducted more than 200 experiments involving over 20,000 individuals that show how exposure to misinformation induces memory distortion. People "recalled" a conspicuous barn in a bucolic scene that contained no buildings at all, broken glass and tape recorders that were not in the scenes they viewed, a white instead of a blue vehicle in a crime scene, and Minnie Mouse when they actually saw Mickey Mouse. In another study, Loftus convinced between twenty percent and forty percent of subjects to pay more for strawberry ice cream after suggesting, falsely, that

79. Loftus, E. (1996) *Eyewitness Testimony*. Cambridge: Harvard U Press.

the subjects loved the flavor as a child. For other examples, go to https://www.youtube.com/watch?v=58AxIGmjEP4.

When Loftus was fourteen, her mother drowned. She had no recollection of viewing the death scene and had always thought that her aunt had discovered the body. Thirty years later, an uncle told her that Loftus herself had found the body. Over the next several days, many details came flooding back—her terror, the police cars, and the stretcher with the white blanket tucked around her mother's body. Several days later, her brother told her that the uncle was wrong. The aunt *had* discovered the body. Several relatives confirmed it.

While interviewing people about a video they had watched, Daniel Gurney and colleagues performed misleading hand gestures to suggest inaccurate information about details in the video.[80] For example, the interviewer stroked his chin to suggest that someone had a beard, although the man in the video did not have one. The interviewees who saw chin stroking were much more likely than those who did not to recall seeing a beard.

Loftus's research sparked interest in the possibility that some people are in prison because the faulty memory of eyewitnesses had led to wrongful convictions. The Innocence Project estimates that in the United States, between 2.3% and five percent of all prisoners are innocent.[81] As of November 17, 2019, the Innocence Project has worked on 189 successful DNA-based exonerations.[82]

If you hear family stories of your childhood often enough, you may come to believe them even if they're not true. If you see a misleading news story or video, your recollection of what a politician actually said or did can be transformed. *Slate* writer William

---

80. British Psychological Society (2012) Influencing others through gestures: Pitfalls for eyewitnesses. *Science Daily*, 4/20.

81. How many innocent people are there in prison? The Innocence Project. Retrieved from *Wikipedia*, 6/1/2020.

82. DNA exonerations in the United States. The Innocence Project. Retrieved from Wikipedia, 6/1/2020.

Saletan showed readers photos of three real events and one doctored image of a fake event from a pool of five fakes. One fake showed President Bush on vacation with a baseball player during Hurricane Katrina. Another showed President Obama shaking hands with Iranian President Mahmoud Ahmadinejad. Readers were asked if they recalled the event and to describe how they felt when first hearing about it.[83]

Half the time, readers said they remembered the fake event and even reported seeing it on the news. When told that one of the events was a fake, they guessed a real event sixty-three percent of the time. Liberals were more likely than conservatives to remember Bush's fake vacation, and conservatives were more likely to recall Obama's fake handshake.

Ulric Neisser questioned 106 university students a few days after the space shuttle Challenger exploded in 1986. He asked them to write down answers about specific aspects of their memories: *How did you hear about it? Where were you? What were you doing? Who was with you?* and *How did you feel?* He also asked them to give 5-point confidence ratings to their memories. Most gave their memories a rating of 5—they recalled exactly where they were and what they were doing when they heard the news. But when questioned again 2.5 years later, although still certain that their memories were accurate, almost half of them gave different answers. Below are two reports from the same person.[84]

> January, 1986: "I was in my religion class and some people walked in and started talking about the explosion. I didn't know any details except that it had exploded."

> September, 1988: "When I first heard about the explosion I

---

83. https://slate.com/technology/2010/05/slate-conducted-a-mass-experiment-in-altering-political-memories-were-you-fooled.html

84. Neisser, U. & Harsch, N. (1992) Phantom flashbulbs: False recollections of hearing the news about Challenger. In Winograd, E. & Neisser, U. (Eds) *Affect and Accuracy in Recall: Studies of 'Flashbulb' Memories* (pp. 9-31). NY: Cambridge U Press.

was sitting in my freshman dorm room with my roommate and we were watching TV. It came on a news flash."

Neisser, like Loftus, devoted his career to studying memory in part because of his own false memory. He described how he learned about the attack on Pearl Harbor: "I recall sitting in the living room of our house – we only lived in that house for one year, but I remember it well listening to a baseball game on the radio. The game was interrupted by an announcement of the attack, and I rushed upstairs to tell my mother." Years later, Neisser realized that this memory was definitely incorrect. Pearl Harbor was attacked on Dec. 7, and there is no baseball on the radio in December.

The philosopher Jean Piaget also wrote about an early incident.[85] He described sitting in his pram and being pushed by his nurse, when a man tried to kidnap him. His nurse "bravely tried to stand between me and the thief…Then a crowd gathered, a policeman came up, and the man took to his heels. I can still see the whole scene and can even place it near the tube station."

Piaget's vivid memory, which persisted into his early adulthood, was of an event that never happened. The nurse wrote to his parents years later saying that she wanted to confess her past sins and return the watch she'd been given as a reward for saving the baby's life. She had made up the entire incident.

Matthew Hutson[86] begins an interesting article by requesting of readers: Read this list of words: table, sit, legs, seat, soft, desk, arm, sofa, wood, cushion, rest, stool. Now count to 30.

You can be a subject. Read the list once more. Then, before reading on, go to footnote 86 and answer the question there.

Huston noted that many people answer yes. Then he notes: If so, I've just implanted a false memory—read the list again. In similar tests using lists such as this, people usually say they saw the

---

85. Piaget, J. (1962) *Plays, Dreams and Imitation in Childhood.* NY: Norton.

86. Hutson, M. (2019) https://www.psychologytoday.com/us/
articles/201903/how-memory-became-weaponized
Did you spot the word chair?

word that is related to the others.

"When I was younger I could remember anything, whether it had happened or not."—Mark Twain

"Each of us is the accumulation of our memories."
—A.L. McGinnis

For a dash of humility, watch as a chimpanzee takes a memory test: https://m.youtube.com/watch?v=TC1nJ61l-h4

"Knowledge" that Comes from Other Sources

Any form of information that comes from other sources may be incorrect because of unintentional error, misguided theory, or deliberate deception. The next sections deal with deception.

When we rely on others for our knowledge, we run the risk that they may try to deceive us. I give many examples in the appendices. If they seem repetitious and excessive, note two points. First, no single example of deception by individuals or organizations will shock anyone who keeps up with current events. The repetitions show that the examples are common occurrences, not isolated incidents. Even so, *they are only a tiny sample of actual cases.* Taken collectively, they indicate that most people are repeatedly deceived about many things that matter to them. Second, undoubtedly many important examples—including many that nobody has detected, yet or forever—have been omitted.

"Men are so simple and so much inclined to obey immediate needs that a deceiver will never lack victims for his deception."—Machiavelli

"Folks everywhere—the shrewd, the simple, the powerful and the weak—have been taken in by hoaxes and scams since the beginning of recorded time."—Carl Sifakis, *Hoaxes and Scams*

"In the big lie there is always a certain force of credibility; because the broad masses of a nation are always more easily corrupted in

the deeper strata of their emotional nature than consciously or voluntarily; and thus in the primitive simplicity of their minds they more readily fall victims to the big lie than the small lie, since they themselves often tell small lies in little matters but would be ashamed to resort to large-scale falsehoods. It would never come into their heads to fabricate colossal untruths, and they would not believe that others could have the impudence to distort the truth so infamously. Even though the facts which prove this to be so may be brought clearly to their minds, they will still doubt and waver and will continue to think that there may be some other explanation. For the grossly impudent lie always leaves traces behind it, even after it has been nailed down, a fact which is known to all expert liars in this world and to all who conspire together in the art of lying.”—Adolf Hitler, *Mein Kampf*

“Those who manipulate the unseen mechanism of society constitute an invisible government which is the true ruling power of our country. We are governed, our minds molded, our tastes formed, our ideas suggested, largely by men we have never heard of. This is a logical result of the way in which our democratic society is organized. Vast numbers of human beings must cooperate in this manner if they are to live together as a smoothly functioning society. In almost every act of our lives whether in the sphere of politics or business in our social conduct or our ethical thinking, we are dominated by the relatively small number of persons who understand the mental processes and social patterns of the masses. It is they who pull the wires that control the public mind.”—Edward L. Bernays, *Propaganda*

By the time they reach adolescence, most people realize that TV commercials and ads in newspapers and magazines often distort the truth. Our world of used car salesmen, pyramid schemes, and politicians gives good reason for generalized suspicion. We are constantly fed inaccurate and misleading information. The stage magician seems to saw the pretty woman in half, Richard Nixon says “I am not a crook,” Bill Clinton says “I did not have sex with that woman,” the Secretary of Defense claims there are weapons of mass destruction in Baghdad and he knows where they are, Pat Robertson proclaims himself a man of God, Donald Trump speaks.

Those are petty deceptions. We are very possibly deceived on a much larger scale, and a veil of unknown but substantial thickness shields us from knowledge imparted by others. Philosophers and science fiction writers often imagine scenarios in which people are perpetually fooled. Paranoid schizophrenics may live in such a world. Or, maybe paranoids see clearly and it's the rest of us who are fooled. Philosopher Rene Descartes conjectured an evil and powerful demon devoted to deceiving humankind and rendering wrong everything we think we know, but a supernatural being is unnecessary. There are people alive today with enough wealth, power, and cleverness to do demonic work. For Descartes' notion to be taken seriously, three conditions must be satisfied. In normal criminal investigations, prosecutors attempt to establish who had the motive, means, and opportunity to carry out the crime. The same strategy applies here.

Motives to Deceive

Any of the powerful human motives could serve as backdrop for a large-scale deceit: love, hate, greed, jealousy. Curiosity is sufficient motivation for many scientists. They bring Descartes' demon to life for millions of laboratory animals each year. For example, biologist Roger Sperry removed the eyes of frogs, rotated them 180 degrees, and placed them back in their sockets. The nerve fibers regenerated and the frogs were able to see again. But when Sperry dangled a fly upwards and to the right, the frogs invariably struck downwards and to the left (which reinforces the view that even seemingly direct perceptions are fallible and can be manipulated by others). Other researchers have raised cats in total darkness and given monkeys powerful mind-altering drugs. PETA (People for Ethical Treatment of Animals) has literature citing hundreds of other examples.

Herodotus wrote of the 7th century B.C. Egyptian pharaoh

Psamtik who wondered how early experience affects language learning. So he isolated two infants and appointed caretakers to provide food and shelter but never to speak in their presence. The Holy Roman Emperor Frederick II conducted essentially the same experiment after taking a group of infants from their mothers. All the children died. He also locked convicts in an airtight room until they suffocated, then tried to watch their souls escape when he opened the door.

There's no need to search the distant past. The atrocities committed in Nazi concentration camps are well known.

The 2018 documentary film *Three Identical Strangers* tells the true story of a set of American identical triplets born to a single mother in 1961. When they were six-months-old, under the auspices of the Jewish Board of Guardians and the Louise Wise adoption agency, they were each placed with a different family—three families that had vastly different parenting styles and economic levels. Neither the adoptive parents nor the sons knew about the siblings. The sons discovered each other purely by accident when they were nineteen. They quickly became very close, but all three struggled with mental health issues and one committed suicide. The separations had been done as part of a large study to track the development of genetically identical siblings raised in different circumstances. The practice of separating twins at birth continued in the state of New York until the 1980s.

Appendix 2 lists a very partial sample of studies conducted within the past 100 years by reputable U.S. scientists: Skip Appendix 2 if you have a weak stomach. Differences between the Nazi and U.S. experiments are subtle at best.

During the 1992 U.S. presidential election campaign, incumbent George Bush declared repeatedly that he would do anything to remain president. Isn't it within the realm of possibility that some future winning candidate really would do anything? An evil dictator could conceivably do frog-like experiments on humans, and the victims would not necessarily be aware. Iraqi dictator Saddam Hussein gassed thousands of his own citizens. Had it served his purposes, he certainly wouldn't have hesitated to use mind-altering substances on them. What if the Nazis had won the war?

One apparent problem with my view is that perpetrator(s) would have to apply immense effort with extraordinary skill to create an entire universe of illusions. But people with special talents often attempt to use those talents to their fullest. Zoo keepers and biology laboratory workers have created elaborate artificial worlds for their subjects and take pride in the correctness of tiny details. Below are a few illustrative examples of people who acted out obsessions. (They may not be true, but they have been detailed in books by reputable authors and publishers. If they are fabrications, they illustrate another of my points.)

- The mathematician Carl Friedrich Gauss tried to solve a problem while his wife was sick. The doctor came to tell him she was dying. Never looking up, Gauss said "Tell her to wait a moment till I'm through."[87]

- The Badwater 135 mile long race starts in Death Valley in *July* and ends on Mount Whitney, covering three mountain ranges for a total of 14,600 feet of cumulative vertical ascent and 6,100 feet of cumulative descent. Double amputee Chris Moon completed the 2013 Badwater, and seventy-five-year-old Jack Denness completed the 2010 in a little more than fifty-nine hours.[88]

- Charles and Ray Eames obsessed with refining the foot/glide on their upholstered wire chair. After introducing it in 1951, they received feedback that the feet of the chair would often crack after years of use. So they worked to refine it and introduced a new metal and rubber foot/glide design in 1953. But this new-and-better version also often deteriorated after years of use. So they tried again and introduced a

---

87. http://datatorch.com/Science/Scientists_Mini_Stories.aspx?id=42

88. https://www.mnn.com/health/fitness-well-being/
stories/11-of-the-most-difficult-ultramarathons-in-the-world

new foot/glide design in 1957.[89]

- Steve Jobs was described as "passionate to the point of obsessive about design." He insisted that his computers look perfect both inside and out.[90]

- In 1959, seventeen-year-old Mauri Rose Kirby spent 211 days, nine hours and thirty-three minutes in a three-by-three-by-six-foot box. She had a phone, a sleeping bag, and an electric heater in her perch. She had issues with subzero temperatures, high winds, and crackpots.[91]

- In May, 1986, Ken Owen lay on a bed of 600 very sharp six-inch nails spaced two inches apart. During that time he had fifty-one concrete blocks smashed on his chest.[92]

- The Watts Towers are a collection of seventeen interconnected sculptural towers, architectural structures, and individual sculptural features and mosaics in Watts, Los Angeles. The tallest tower is 107 feet high. The entire collection was designed and built solely by construction worker and tile mason Sabato Rodia over a period of thirty-three years from 1921 to 1954. He used salvaged steel rods, bed frames, and cement for the framework; and glass bottle fragments, ceramic tiles, and seashells for the thick coral-like surface. The Watts Towers were designated a National Historic Landmark and a California Historical Landmark in 1990.[93]

- Actress Colleen Moore enlisted the help of more than 700 talented professionals, including surgical instrument lighting

89. https://jkglei.com/obsession/

90. https://www.smithsonianmag.com/arts-culture/how-steve-jobs-love-of-simplicity-fueled-a-design-revolution-23868877/

91. https://www.indystar.com/story/news/history/retroindy/2015/03/09/mom-daughter-record-pole-sitters/24638079/

92. https://babylonwales.blogspot.com/2009/01/youve-made-your-bed-of-nails.html

93. https://en.wikipedia.org/wiki/Watts_Towers

specialists, Beverly Hills jewelers, and Chinese jade crafts-men, to build an astonishing miniature world. It took nine years and nearly $500,000 in 1930s dollars to complete the eleven-room aluminum castle. Housed in Chicago's Muse-um of Science and Industry, the nine-feet square aluminum two-story structure weighs about a ton and contains more than 2,000 miniatures. All the appliances are functional.[94]

But a motive isn't really necessary. Descartes' demon would not have to be perverse or even alive. Suppose, for example, that some atmospheric element distorts human perceptions.

Means

Individuals perverse enough to do terrible things would not have to be all-powerful—just powerful enough—and that includes a great many people. The likely existence of non-terrestrial intelli-gent life increases the possibilities considerably. Some deception tactics require sophisticated technology. Others do not. Below are some possibilities.

Drugs

At a dose of about fifty to 100 micrograms, the drug LSD pro-foundly distorts perceptions and cognition. The small spice tins sold in supermarkets hold about 28 million micrograms, so a spice tin could hold enough LSD for 280,000 100-microgram trips. LSD was first synthesized in 1938. In 1953, the CIA authorized project MK-ULTRA, designed to test LSD and other drugs for possible wartime use. The idea was to find substances that would allow the CIA to control people's minds and make them do things that they would never otherwise do. So, drugs were administered to unsuspecting prisoners and others. The mobster Whitey Bulg-er was injected with LSD over fifty times when he was a young

---

94. https://www.thevintagenews.com/2018/04/06/colleen-moore-dollhouse-2/

prison inmate. Bulger went on to terrorize South Boston as the notoriously violent leader of the Winter Hill Gang.[95]

Chemists with the Army Chemical Corps developed quinuclidinyl benzilate (BZ), which causes symptoms such as headaches, giddiness, disorientation, auditory and visual hallucinations, and maniacal behavior that usually lasts about three days but in some sensitive people persists for as long as six weeks. Nowadays, computers help chemists synthesize new drugs that act on highly specific parts of the brain. Articles published in reputable scientific journals describe new drugs far more powerful than LSD. Who knows about classified research in government laboratories!

Electrical Stimulation of the Brain

More than half a century ago, flamboyant neurophysiologist Jose Delgado implanted electrodes into a bull's brain. Delgado passed an electric current through the medial region of the hypothalamus, and that induced the bull to charge him. When it got within a few feet, he stimulated a different area that caused the bull to stop dead in its tracks. Today, graduate students in physiology, psychology, and various other fields routinely implant electrodes and cause animals to start or stop eating, drinking, copulating, sleeping, waking, nest building, nursing, and fighting. The animals can be controlled from a distance. Several species have been controlled remotely including moths, cockroaches, rats, mice, and pigeons. In 2002, scientists remotely controlled rats from a laptop 500 yards away. The rats could be instructed to turn left or right, climb trees and ladders, navigate piles of rubble, and jump from different heights. They could even be commanded into brightly lit areas, which rats usually avoid.[96]

---

95. Isikoff, M. (2020) *Yahoo News*. https://www.yahoo.com/news/did-the-ci-as-notorious-mind-control-program-create-an-infamous-killer-145804316.html

96. Talwar, S. *et al.* (2002) Rat navigation guided by remote control. *Nature* 417: 37–38 https://doi.org/10.1038/417037a

Yukiyasu Kamitani and his team had human subjects lie in a functional magnetic resonance imaging (fMRI) scanner while connected to an electroencephalography (EEG) machine. As soon as the EEG machine indicated that they were dreaming, they were awakened and asked to recall what their dream was about. This process was repeated nearly 200 times for each subject. The team recorded dream appearances of twenty key objects, such as "male" or "room," and then developed an algorithm to find patterns between any of the objects that the person had seen and specific brain activity. They eventually became able to guess with seventy-five to eighty percent accuracy whether any of the twenty objects had occurred in a subject's dream.[97]

Computer scientists and cognitive neuroscientists put volunteers in an fMRI scanner, showed them drawings of ten different objects, and asked them to think about the objects. Each object activated many brain locations. For instance, thinking about swinging a hammer activated the motor area whereas thinking what a hammer is used for and its shape activated other areas. The researchers were able, from the characteristic activation patterns, to accurately determine which of the ten drawings a participant was viewing. From these last two achievements, it's a small step to stimulating the appropriate brain areas to induce specific dreams and other activities.[98]

FakeApp

In recent years an extremely powerful and frightening method for deceiving large numbers of people has been developed. FakeApp, which can be downloaded for free, allows users to manipulate digital media. For example, they can take a picture of a face and put

97. Akst, J. (2012) Decoding Dreams. https://www.the-scientist.com/notebook/decoding-dreams-39990

98. https://www.cnet.com/news/60-minutes-video-tech-that-reads-your-mind/

it on a different body. It takes only a little skill to combine fake images with fake, realistic, audio. So, FakeApp has been used to put celebrities into pornographic films. From there it's a short step to smearing politicians or framing people for crimes or even having a world leader declaring war on another country. FakeApp gives ample reason for doubting what we see with our own eyes. In May, 2019 a video went viral of Democratic Speaker of the House Nancy Pelosi giving a speech while apparently drunk. It was a doctored video. Holland Cotter of *The New York Times* wrote, "The time was, we thought of photographs as recorders of reality. Now we know they largely invent reality."[99] To see FakeApp in action, go to https://www.youtube.com/watch?v=T76bK2t2r8g.

Computer scientist Hany Farid said, "You have the technology to create sophisticated and compelling fakes. You have a delivery mechanism with unprecedented speed and reach. You have a polarized public willing to believe the worst about adversaries. And then you have bad actors, whether state-sponsored agents disrupting a global election, people trying to incite violence, or those looking to monetize fake news for personal gain. This is the perfect storm of an information war. It is a war our memories have not evolved to win."[100]

Other forms of social media that reach large numbers of people can be manipulated for nefarious reasons. A Twitter account that claimed to represent a national antifascist organization urged protesters to loot white neighborhoods. It was actually run by a white nationalist group. The account falsely aligned itself with ongoing *Black Lives Matter* protests nationwide. One of its messages that was retweeted hundreds of times called for protesters to "move into residential areas" and "take what's ours."[101]

---

99. Cotter, R. (2008). Well, it looks like truth. *New York Times*, Jan 18.

100. https://www.psychologytoday.com/us/articles/201903/
    how-memory-became-weaponized

101. https://www.yahoo.com/news/antifa-twitter-account-called-loot-
    ing-141834707.html

Opportunity

Dictators, neuroscientists, chemists, reclusive billionaires, television executives, computer programmers, artificial intelligence experts, and many others have many opportunities to deceive people on an enormous scale.

Natural Selection

In a 1940 book, biologist H.B. Cott drew parallels between Darwinian evolution and international arms races. Cott wrote:

> Before asserting that the deceptive appearance of a grasshopper or butterfly is unnecessarily detailed, we must first ascertain what are the powers of perception and discrimination of the insects' natural enemies. Not to do so is like asserting that the armour of a battle cruiser is too heavy, or the range of her guns too great, without inquiring into the nature and effectiveness of the enemy's armament.

> Just as greater speed in the pursued has developed in relation to aggressive weapons, so the perfection of concealing devices has evolved in response to increased powers of perception.

Evolutionary arms races are costly, and the biochemical machinery used to locate prey or avoid predators is unavailable for mating or resisting disease. Sometimes the cost of avoiding predation is too high. If a predator exploits but doesn't kill its prey, the prey may never learn. If a prey species greatly outnumbers the predators, only a small percentage of the prey fall victim and the survivors never evolve countermeasures. For example, bolas spiders dangle on strands from overhangs and produce an odor that mimics the odor of female moths. Male moths are attracted, and the bolas spider swings a second strand like a lasso. If the spider misses, the moth typically flies back within range. Male moths that didn't respond to the odor of females would not leave any descendants.

Biologist Niko Tinbergen noted that black headed gulls always carry empty egg shells out of their nests and drop the shells some distance away. Tinbergen conducted a series of experiments which showed that nests that contain empty eggshells are more likely to be attacked by predators. The farther away the eggshell was carried, the safer were the remaining unhatched eggs still in the nest. Tinbergen's work earned him a Nobel Prize, and many current scientists follow his lead. They assume that if all animals of a species engage in a certain behavior, the behavior must have an important function for members of that species.

Biologist Richard Dawkins showed that the matter is not so simple. He wrote that when scientists such as Tinbergen see an animal performing behavior pattern A in situation P, their immediate reaction is to ask: "In what way is behavior pattern A good for the animal in situation P?" According to Dawkins, that might be the wrong question. Some other animal or plant may be manipulating the animal, perhaps behind the scenes, for its own purposes.[102] Below are examples:

- Certain flukes have a snail as a host. To reach the next stage of their life cycle they must pass from inside the snail to a bird. For this to happen, a bird must eat the snail. The flukes burrow up into the snail's tentacles and can be seen through its skin, pulsating conspicuously. Snails normally avoid light and therefore do not approach the tops of plants. But infected snails actively seek light. This carries them up to the open tops of the plants and makes them more likely to be seen by birds. Birds are attracted by the tentacles, eat them, and send the flukes to their next stage. The change in snail behavior benefits the parasites, not the snails. A scientist who asks: "In what way does its light-seeking behavior benefit the snail?" will not find a correct answer. A fluke is manipulating the snail from behind the scenes.

---

102. Dawkins, R. (1982) *The Extended Phenotype: The Long Reach of the Gene*. Oxford U Press.

- Adult hairworms breed in water and somehow get their young inside of grasshoppers, possibly when the insects drink larvae-infested water. The hairworms pump the insects with chemicals that cause the grasshoppers to leap into water and drown. When the grasshopper hits the water, the worm comes out of its rear end and swims off to find a mate. Hairworms target many other land-based insects.

- Bacteria within our bodies, collectively known as the gut microbiome, outnumber our own cells about 100-fold. They may influence dietary choices by releasing signaling molecules into the gut.[103] The gut links with the immune, endocrine, and nervous systems, so the signals may influence many physiologic and behavioral responses. Microbes may alter the neural signals in the vagus nerve, changing taste receptors to produce toxins to make us feel bad or chemical rewards to make us feel good. The results are not always aligned with our own dietary needs or other interests.

- Parasites do not have to live inside their hosts. Cuckoos lay eggs in the nests of their hosts. The newly hatched cuckoo pushes the host's eggs out of the nest and induces the host to feed it.

- *Toxoplasma gondii* is a microscopic protozoan that causes a disease called toxoplasmosis. Cats, the primary host, transmit the parasite through their feces. Rats that pick up the parasite through soil contaminated with cat feces become fearless near cats and are likely to be eaten by a cat, which starts the cycle all over again. Humans can get infected if they eat undercooked, infected meat; ingest water, soil, or anything else contaminated with cat feces (which can easily occur from changing a cat litter box); or through transmission from a pregnant woman to her unborn baby. Some researchers estimate that more than thirty percent of the human population

---

103. Alcock, J. et al. (2014) Is eating behavior manipulated by the gastrointestinal microbiota? Evolutionary pressures and potential mechanisms. *Bioessays*, DOI:10.1002/bies.201400071.

is infected and has some behaviors manipulated by the parasite. Schizophrenics are more likely than non-schizophrenics to have toxoplasmosis. Infected married women are more likely than noninfected to have affairs. Infected men tend to be more aggressive, and infected humans of both genders tend to have slower reaction times.[104] *Toxoplasma gondii* is one parasite. It seems reasonable to assume that undiscovered others also affect human behavior. Janice Moore's 2002 book, *Parasites and the Behavior of Animals*, has a sixty-page annotated appendix of published studies documenting many kinds of associations between parasites and host behaviors. Below are two additional examples:

A virus called ATCV-1 showed up in human brain tissue several years ago. Researchers checked for it in ninety-two healthy people and found it in forty-three percent of them. Those infected with the virus had shorter attention spans and performed ten percent worse than uninfected people on tests requiring visual processing.[105]

The flu, like many viruses, travels from one host body into another. So, from the flu virus perspective, there is a benefit in having carriers be highly sociable. For the first twenty-four to forty-eight hours after having the flu, people don't show symptoms but *can* transmit it to others. Reiber and colleagues collected data from thirty-six adults who had recently received a flu shot.[106] The flu shot gives recipients a small dose of the virus, so the researchers knew exactly when each individual was exposed. The researchers asked each participant to document the number of individuals that he or she interacted with for the two days prior to obtaining the

---

104. McAuliffe, K. (2012) How your cat is making you crazy. *The Atlantic*, March.

105. Yolken, R. et al. (2014). Chlorovirus ATCV-1 is part of the human oropharyngeal virome and is associated with changes in cognitive functions in humans and mice. *Proc Natl Acad Sci*, 111 (45): 16106–11.

106. Reiber, C. et al. (2010) Change in human social behavior in response to a common vaccine. *Annals of Epidemiology*, 20: 729-33. DOI: 10.1016/j.annepidem.2010.06.014

vaccine and then for two days immediately after receiving it. The number of people with whom the participants interacted during the post-vaccine period was nearly *double* the number they had interacted with during the pre-vaccine period.

As noted above, neurophysiologists can manipulate the behavior of animals by passing current through implanted electrodes. Dawkins asked, "If the brain is vulnerable to such manipulation, should not natural selection, working on other animals, have perfected the power to manipulate?" Our eyes, ears, and noses open into deep parts of our brains, predisposing the brains to be manipulated. Dawkins wrote, "Natural selection would surely favor animals that succeed in manipulating the nervous systems of other animals."

Secret Experiments?

Historian of science Robert Root-Bernstein claimed that ninety percent of scientists who ever lived are alive today, ninety percent of the scientific literature has been written by scientists now alive, and more than ninety percent of research money for science has been spent in the last generation. Since 1660, when the Royal Society was founded in England, the total size of science has increased about a millionfold. The technology for facilitating scientific discovery has been increasing exponentially. An implication of these figures is that for every major discovery made in 1665, about a million should be made each current year. Yet the number of major discoveries per century has remained fairly constant. Root-Bernstein concluded that scientists today aren't being trained properly.[107] A more provocative conclusion is that revolutionary discoveries are being made at the seventeenth century pace and the vast majority of citizens are kept ignorant of them. Imagine a scientist who discovered that a readily available chemical reverses aging. Going public would be disastrous, because nobody would

---

107. Root-Bernstein, R. (1989) *Discovering: Inventing and Solving Problems at the Frontiers of Science.* Cambridge: Harvard U Press.

die and births would continue until all habitable space was used up. Other discoveries might be even more sinister.

Psychologists estimate that Einstein's IQ was about 180. According to the probability distribution of the normal curve, an intelligence of his magnitude occurs only once in 10 million births. Extremely rare. On the other hand, the population of the earth is 7 billion. Probably about 700 people with Einsteinian IQs are alive today. Strange that we haven't heard of them.

Could we all be part of a sophisticated worldwide deception experiment? What if the Nazis did win the war?

Individuals

Other people occasionally lie. Have you ever distorted the truth to parents, siblings, friends, lovers, teachers, employers, or customers? Of course you have, and others have deceived you. We can never be certain of the feelings or intentions of others. As you continue to read, accept that the word 'certain' can justifiably be changed to the phrase 'even mildly confident.' Did I say that people occasionally lie? Let me amend that. Polygraph expert Leonard Saxe said, "Lying has long been a part of everyday life. We couldn't get through the day without being deceptive."[108] Almost ninety percent of college students admitted to having lied to a romantic partner.[109] Feldman and colleagues asked college students, strangers to each other, to talk for ten minutes.[110] They were unaware that the session was being videotaped. Afterwards, they watched the video and identified all lies they had told. Sixty percent admitted to having told at least one lie, and they admitted to an average of 2.92. The students were surprised at the results.

---

108. Kornet, A. (1997) The truth about lying. *Psychology Today*, 5/1.

109. Knox, D. et al. (1993) Sexual lies among university students. *College Student Journal*, 27: 269-72.

110. Feldman, R. (2002) Self-presentation and verbal deception: Do self-presenters lie more? *Basic and Applied Social Psych*, 24: 163-70.

Ariely and colleagues performed several ingenious experiments and looked at a huge amount of data sets—from insurance claims to employment histories to the treatment records of doctors and dentists—to study the extent to which people cheat. They concluded that almost everybody cheats.[111] DePaulo and colleagues asked people between the ages of eighteen and seventy-one to keep a diary of all the lies they told. Most admitted to lying once or twice a day and in about twenty percent of their social exchanges lasting ten or more minutes. Each week they deceived about thirty percent of those with whom they interacted one-on-one, not including trivial comments such as "I'm fine" or "No trouble at all."[112]

The vast majority of big lies—deep betrayals of trust—occur between people in intimate relationships.[113]

> "By the time you swear you're his,
>   Shivering and sighing.
> And he vows his passion is,
>   Infinite, undying.
> Lady make note of this —
>   One of you is lying."
> —Dorothy Parker

Jones and Sigall convinced survey participants that they were connected to an infallible lie detector. Their responses were compared with those from a control group who were asked the same questions but not attached to the device. The responses were considerably different for the two groups.[114]

---

111. Ariely, D. (2012) Why we lie. *Wall Street Journal*, 5/26, p. C1.

112. DePaulo, B. et al. (2004) Serious lies. *Basic & Applied Social Psych*, 26: 147-67.

113. DePaulo, B. et al. (1996) Lying in everyday life. *J Personality Social Psych*, 7: 979-95.

114. Jones, E. & Sigall, H. (1971) The bogus pipeline: A new paradigm for measuring affect and attitude. *Psych Bull*, 76: 349-64.

"Fiction was invented the day Jonah arrived home and told his wife that he was three days late because he had been swallowed by a whale."—Gabriel García Márquez

The poet E.A. Robinson understood our inability to know the true feelings of others.

"Richard Cory" (by E.A. Robinson)

Whenever "Richard Cory" went down town,
We people on the pavement looked at him;
He was a gentleman from sole to crown,
Clean favored, and imperially slim.

And he was always quietly arrayed
And he was always human when he talked;
But still he fluttered pulses when he said,
"Good morning" and he glittered when he walked.

And he was rich—yes, richer than a king,
And admirably schooled in every grace;
In fine, we thought that he was everything
To make us wish that we were in his place.

So on we worked, and waited for the light,
And went without the meat, and cursed the bread;
And "Richard Cory", one calm summer night,
Went home and put a bullet through his head.

The wretched widow grieving at her loved one's grave may actually be rejoicing at her inheritance or thinking of an ice cream sundae. There is no way to find out. You can ask her, but she may lie. Torture her, probe her brain with tiny electrodes, hook up your brain to hers: it makes no difference. There are no infallible methods of verification. You cannot apprehend her sensations. Even two brains hooked together and exposed to identical stimuli would not experience identical feelings; otherwise, a snail could be made to feel sublime love.

The worst is still to come. You may believe that, although you can never be sure of another's emotions, you can make intelligent guesses about them. But to do that, you must have some way of knowing when your guess is correct. And that is impossible.

Self-Deception

So, we have no reason to be confident that we know what another person is thinking. Far more disconcerting, we don't know ourselves very well.[115] Freud famously compared the mind to an iceberg, with nine tenths of it hidden below the surface, i.e., unconscious. Although his ideas were largely untestable, psychologists have since shown that many of our decisions and behaviors are deeply influenced by unconscious thought.

Psychologists Shelly Taylor and Jonathon Brown claimed that positive self-deception is both normal and beneficial.[116] They argued that most people view themselves in unrealistically positive terms; believe they have more control over their environment than they actually do; and have unjustifiably positive expectations about the future.

> *"No man is happy without a delusion of some kind. Delusions are*
> *as necessary to our happiness as realities."*
> —Christian Nevell Bovee

North and colleagues played French and German music on separate days in a supermarket.[117] They used either accordions (French) or an oompah band (German) to prime notions of 'Frenchness' or 'Germanness.' On French music days, French wines

---

115. "Knowledge of the self is the mother of all knowledge. So it is incumbent on me to know myself, to know it completely, to know its minutiae, its characteristics, its subtleties, and its very atoms."—Khalil Gibran

116. Taylor, S. & Brown, J. (1988). Illusion and well-being: A social psychological perspective on mental health. *Psych Bull*, 103: 193—210.

117. North, A. et al. (1997) In-store music affects product choice. *Nature*, 390: 132.

outsold Germans by five bottles to one; on German music days, German wines outsold French by two bottles to one. Only one of forty-four customers who answered questions at the checkout counter mentioned music as affecting their wine buying. When asked specifically if they thought that the music affected their choice, eighty-six percent said that it hadn't. Areni and Kim conducted a similar study.[118] They played either classical or top forty music in a wine cellar. They assumed that classical music evokes thoughts of sophistication and affluence. Sure enough, customers who heard classical music bought more expensive wines than did those who heard the top 40.

Custers and Aarts reviewed recent literature on unconscious influences.[119] Following are a few examples:

- Student volunteers worked on two seemingly unrelated puzzles. The first exposed some students to words related to achievement, such as win and achieve, while others saw neutral words. On the second puzzle, the achievement group showed greater persistence and outperformed the others—but denied that the first task influenced their responses to the second.

- Subjects who read words related to cooperation were more cooperative than controls in economic games.

- Subjects exposed to words describing occupations associated with making money, such as stockbroker, worked harder when money was at stake.

- When people enter an office with a leather briefcase on the desk, their competitiveness increases.

- People talk more softly when looking at a library picture on the wall.

---

118. Areni, C. & Kim, D. (1993) The influence of background music on shopping behavior: classical versus top-forty music in a wine store. *Advances in Consumer Research*, 20: 336-40.

119. Custers, R. & Aarts, H. (2010) The unconscious will: how the pursuit of goals operates outside of conscious awareness. *Science*, 329: 47-50.

- They do a better job of cleaning when a cleaning agent scent is in the air.

- Stimuli can be presented at an intensity just below the threshold of conscious awareness. These subliminal stimuli may influence motivations and behaviors. So, for example, people primed with subliminal drinking-related words drank more fluids during a taste task. After being subliminally primed with words related to helping occupations such as nurse, subjects were more likely to help another person.

- Korean moviegoers were exposed to a subliminal video of people getting full chest tattoos of Korean leader Kim Jong-II. During the following month, more than 25,000 Koreans had their entire chests tattooed with Kim Jong-II's image.[120] For more on self-deception, see p. 53.

Corporate

Many companies have distorted or suppressed findings that might have caused them to lose profits. Some have knowingly promoted hazardous products, sold outdated and contaminated foodstuffs, and illegally disposed of waste products that polluted water and air. The 2001 book *Trust Us, We're Experts*, gives a bookful of examples.[121]

The September 10, 2006 *St. Petersburg Times* of Florida wrote about corporate (plus journalistic) deception:

"...James K. Glassman, a prominent syndicated columnist, denounced *Super Size Me*, a movie critical of McDonald's. Readers were not told that McDonald's is a major sponsor of a Web site hosted by Glassman. ... Steven Milloy wrote a column in the *Washington Times* that sided with the oil industry against windfall profits taxes. Readers weren't

---

120. This last one never happened. As noted previously, you can't believe everything you read.

121. Rampton, S. & Stauber, J. (2001) *Trust Us, We're Experts*. NY: Tarcher/Putnam.

told that groups closely affiliated with Milloy have received at least $180,000 from ExxonMobil. John Stauber, whose *Center for Media and Democracy* tracks corporate front groups, said that having others deliver their talking points lets companies stay above the fray. 'What these companies are doing is paying somebody else to attack their critics while keeping their fingerprints off the attack.'"

The American Association for Justice gave more recent examples:[122]

- Agrochemical company Monsanto hired ghostwriters to write scientific reports that led the U.S. Environmental Protection Agency (EPA) to conclude that glyphosate, a chemical in its Roundup weed killer, does not cause cancer. Emails discussing the ghostwriting were revealed as part of a class action lawsuit claiming that Monsanto failed to warn that Roundup could cause non-Hodgkin's lymphoma. In one email, a Monsanto executive stated, "We would be keeping the cost down by us doing the writing" while researchers "would just edit & sign their names so to speak." Monsanto worked with an EPA official to stop the U.S. Department of Health and Human Services (HHS) from beginning its own review. One Monsanto executive wrote in an email that the EPA official had told him, "If I can kill this, I should get a medal." HHS did not go forward with the review.

- Wells Fargo charged more than 800,000 customers for auto insurance they didn't need and often didn't know about. As many as 274,000 customers were forced into delinquency by the expense of the unneeded insurance, and almost 25,000 had their cars wrongfully repossessed.

- Johnson & Johnson (J&J), the world's biggest health care products company, is facing more than 5,000 lawsuits over allegations that its talc products cause ovarian cancer.

122. https://www.justice.org/sites/default/files/file-uploads/Corporate_Misconduct_2017_FINAL_0.pdf

Documents unsealed during litigation allegedly show that J&J was concerned about asbestos fibers contaminating its talc products as early as the 1970s. Nevertheless, J&J trained its employees to maintain that the cancer-causing substance "has never been found and it never will."

- J&J faces at least 18,500 lawsuits over its antipsychotic drug Risperdal, which can cause young boys to suffer gynecomastia—the development of female breast tissue. J&J has been accused of hiding evidence as early as 2003 that the rate of gynecomastia associated with Risperdal was far higher than the company let on.

- Japanese auto parts maker Takata admitted that as many as 70 million of its air bags were prone to exploding and imbedding metal shrapnel into front seat occupants. Takata and its biggest customer, Honda, were allegedly aware of the problem as early as 2004, but neither company alerted the public until 2008.

- In 2018, New York City sued the world's five largest publicly traded oil companies alleging that the companies together were responsible for eleven percent of the world's global warming gases and that they have long known about their environment impact. The New York Attorney General's office also sued ExxonMobil in 2018, claiming that it had misled investors about the financial risks climate change entailed. Internal documents from the 1980s reveal that Shell's researchers believed global warming "mainly due to fossil fuel burning and deforestation" would "create significant changes in sea level, ocean currents, precipitation patterns, regional temperature and weather." The researchers concluded: "Such relatively fast and dramatic changes would impact on the human environment, future living standards and food supplies, and could have major social, economic and political consequences... By the time global warming becomes detectable it could be too late to take effective countermeasures to reduce the effects or even to stabilize the situation." By 1990

Exxon had embarked on a massive disinformation campaign, launching ad campaigns questioning global warming and using influence to shut down critical research and "emphasize uncertainty." Exxon took out full-page ads denying climate change, even as they simultaneously factored climate change into their operations.

Some corporations award research funds on condition that results cannot be published without their approval. Then they suppress unsatisfactory results. The British pharmaceutical company Boots manufactures Synthroid, the first synthetic thyroid drug. Introduced in 1958, Synthroid had by the 1990s captured eighty-four percent of the U.S. market for drugs to control hypothyroidism. Then three much cheaper generics began making inroads into Boots's sales, so Boots awarded a $250,000 grant to a team of researchers to compare Synthroid with the rivals. The grantors expected Synthroid to come out on top. But the researchers found that all four drugs were essentially interchangeable. Boots cited the contract forbidding publication of the findings without Boots's approval. And Boots refused to approve.[123] Fortunately for the many people who need hypothyroid medication but can't afford Synthroid, the researchers braved legal threats and reported their findings to the *Wall Street Journal*. That's a success story, but many other companies have managed to prevent publication of studies that show their products in a negative light. See, for example:[124]

---

123. UCSF thyroid study pulled from journal/drugmaker-sponsor didn't like results (1996). https://www.sfgate.com/news/article/UCSF-Thyroid-Study-Pulled-From-Journal-2984817.php

124. Dickersin, K. (1990) The existence of publication bias and risk factors for its occurrence. *JAMA*, 263:1385–9; Easterbrook, P. & Matthews, D. (1992) Fate of research studies. *J R Soc Med*. 85:71-6; Lexchin, J. et al. (2003) Pharmaceutical industry sponsorship and research outcome and quality: systematic review. *BMJ*, 326:1167–70. doi:10.1136/bmj.326.7400.1167; Dwan, K., et al. (2008) Systematic review of the empirical evidence of study publication bias and outcome reporting bias. *PLoS One*. 3(8):e3081. doi:10.1371/journal.pone.0003081.

Governmental and Political

Machiavelli gave advice to would-be rulers. He wrote in *The Prince*: "Everyone admits how praiseworthy it is in a prince to keep his word, and to behave with integrity rather than cunning. Nevertheless our experience has been that those princes who have done great things have considered keeping their word of little account, and have known how to beguile men's minds by shrewdness and cunning. In the end these princes have overcome those who have relied on keeping their word."

Stephen Knott wrote that the founding fathers of the United States practiced frequent deceptions, and the American Revolution would probably have failed without them.[125] George Washington used his personal funds to pay for clandestine operations that were essential to winning the war. He withheld information from the Continental Congress. For the 1781 Yorktown campaign he wrote, "pains [were] taken to deceive our own army." Thomas Jefferson authorized the Lewis and Clark expedition, ostensibly an effort to discover new species of flora and fauna but primarily an intelligence operation. James Madison conducted covert operations designed to secure parts of Florida by inciting "spontaneous" uprisings in Spanish-held territory. He provided misleading accounts to Congress and to foreign governments of his administration's actions. James Monroe lied to Congress about military activities in the then territory of Florida. James Polk lied about the incidents leading the United States to engage in war with Mexico.

In more recent times, every U.S. president going back at least to Franklin Roosevelt and the Manhattan project has either kept matters of grave importance hidden or successfully deceived most of the population about them. Following are a few examples:

- The Manhattan Project was a U.S. program begun shortly before the U.S. entered World War II. Its objective was to

---

125. Knott, S. (2016) Espionage, kidnapping, and the dark art of spycraft is as American as George Washington. *Foreign Policy*, 2/15.

develop nuclear weapons. It employed more than 130,000 people at several production and research sites. The objective was kept secret from the vast majority of Americans including most of the project workers.

- Dwight Eisenhower denied that U.S. spy planes were flying over the Soviet Union. They were. One was shot down, provoking an international incident.

- In 1961, 1,400 American-trained Cuban exiles began the "Bay of Pigs" invasion of Cuba. One week earlier, John Kennedy had said that "...there will not be, under any conditions, an intervention in Cuba by the United States Armed Forces."

- Lyndon Johnson campaigned actively for peace in late 1968. According to the Congressional Record, 147,786 tons of bombs were dropped over Laos during the first ten months of 1968. During the peace initiative in November and December, 91,831 tons were dropped.

- Concerning Richard Nixon, William Zinsser noted, "It is a fitting irony that under Richard Nixon, 'launder' became a dirty word."

- Ronald Reagan denied lying. Reagan said, "A few months ago I told the American people I did not trade arms for hostages. My heart and my best intentions still tell me that's true, but the facts and the evidence tell me it is not."

- George Bush misrepresented scientific findings to justify various administration policies. Sixty-two scientists including twenty Nobel laureates, nineteen recipients of the National Medal of Science, and advisors to the Eisenhower and Nixon administrations signed a statement highly critical of the administration's distortions. In 2008, Bush's press secretary Scott McClellan published a book in which he confessed to regularly and routinely, but unknowingly, passing on lies to the media, following the instructions of his superiors. The media reported the lies as facts.

On October 10, 1990, a fifteen-year-old girl named Nayirah testified before the Congressional Human Rights Caucus. She stated that after the Iraqi invasion of Kuwait she had witnessed Iraqi soldiers take babies out of incubators in a Kuwaiti hospital and leave the babies to die. The testimony was widely publicized and used by President George H. W. Bush as part of the rationale to back Kuwait in the Gulf War. More than a year later, it was revealed that she was the daughter of the Kuwaiti ambassador to the United States and that her testimony was organized as part of the Citizens for a Free Kuwait campaign run by an American public relations firm for the Kuwaiti government. An *ABC* report found that Iraqi troops "almost certainly had not stolen hospital incubators and left hundreds of Kuwaiti babies to die."

- Donald Trump has set a record for number of lies told in office that will probably stand longer than Joe Dimaggio's consecutive game hitting streak. *Time Magazine* reported that in his first 347 days in office he made 1,950 false or misleading claims. Then he picked up the pace—according to the April 3, 2020 *Washington Post*, he made 18,000 false or misleading claims in his first three years in office. On July 9, he crossed the 20,000 mark after averaging twenty-three claims a day over the previous fourteen months.

Despite the above, the United States is perhaps the most open society ever known. Yet, U.S. government agencies have systematically deceived and mistreated thousands of citizens. For example, William Albertson was a leading figure in the Communist Party. In 1964, his friends found a secret informant's report to the FBI in Albertson's handwriting, signed "Bill." He swore he hadn't written it, but the party expelled and ostracized him and he lost his job. Twelve years later, an internal FBI memorandum mistakenly made public detailed how the department's counterintelligence division had planted a fake report. The government paid $170,000 to Albertson's widow.[126]

---

126. Lewis, A. (1989) ABROAD AT HOME; Rule of Law? NY *Times*, 10/26.

Lies and deceptions have been perpetrated on a much larger scale. Starting in the 1930s and continuing for four decades, 399 African American men with syphilis were led to believe they were being given excellent medical treatment when in fact they were deliberately not treated; penicillin, effective against syphilis, was withheld so scientists could study the course of the disease. The disgraceful sham was supported by government agencies.[127] Government officials lied to justify the internment of thousands of Japanese American citizens during World War II. High government officials knowingly presented the Supreme Court with false records that misled the Court and resulted in decisions that deprived the petitioners of their rights to fair hearings.[128]

A water crisis in Flint, Michigan began when the city's water source was switched from the Detroit water system to the Flint River without adding corrosion controls. This act of negligence allowed lead to leach from the pipes. Although health experts warned of the danger of Legionnaires' disease and the possible link to the change in the city's water source as early as October 2014, their efforts to investigate the situation were blocked by high-placed officials in state and federal agencies. Harvey Hollins, an appointee of Governor Rick Snyder, contradicted Snyder's repeated claims that he did not learn of a deadly outbreak of Legionnaires' disease until January 12, 2016.[129] Hollins stated that he told Snyder about the outbreak of Legionnaires' disease in December 2015.

Documents show that Nick Lyon, the director of the state's Department of Health and Human Services, failed to alert the public about the deadly disease although he was aware of the outbreak as early as January 2015. A study by David Slusky and Daniel

---

127. Gray, F. (1998) *The Tuskegee Syphillis Study: The Real Story and Beyond.* Montgomery, AL: NewSouth Books.

128. Norton, H. (2015) The government's lies and the constitution. https://scholar.law.colorado.edu/articles/54/

129. Brehm, S. (2017) Court testimony exposes governor's lies about Flint water crisis. https://www.wsws.org/en/articles/2017/10/09/flin-o09.html

Grossman found that fetal death rates increased by fifty-eight percent and fertility rates decreased by twelve percent after the April
2014 change in the city's water source.[130] Ingesting lead by young
children causes brain damage and behavioral disorders. An estimated 9,000 Flint children suffered permanent damage.

Top of State agencies have lied about when polls would close in
hopes of suppressing the votes of minorities; and about unemployment rates, to improve the incumbent's prospects in an upcoming
election. Some government lies are not easily rebutted. Examples
include lies about matters on which the government has special
access, e.g., executive branch lies about certain national security
and intelligence topics.

Whether one views Bradley Manning, the source of the massive WikiLeaks trove of state secrets, as a hero or a traitor, there is
no denying that he revealed important information that had been
kept from the American public. For example:

- Out of 109,000 Iraqi deaths logged in a six year period,
  66,081 were unarmed civilians.

- U.S. Soldiers committed horrific acts of torture on Iraqi
  prisoners. Despite hundreds of filed complaints, authorities
  never investigated.

- U.S. defense contractor DynCorp was involved in child
  trafficking.

In March, 2013 Director of National Intelligence James Clap-
per denied that the National Security Agency was collecting any
type of data on millions of Americans. About three months later,
Edward Snowden leaked documents revealing that the NSA was
conducting sweeping domestic and international communications
dragnets. Virtually every U.S. telephone company made customers' phone records available to NSA.

---

130. Grossman, D. & Slusky, D. (2017) The effect of an increase in lead in the
water system on fertility and birth outcomes: The case of Flint, Michigan. https://econpapers.repec.org/paper/kanwpaper/201703.htm

As a run-up to the 2020 presidential election, McKay Coppins wrote that the Trump campaign was planning to spend more than $1 billion on an extensive disinformation campaign. They planned to be aided by a vast coalition of partisan media, outside political groups, and freelance operatives. They were expected to use Facebook to send customized propaganda with hundreds of variations specific to individual voters.[131]

The 2020 coronavirus gave rise to dozens of conspiracy theories, disinformation, and propaganda. The World Health Organization warned of an "infodemic," and Snopes, a fact-checking site, wrote that "The magnitude of misinformation spreading in the wake of the Covid-19 pandemic is overwhelming our small team."

Donald Trump dismantled the National Security Council's pandemic response unit in 2018. Asked about the decision by a reporter, Trump said he didn't know anything about it. He did know. See https://video.search.yahoo.com/yhs/search?fr=yhs-avast-secure-browser&hsimp=yhs-securebrowser&hspart=avast&p=trump+dis-mantling+pandemic+youtube+video#id=21&vid=f2fbfc4efc-861de3cf69cb9d511ad9ec&action=viewl

A YouTube video claimed that the cause of the disease is not a virus but rather 5G cellular networks. It received 1.9 million views as of 4/10/20. Other claims mentioned secret cures such as diluted bleach, turning off electronics, and bananas.

A Chinese official claimed that the virus was introduced to China by members of the United States Army. Venezuelan President Nicolás Maduro agreed, saying that it was an American bioweapon aimed at China. Officials in Iran also called it a Western plot. So did outlets that back the Russian government, including branches in Western Europe. They promoted claims that the U.S. engineered the virus to undermine China's economy. Instagram posts blamed Bill Gates. Senator Tom Cotton, an Arkansas

131. Coppins, M. The 2020 Disinformation war: deepfakes, anonymous text messages, potemkin local-news sites, and opposition research on reporters – a field guide to the year's election and what it could do to the country. *The Atlantic March, 2020*

Republican, fought back for the U.S. He suggested that the virus was produced by a Chinese weapons lab.

On March 30, 2020, Trump was asked about a *Washington Post* editorial condemning Russia and China for spreading misinformation about the virus. Trump responded, "Number one, you don't know what they're doing. And when you read it in the *Washington Post*, you don't believe it." Then, speaking about governments spreading outrageous lies, he added, "They do it and we do it...Every country does it."[132]

The bottom line: Possibly nobody knows the truth. Ordinary citizens definitely do not.

Many sources of disinformation are motivated by financial rather than ideological reasons. The *Global Disinformation Index* is a nonprofit that defines disinformation as inaccurate information spread purposefully and/or maliciously. The organization surveyed 20,000 domains it suspected of disinformation, looking at the websites' traffic and audience information, what kinds of ads they were running, and how much they made per visitor on advertisements. It concluded that at least $235 million in revenue is generated annually from ads running on extremist and disinformation websites. Danny Rogers, chief technology officer at the *Global Disinformation Index*, said that the findings reflect just the tip of the iceberg.[133]

Pope Francis criticized disinformation in a 2016 interview. He had been falsely accused by a fake news website of supporting Donald Trump for U.S. President.

Of course, fraud goes in both directions. Both individuals and corporations commit fraud against the government. The Department of Justice obtained more than $3 billion in settlements and judgments from civil cases involving fraud and false claims against

---

132. https://www.vanityfair.com/news/2020/03/donald-trump-coro-navirus-lies-china

133. https://www.cnn.com/2019/08/18/tech/advertising-disinforma-tion-money-reliable-sources/index.html

the government in the fiscal year ending Sept. 30, 2019.[134]

One final note: as of March 25, 2020 *Wikipedia* devoted fifty-nine pages to the category "Politicians convicted of mail and wire fraud."

The Military

In the *New Yorker* magazine,[135] Rachel Monroe wrote, "Politicians lie to get us into wars; generals lie about how well things are going; soldiers lie about what they did during their service." Vietnam veteran B. G. "Jug" Burkett was the first to expose military imposters on a large scale. Since the mid-1980s, Burkett has investigated more than 3,000 people and exposed hundreds of veterans who claimed disabilities from wartime service they didn't perform and civilians who invented service records to collect disability benefits. The imposters include a city-council member, the head of a Vietnam Veterans of America chapter, and a U.S. congressman. The websites http://www.stolenvalor.com/target.cfm?source=link&sort=order and https://www.pinterest.com/pin/342836590366544384/ list many more imposters.

The Media

The media includes radio, television, magazines, and newspapers, encompassing everything from the staid *New York Times* to the *National Enquirer*. Sophisticated people may scoff at the gullibility of *Enquirer* readers (real headlines: FBI Captures Bat Child; Gay Aliens Found in UFO Wreck; and Man's 174-mph Hour Sneeze Blows Wife's Hair Off!), but *Enquirer* subscribers may scoff back at the close-mindedness of the *Times* readers. *Business Insider* listed "11 Crazy *National*

---

134. https://www.justice.gov/opa/pr/justice-department-recovers-over-3-billion-false-claims-act-cases-fiscal-year-2019

135. Monroe, R. (2020) Stolen Valor, *New Yorker*, 10/26 p. 26-31.

Enquirer Stories That Turned Out To Be True."[136] Next time you see a bald woman, you should ask if her husband has a cold.

In a 1978 speech, Aleksandr Solzhenitsyn said, "The press has become the greatest power within the Western countries, more powerful than the legislature, the executive, and the judiciary." That was then. With deception, lies, and suppression of information coming from all directions, independent members of the media are sorely needed to provide checks on the claims of politicians, corporate executives, and others. But many problems limit the extent to which media reports can be trusted. First, members of the media cannot report all available stories and facts; they have to select and often do so on ideological grounds. Furthermore, many business, military, and other government policies are conceived and implemented behind closed doors, so media people have limited access to the events they cover. Media blackouts and limited access to conflict zones are common. In February, 2017, journalists from the *New York Times*, the *Los Angeles Times*, *Politico*, and *CNN* were blocked from attending a media briefing at the White House. In June, 2017, reporters were told they could no longer film interviews with senators in Capitol hallways. *New York Times* reporter Steven Greenhouse tweeted, "It is dangerous for democracy and for holding politicians accountable when a White House excludes tough-minded journalists who criticize them."

Another problem is that some media personnel are lazy, have limited resources to do proper investigative work, or are on tight deadlines. So, they focus on stories that can be summarized succinctly, which crowds out ones that take time to explain. Many television outlets regularly use video news releases (VNRs). A VNR is a video segment made to look like a news report but which has been created by a PR firm, advertising agency, marketing firm, corporation, or government agency. It has a script so the television station crew can put together and edit the story as if they had

---

136. https://www.businessinsider.com/national-enquirer-stories-that-were-true-2013-2.

shot it themselves. VNRs are generally dramatic, slick, and more compelling than the local reporters' best efforts. TV stations save money by airing VNRs instead of sending reporters into the field, and they pass the videos along to viewers without acknowledging their source. The videos often include interviews with actors or experts with biased views, and they are frequently nothing more than lengthy commercials or political propaganda masquerading as news. They were used by all the presidential candidates in the 1992 elections. A 1992 survey found that eighty percent of U.S. news directors use VNRs a few times each month.[137]

The Center for Media and Democracy reported that seventy-seven local stations that collectively reach more than half of the U.S. population had slipped corporate sponsored VNRs into their regular news programming. In each case, the stations actively disguised the sponsored content to make it appear to be their own reporting. See http://www. sourcewatch.org/index.php/Video_news_releases for examples. In 2011, the FCC fined a Minneapolis TV station $4,000 for airing a VNR without sponsorship identification. In May, 2020, Amazon issued a VNR that included footage from its warehouses and a script for news anchors. The segment includes interviews with warehouse workers praising the company's efforts to combat COVID-19. At least eleven TV news stations ran the video as news with few, if any, changes.[138]

John Stauber said, "Half of everything in the news actually originates from a PR firm. If you're a lazy journalist, editor, or news director, it's easy to simply regurgitate the dozens of press releases and stories that come in every day for free from PR firms."[139]

Members of the media often promise confidentiality to sources

---

137. https://www.herinst.org/BusinessManagedDemocracy/culture/media/VNRs.html

138. https://www.cbsnews.com/news/amazon-covid-19-publicity-video-airs-as-news-on-local-tv-stations/

139. Stauber, J. (1999) WAR ON TRUTH: The secret battle for the American mind. *The Sun*, March.

who provide important information but risk retaliation if exposed. In a study of more than 2,400 cases of fraud in 114 countries, about forty percent of cases were uncovered by whistle-blowers. So, legal efforts to compel journalists to reveal confidential sources is a major concern. Without a federal shield law, journalists facing a federal subpoena confront the prospect of jail. Police reporter Brian Karem spent two weeks in jail after he refused to disclose a confidential source. Judith Miller was jailed for more than two months for refusing to appear before a grand jury investigating a government leak involving CIA operative Valerie Plame. *Los Angeles Times* reporter William Farr was jailed for forty-six days for refusing to reveal sources for a story about the Charles Manson trial. Josh Wolf was jailed for 226 days after he refused to hand over video footage of a protest in San Francisco. President Trump said that then FBI director James Comey "should consider putting reporters in prison for publishing classified information." The U.S. Justice Department has also sought to imprison government employees for leaking classified information to the media. See a comprehensive list of federal cases at https://www.rcfp.org/resources/leak-investigations-chart/.

Members of the media as much as other people are motivated by opportunities for power, prestige, and money. So, another reason for being wary of media reports is that some journalists have succumbed to temptation and committed fraud. They have described heart-wrenching events and personal sagas that never happened. For descriptions of a few high-profile cases, see https://longreads.com/2014/01/22/famous-cases-of-journalistic-fraud-a-reading-list/.

Media executives, like executives in other businesses, are concerned with profits. Much of their revenues, an average of seventy-five to eighty percent for both elite and non-elite American newspapers, comes from advertising. Benson wrote that the need to attract new sources of advertising has led to the creation of news sections such as travel, lifestyle, and food. These sections have proliferated as hard local, national, and international news sections have dwindled.

Editorial content has been nearly universally watered down.[140]

Skinner described a 2012 incident in Dearborn, Michigan, where a racist pastor tried to inflame anti-Muslim sentiment. Fewer than thirty people showed up to join or counter him, but the media covered the event in great detail. Skinner speculated that they anticipated a large viewership because of the threat of violence that would translate to profit.[141]

Media executives tread very carefully when considering stories that might offend the advertisers. An internal review by *BuzzFeed* found three instances when editors deleted posts after an advertiser or employees from the company's business side complained about their content.[142] In a poll of 250 daily newspaper editors, ninety-three percent of respondents answered that an advertiser had threatened to withdraw advertising because of the content of news stories; fifty-five percent reported pressure from within their newspaper to write or tailor news stories to please advertisers; thirty-seven percent admitted to having caved in to the pressures; and eighty-nine percent said that advertisers had followed through on their threats.[143]

Editors are reluctant to be critical of local politicians who control licensing and enact laws that affect the media. They encourage controversy to give the impression of open debate, but only within a narrow range of opinion. They do not report on news that falls outside that range. Between January and August 2014, no representatives for organized labor made an appearance on any of the high-profile Sunday morning talk shows despite episodes

140. Benson, R. Profit pressures transform American media; but journalists' debate over the 'Wall' obscures systemic problems. https://www.irle.berkeley.edu/culture/papers/Benson.pdf

141. Skinner, D. When news media's bottom line is profit. https://chicagomonitor.com/2012/11/when-news-media-is-driven-by-profit-not-informing-the-public/

142. https://www.nytimes.com/2015/04/20/business/media/buzzfeed-says-posts-were-deleted-because-of-advertising-pressure.html

143. Soley, L. & Craig, R. (2013) Advertising pressures on newspapers: A survey. *J Advertising*, 21: 1-10.

that covered topics such as labor rights and jobs. Over that same period, current or former corporate CEOs made twelve appearances.[144] (In a related study, a five week survey of six primetime TV interview/discussion programs found that eighty-four percent of the 1,015 guests were white and seventy-two percent were men.)[145]

Writers and editors who report the news select and organize each day's flood of information in a way that makes sense to them and their audiences. This process is called framing. They frame issues in ways that depend on their location and political ideology. Fryberg and colleagues studied arguments supporting and opposing an anti-immigration bill from three weeks of newspaper articles in two Arizona newspapers (one conservative, one liberal) and five national newspapers (three conservative, two liberal).[146] Both location and political ideology influenced the framing. The national more than Arizona newspapers framed arguments supporting the bill in terms of threats to economic and public safety; and they framed arguments against the bill in terms of civil rights issues. Conservative newspapers were more likely than liberal newspapers to frame the bill in terms of economic and public safety threats, but they did not differ in mentions of civil rights issues.

The Internet

The internet is an incredible and much used source of almost instantaneously available information. According to a Pew Research Center study, sixty-two percent of U.S. adults get news on social

---

144. Hart, P. (2014) Labor almost invisible on TV talk: Sunday chat shows skip worker representatives. https://fair.org/take-action/media-advisories/labor-almost-invisible-on-tv-talk/

145. Hart, P. https://fair.org/press-release/study-cable-news-a-white-mans-world/

146. Fryberg, S. (2012) How the media frames the immigration debate: The critical role of location and politics. *Analysis of Social Issues and Public Policy*, 12: 96-112.

media and eighteen percent do so often.[147] But much of the information is wrong. Internet sites can be found that support even the most wildly imagined ideas, and the most popular fake news stories are more widely shared on Facebook than the most popular mainstream stories.[148] Powerful algorithms suggest sites to individuals based on their viewing habits, and confirmation bias, the tendency to ignore contradictory evidence, means that misinformation often goes uncorrected. Many people who read fake news stories believe them.

The Internet's wildly untrue claims (probably—but the point is that we can't know for sure) include such as that the coronavirus was created as a bioweapon or was funded by the Bill & Melinda Gates Foundation to further vaccine sales, or that it can be cured by eating garlic or drinking a bleach concoction. According to the *New York Times*, hundreds of thousands of people have consumed dozens of documented falsehoods about the coronavirus on social media websites.[149]

Safiya Umoja Noble, in *Algorithms of Oppression*, showed that Internet searches are biased.[150] Search results are ranked, and results on the first page are much more likely to be explored than results on later pages. Noble reported that a 2014 Google search for "black girls" put sexually explicit terms on the first page, but a

147. Gottfried, J. & Shearer, E. News use across social media platforms 2016. https://www.journalism.org/2016/05/26/news-use-across-social-media-platforms-2016/

148. Silverman, C. (2016) This analysis shows how fake election news stories outperformed real news on Facebook. *BuzzFeed News*, November 16.

149. https://www.nytimes.com/2020/02/06/health/coronavirus-misinformation-social-media.html?auth=login-email&can_id=52e33918b30442606fa2a720c190feb4&email_referrer=email_763392&email_subject=re-coronavirus-info-in-statefull-default-your-state&link_id=2&login=email&source=email-re-coronavirus-info-in-statefull-default-your-state-3

150. Noble, S. (2018) *Algorithms of Oppression*. NY: NYU Press.

search for "white girls," gave radically different results. More generally, Noble showed, the search algorithms used by Google and others discriminate against people of color, especially women of color.

And then there is fake news. Unlike news satire, which is presented for humor, many Internet sites intentionally publish hoaxes and disinformation. Their goal is to mislead and sometimes profit financially from readers' gullibility. The *Daily Dot* listed 176 fake news sites. See https://www.dailydot.com/layer8/fake-news-sites-list-facebook/. According to a *BuzzFeed* News report, the top 50 fake news stories on Facebook of 2018 generated around 22 million total shares, reactions, and comments.[151]

Denise-Marie Ordway wrote that fabricated stories posing as serious journalism have become a means for some writers to make money and influence public opinion. As a result, much of the public is seriously misinformed about important issues.[152] The *Pew Research Center* survey suggests that twenty-three percent of U.S. adults have shared fake news with friends and others—even when they knew the news was false. And, studies have shown that mere repetition of statements increases their believability.

Vosoughi and colleagues investigated the diffusion of all of the verified true and false news stories, about 126,000, distributed on Twitter from 2006 to 2017.[153] The stories were tweeted by about 3 million people more than 4.5 million times. The news was classified as true or false using information from six independent fact-checking organizations that exhibited ninety-five to ninety-eight percent agreement on the classifications. The top one percent of false news diffused to between 1,000 and 100,000 people, whereas the truth rarely diffused to more than 1,000. Falsehoods

---

151. https://www.buzzfeednews.com/article/craigsilverman/
     facebook-fake-news-hits-2018

152. Ordway, D. (2017) Fake news and the spread of misinformation.
     https://journalistsresource.org/studies/society/internet/fake-news-conspiracy-theories-journalism-research/

153. Vosoughi, S. et al. (2018) The spread of true and false news online.
     Science, 359: 1146-51.

diffused significantly farther, faster, deeper, and more broadly than the truth in all categories of information.

Hunt and Gentzkow presented evidence that social media was an important source of news in the run-up to the 2016 presidential election.[154] Fourteen percent of Americans called social media their most important source of election news. Of the known false news stories that appeared in the three months before the election, those favoring Trump were shared a total of 30 million times on Facebook, and those favoring Clinton were shared eight million times. The average American saw and remembered 0.92 pro-Trump fake news stories and 0.23 pro-Clinton fake news stories. Slightly more than half of those who recalled seeing fake news stories believed them.

Historical

> *"What did you learn in school today, dear little boy of mine?*
> *I learned our government must be strong.*
> *It's always right and never wrong....*
> *That's what I learned in school."*
> —Song by Tom Paxton, 1963

> *"Until lions have their historians, tales of the hunt shall always glorify the hunters."*—African Proverb

> *"History will be kind to me for I intend to write it."*
> —Winston Churchill

History is a discipline that combines reason, empiricism, and faith. To some extent at least, most people probably trust history books. But even when supported by impressive documentation, chronicles of historical events may be inaccurate. Disraeli wrote that "all great events have been distorted, most of the important

---

154 Hunt, A. & Gentzkow, M. (2017) Social media and fake news in the 2016 election. Working paper for the *National Bureau of Economic Research*, No. 23089.

causes concealed, some of the principal characters never appear, and all who figure are so misunderstood and misrepresented that the result is a complete mystification." Voltaire, more succinctly, called histories "fables that have been agreed upon."

Howard Zinn used a book full of examples to illustrate Voltaire's point. For example, Christopher Columbus has been portrayed to U.S. schoolchildren as a brave and skillful hero. Zinn wrote that almost every textbook in every school in the United States omits crucial material: "Columbus, in his greed for gold, mutilated, enslaved, and murdered the Indians who greeted him in friendly innocence, and this was done on such a scale as to deserve the term 'genocide'—the destruction of an entire people."[155]

Zinn cited documents, some written by Columbus himself, to support his claim. Then he showed that historians' treatment of Columbus is typical of their approach to most topics. They emphasize the doings of the rich and powerful—political and military leaders and industrial barons—while ignoring the life-and-death struggles of ordinary people. Claiming to be objective in chronicling the past, they always serve some present interest. Their biases are especially pronounced in wartime. Their country is portrayed as good, the enemy as evil. They paint no shades of gray.

Most U.S. history textbooks either sanitize or completely ignore the terrible crimes perpetrated against African-Americans. Bennett Minton[156] wrote that textbooks written for Virginians in the fourth, seventh and 11th grades gave a whitewashed account of Virginia's history. For example, one textbook wrote that a feeling of strong affection existed between masters and slaves in most

---

155. Zinn, H. (2003) *A People's History of the United States*. NY: Perennial Classics.

156. Minton, B. (2020)The lies our textbooks told my generation of Virginians about slavery https://www.washingtonpost.com/outlook/slavery-history-virginia-textbook/2020/07/31/d8571eda-d1f0-11ea-8c55-61e7fa5e82ab_story.html?hpid=hp_opinions-for-wide-side_opinion-card-b%3Ahomepage%2Fstory-ans&fbclid=IwAR12sABJTa8uSNCI-qPwp7XKXa38HJJmhugTfyxjNL8JodeqFCFcgwPfVpeU

Virginia homes. The authors added that masters knew that the best way to control their slaves was to win their confidence and affection; and that enslaved people "went visiting at night and sometimes owned guns and other weapons." Illustrations featured masters and slaves all dressed smartly, shaking hands amiably.

Textbook writers have also ignored many African-American achievements, such as that of the three brilliant women at NASA who were instrumental in astronaut John Glenn's launch into orbit. To learn about other highly accomplished African-American scientists who you probably never heard of, go to https://www.pbs.org/education/blog/ten-black-scientists-that-science-teachers-should-know-about-and-free-resources. For more, see[157].

In 2010, the Albert Shanker Institute issued a report, "American Labor in U.S. History Textbooks: How Labor's Story Is Distorted in High School History Textbooks."[158] The report reviews widely used high school U.S. history textbooks for their treatment of unions in American history. The authors conclude that the history of the U.S. labor movement is largely "misrepresented, downplayed or ignored." The textbooks "often implicitly (and at times explicitly) represent labor organizing and labor disputes as inherently violent."

"History is a set of lies agreed upon."—Napoleon

"History isn't what happened. It's who tells the story."
—author Sally Roesch Wagner

Appendix 3 describes several historical events that did not

---

157. Raphael, R. (2007) Are U.S. history textbooks still full of lies and half-truths? https://historynewsnetwork.org/article/7219; Finger, B. (2015) Here's how new texas public school textbooks write about slavery. https://jezebel.com/heres-how-new-texas-public-school-textbooks-write-about-1726786557

158. (2011) https://www.aft.org/news/labors-story-left-out-high-school-history-textbooks#:~:text=%22American%20Labor%20and%20U.S.%20History%20Textbooks%3A%20How%20Labor%27s,while%20giving%20little%20or%20no%20attention%20to%20

happen the way they are told in most classrooms and textbooks.

You may or may not believe that Lee Harvey Oswald was the lone assassin of President John F. Kennedy, but you're probably certain that Oswald was at least somewhat involved. And that, whoever the perpetrator, Kennedy is dead. But straightforward explanations are not more likely true than complex ones, and even the most obvious inferences can be challenged by an infinite number of alternatives. The scenario below explains the events in Dallas as adequately as does your version. Do you assign it a zero probability? On what grounds?

October 28, 1963

"Mr. President, there's a message for you. I think you should read it."

President John F. Kennedy rose slowly from his rocking chair, athletic frame contorted by the persistent pain in his back. He took the letter from his press secretary, Pierre Salinger, and slowly read.

Hi Lieutenant,

It's been a long time. You've sure done well since our navy days. Hey, remember when you called me the most unprincipled man you'd ever known. Wait till you see how right you were. You've irritated certain powerful business interests, and they offered me a huge contract to get you out of office by next month. Naturally, I accepted. They gave me a staff of exceptionally well-trained assassins, and of course I have my own people.

Part of your character assessment was that I have a great capacity for attracting a loyal following of lunatics. The peasants think you're well-protected, but you know as well as anybody that any security can be breached. Remember the incident with the keys. You were always impressed with my efficiency (admit it, you loved having me on your staff), and I've got an amazing arsenal at my disposal. My sponsors have been very generous.

I'm writing because I always liked you. You have style and charm, and Jackie looks great in a bathing suit. So I'd rather not hurt you. But you must leave office. For various reasons resignation wouldn't work, but there is a way. I've explored the feasibility of setting up an immense deception. If you accept, we'll use plastic surgery to give you a brand new face even handsomer than the present one. (Incidentally, your medical care stinks. One of my doctor friends says he can cure your back problems in no time.) You'd be able to use your money however you want, within certain limits of course. You could sip martinis on tropical beaches while the world grieves at your martyrdom.

Who knows, with my new wealth, maybe I'd join you. We could continue our chess series. I've gotten much better.

My offer is generous. If you refuse, my sponsors are prepared to use far more drastic measures and you wouldn't be their only target. The list includes Jackie, Rose, Bobby, Ted, John-John, Caroline and the rest of the clan. So, I know you'll appreciate that you've got to accept. Just put an ad in the Post in the personals section. Have it read "Howie, I love it. John. Then I'll have my friend Martin contact you.

Best wishes,
Ensign HCW

The President reread the letter, then started laughing. Pierre," he said at last, "call up the classified department at the *Post*. And you'd better start looking for a new job."[159]

Appendix 4 describes three other products of my crazy imagination. But what are your reasons for thinking they are only imaginary?

Censorship

Some deception involves acts of omission rather than commission. Carl Jensen, a professor at Sonoma State University, found

---

159. John (November 9, 1963) *Washington Post*.

that the media often featured trivial and non-newsworthy stories rather than newsworthy ones. So he founded Project Censored, a research group that tracks the news published in independent journals and newsletters. From these, Project Censored compiles an annual list of socially significant news stories that have been overlooked, under-reported, or self-censored by the country's major national news media. The goal is to report stories that are timely, ongoing, backed with verifiable documentation, and with implications for a significant number of U.S. residents. Table 3 lists headlines for the top ten underreported stories of 2019. To read more, go to https://www.citybeat.com/news/news-feature/article/21109045/project-censored-reveals-its-top-10-most-important-underreported-stories-of-2019.

Table 3: The Top Ten Underreported Stories Of 2019

- Justice Department's Secret FISA Rules for Targeting Journalists
- Think Tank Partnerships Establish Facebook as a Tool of U.S. Foreign Policy
- Indigenous Groups from the Amazon Propose Creation of Largest Protected Area on Earth
- U.S. Oil and Gas Industry Set to Unleash 120 Billion Tons of New Carbon Emissions
- Modern Slavery in the United States, Around the World
- Survivors of Sexual Abuse and Sex Trafficking Criminalized for Self-Defense
- Flawed Investigations of Sexual Assaults in Children's Immigrant Shelters
- US Women Face Prison Sentences for Miscarriages
- Developing Countries' Medical Needs Unfulfilled by Big Pharma
- Pentagon Aims to Surveil Social Media to Predict Domestic Protests

Major Conspiracies

Catastrophes of human making often give rise to conspiracy theorists who cry cover up and try to expand the list of possible perpetrators. (Not one JFK assassin but several. Not foreign terrorists on 9/11 but the CIA.) Mainstream media typically expose flaws in the accusers' arguments and ridicule them. But ridicule, even if justified, has a serious negative consequence—it reduces the likelihood that people will give credence to evidence of real conspiracies. Psychologist William McGuire showed that resistance to persuasion has much in common with resistance to disease. When people are exposed to a weak version of a virus, their immune systems produce antibodies that enable them to withstand stronger forms of the virus. Analogously, people exposed to weak (easily refutable) attacks on their attitudes resist subsequent evidence that might otherwise have persuaded them.[160] Appendix 5 gives brief descriptions of a few notorious conspiracies and cover ups. Although there is no consensus on any of them, the versions in the appendix are probably roughly accurate. However, the whole point of the discussion is to indicate the impossibility of knowing for sure.

Deception—A New Dimension

Deceptions don't always succeed, at least in the long-term. Diligent investigative reporters keep careful watch over powerful people and corporations. They use the Freedom of Information Act, follow paper trails, and encourage whistle blowers. But readers should not conclude that conspiracies, cover ups, and other forms of deception are likely to be caught. Just the opposite. The moral standards of powerful politicians and corporate CEOs are

---

160. McGuire, W. (1961) Resistance to persuasion conferred by active and passive prior refutation of same and alternative counterarguments. *J Abnormal Psychology*, 63: 326–332

probably no higher than those of the rest of us. They must surely make their most important decisions behind closed doors, and the likelihood of getting caught in lies and cover ups is probably quite small. For every one uncovered, dozens may never be known.

Some hopelessly naïve people may be fooled when foreign dictators make outrageous statements about their abilities or claim to have received 100% of the vote. Cynics merely snigger. They ridicule statements from North Korea's rigidly controlled media that the country has never suffered famine or poverty; or that leader Kim Jong II was so beloved that after a munitions train explosion people ran into buildings to save his portraits before they rescued their own family members. The cynics recognize that a substantial percentage of people in powerful, influential positions regard deception as a valuable, even essential, tool of their trade. Philosophically open-minded cynics may go further and acknowledge that ordinary people may be currently deceiving even them about a matter of great personal importance. Get them drunk enough and perhaps they'll concede the remote possibility that someone they know and admire is a secret adulterer, embezzler, or mass murderer.

But even open-minded people have limits on the possibilities they will consider. "Yes," they might say, "it's true that adulterous relationships are often covered up, Congressional Committees lied to, and documents forged." But they'll refuse to believe that the dishonesty of governments and corporations has any bearing on the trustworthiness of millions of bits of personal knowledge. They know there's a country called France and Paris a city within it; that water at sea level boils at 212 degrees Fahrenheit; what goes up must come down; and a ripe apple plucked from a tree tastes better than freshly poured cement. They think it absurd to leap from a heterogenous grouping of examples of dishonesty to the radical skeptic position that the entire universe may be an illusion, including rhinoceroses, jelly donuts, and the Andromeda nebula.

The "open-minded" people are comparable to lifelong desert dwellers trying to assess the world's quantity of water. Imagine showing a Kalahari bushman an Olympic-sized swimming pool.

He'd be awestruck and eventually realize that water is vastly more abundant than he'd thought. Yet his new worldview, even modified to include the pool, would be far closer to his original view than to the truth. Doubt for the open-minded is like water for "enlightened" bushmen. The truly open-minded should accept that they have no basis for estimating the incidence and magnitude of major deceptions and other barriers to knowledge. Only radical skeptics say there is no way of knowing how much of our world is illusory.

Textbooks claim that the universe is 15 billion years old and our separation from amoebas began less than 1 billion years ago. That leaves billions of years for vastly superior intelligent life to have already evolved, either on this planet or elsewhere. They may not want us to know. Could we be the frogs to some superintelligent scientist? Could we be unaware of a superior earth life form or merely unaware of its superiority? Could there be beings from the distant future?

Given the vastness of space and time and our infinitesimally tiny part in it, any presupposition seems unwarranted. Consider: The nearest star to our sun is about 24 trillion miles away. There are two trillion galaxies in the observable universe, each with incalculable billions of stars. One study suggested that there are 300 sextillion stars (3 followed by 23 zeros).[161]

An exoplanet is a planet that orbits a star outside our solar system. By New Year's Day 2018, NASA had confirmed the existence of 3,572 exoplanets, with 5,078 more awaiting final verification. Astronomers estimate that the Milky Way galaxy contains between 100 billion and 400 billion stars, and that the vast majority of stars have at least a few planets around them. So, there are probably hundreds of billions of planets in the Milky Way alone. Estimates of the percentage of planets that have both water and a moderate surface temperature are generally between five and

---

161. Van Dokkum, P. & Conroy, C. (2010) A substantial population of low-mass stars in luminous elliptical galaxies. *Nature*, 468: 940-2.

fifteen percent. So, probably tens of billions of planets in the Milky Way galaxy have some potential for life.

The speed of light is somewhat over 186,000 miles per second, so light travels from the earth to the moon in about 1.3 seconds. Yet a light beam would take about 14 billion years to travel from one end to the other of the known universe. Some people may conceive effortlessly of a universe infinite in size and duration, and they may with equal ease imagine a universe with boundaries. Both possibilities strike me as wildly improbable, yet I can't even conceive of a third alternative. With that in mind, discussions of eternal universal laws seem preposterous. How can anyone look at Figure 10 and continue to believe otherwise? How can people be even mildly confident that their interpretations of what they see are correct?

Figure 10: Arcturus compared to Sun
(Betelguese is much bigger than Arcturus and
Antares is much bigger than Betelguese).

Einstein believed that time travel is impossible. Be tolerant toward his memory. The paradoxes of time travel would not bother an advanced species any more than Zeno's paradoxes bother rocket engineers. For historical reasons, curiosity, nostalgia, or an interesting vacation idea, *H. Superiorus* might visit the twenty-first century. (If a time machine will be built in the distant future, doesn't it make sense to assume that travelers from that future will someday visit our present time? In that case, they're probably here.) What about their morals? Here is a reasonable guess. They would regard themselves as more important than other species and would keep representative others in zoos. They would face tough decisions. For example, should exhibits be arranged according to phyletic status, in which case humans should cohabitate with chimpanzees; or should they be arranged according to natural habitat, which would place humans with dogs, cats, rats, and cockroaches? Some humans might be sent to circuses (they learn tricks fast and look cute when riding a bicycle), labs, or slaughterhouses, or used as beasts of burden. Our own history in dealing with other species and races gives no solace in this regard. Some future *H. Superiorus* soccer team might be called the Grandmas or Buddhists or Entomologists. Alternatively, they might fumigate the planet.

Humans would no more understand the morals of *H. Superiorus* than a dog understands those of its master. Fido praised for killing mice might think he knows, but only so long as he's denied the opportunity to attack birds and hamsters. If Fido could talk, he'd probably acknowledge that he finds the burglar/postman/friend distinction arbitrary and capricious.

So, consider that your senses, whether through their natural limitations or because of intentional deception, have misled you on a much greater scale than you previously imagined possible. Consider the possibility that you are incorrect in thinking you know where you came from, why you are here, what your capabilities are, and what your final fate will be. I do NOT say that is the case; only that it is conceivable and we have no way of estimating the likelihood.

Chapter 11

REASON AND
SCIENCE IN OPPOSITION

Science is empiricism at its most sophisticated. Not widely appreciated is that science and careful reasoning are often at odds with each other, and the question arises about which takes precedence. Philosophers, unsurprisingly, opt for reason.

Plato denied that there can be any knowledge based upon the world of sights and sounds. For him, the only objects of knowledge are certain abstract entities not perceptible by the senses. Friedrich Nietzsche and Immanuel Kant expressed similar views. Nietzsche wrote that we can get no closer to reality than our own sense experience and have no way of evaluating its correspondence with the real world. Kant distinguished between noumena and phenomena. External reality is comprised of noumena, but we perceive only appearances (phenomena). The three great philosophers all concluded that knowledge not filtered by our mental faculties is impossible.

The ancient Greeks viewed observations of the physical world as a valid way to learn, but they preferred seeking truth through logic alone. Aristotle maintained that women have fewer teeth than men. He apparently did not think it necessary to verify this assertion by examining any mouths. He proposed several laws of motion. One is that heavy objects fall faster than lighter ones. He didn't test that proclamation either, and it is wrong. He also gave the wrong answer to the following question: Suppose that you are in a moving vehicle and throw a ball straight up in the air. Will it land behind you or back in your hand? Can you do better than Aristotle? The answer is in footnote 162.[162]

Although Aristotle did not have a great batting average, even great scientists sometimes defer to reason. Isaac Newton refused to believe that the earth could be much older than 6,000 years on the strength of the reasoning that led Archbishop Usher to place the date of creation at 4,004 BC. Johannes Kepler was an astronomer and mathematician and a key figure in the seventeenth-century scientific revolution. He claimed to answer the question: Why are there six planets? Kepler proposed that the distance relationships between the six planets known at that time could be understood in terms of the five Platonic solids enclosed within a sphere that represented the orbit of Saturn. The six spheres each corresponded to one of the planets (Mercury, Venus, Earth, Mars, Jupiter, and Saturn).

Francis Bacon was a brilliant man who made important contributions to law, literature, philosophy, and science. He challenged the authority of Aristotle and insisted that investigations should begin with observations. Yet Bacon also challenged Galileo's claim to have seen four moons around Jupiter. Bacon's strategy was to use pure reason. Seven bodies in space were known at that time, and he argued that there must be exactly seven.

> There are seven windows given to animals in the domicile of the head, through which the air is admitted to the tabernacle of the body, to enlighten, to warm and to nourish it. What are these parts of the microcosmos: Two nostrils, two eyes, two ears and a mouth. So in the heavens, as in a macrocosmos, there are two favourable stars, two unpropitious, two luminaries, and Mercury undecided and indifferent. From this and many other similarities in nature, such as

---

162. The ball will come straight back down. You, the car, the air in the car, and the ball are all moving at the same speed.

the seven metals, etc., which it were tedious to enumerate, we gather that the number of planets is necessarily seven.[163]

Another of Galileo's contemporaries, astronomer and scholar Francesco Sizi, used very similar wording in attempting to refute him:

There are seven windows in the head, two nostrils, two ears, two eyes and a mouth; so in the heavens there are two favorable stars, two unpropitious, two luminaries, and Mercury alone undecided and indifferent. From which and many other similar phenomena of nature such as the seven metals, etc., which it were tedious to enumerate, we gather that the number of planets is necessarily seven... ancient nations, as well as modern Europeans, have adopted the division of the week into seven days, and have named them from the seven planets; now if we increase the number of planets, this whole system falls to the ground...moreover, the satellites are invisible to the naked eye and therefore can have no influence on the earth and therefore would be useless and therefore do not exist.[164]

Bacon and Sizi were certainly not stupid, nor were they irrational. Newton-Smith noted that Bacon's web of belief included the ideas that God created a harmonious universe and that harmony involves a mirroring of man and cosmos.[165] It follows, then, that facts about men can be reasons for hypotheses about the cosmos. Seven windows of the head give reason for inferring seven planets.

---

163. Goehring, C. (1978) The reception of the telescope. *Astronomy Quarterly*, 2:139-52.

164. http://www.anvari.org/fortune/Miscellaneous_Collections/408039_the-astronomer-francesco-sizi-a-contemporary-of-galileo-argues-that-jupiter-can-have-no-satellite.html

165. Newton-Smith, W. (1989) Relativism and the possibility of interpretation. In Hollis, M. & Lukes, S. (Eds) *Rationality and Relativism*. Cambridge, MA: MIT Press.

"Philosophy of science is as useful to scientists as ornithology is to birds."—Richard Feynman

The Aristotle/Sizi/Bacon example shows that rationally derived conclusions vary with the intellectual background and values of the reasoner; and it suggests that philosophers are naïve and empiricists win the day. But empiricist Galileo showed that pure reason can sometimes be enough for understanding physical phenomena. To test Aristotle's claim that heavy bodies fall faster than light ones, Galileo imagined a heavy cannon ball and light musket ball attached together to form a compound object. Aristotle would have predicted that the compound object would fall faster than the cannon ball alone. But it would also fall slower, since the light part would be a drag on the heavy part. Galileo's reasoning showed that all bodies fall at the same speed (at least in a vacuum).

There is a more modern—and successful—counterpart to Aristotle/Sizi/Bacon. Paul Dirac used complex mathematical calculations to develop an equation that combined quantum mechanics with special relativity theory. The equation works for electrons, which have a negative charge, and suggests the existence of particles that behave like electrons but with positive charge. Based purely on the equation, with no experimental evidence to back it up, Dirac in 1931 predicted something entirely new to science—antiparticles. He speculated that every particle has a mirror-image antiparticle with identical properties except for an opposite electric charge; and further, that there may even be a mirror universe of antimatter. In 1932, Carl Anderson discovered the positron. Dirac was awarded the Nobel Prize for physics in 1933.

Some philosophers claim that theirs is the only valid approach to knowledge, because the entire scientific approach is flawed. To appreciate their perspective, imagine that your friend claims that low doses of cyanide are healthful. You ask him to prove it, and he agrees to do an experiment on rats. When the local chemist refuses to sell him cyanide, he uses cyanocobalamin as a substitute. Cyanocobalamin is a cyanide ion substituted cobalamin derivative. He predicts that, if his claim is correct, rats with cyanocobalamin-supplemented diets will live longer than rats without supplementation. Months later, he happily reports that a careful double-blind experiment has upheld his prediction. What's more, he just obtained a vial of pure cyanide and spread some on a delicious-looking sourdough roll. He offers you the first bite. Should you accept? Before answering, consider two syllogisms.

1. Theory T predicts that, under carefully specified conditions, outcome O will occur. I arrange for the conditions, and O occurs. Therefore, I have proven theory T. In shorthand: If T, then O. O. Therefore, T.

2. Theory T predicts that, under carefully specified conditions, outcome O will occur. I arrange for the conditions but fail to obtain the predicted outcome. Therefore, theory T is false. In shorthand: If T, then O. Not O. Therefore, not T.

The second syllogism is valid. If the premises are true, the conclusion must also be true. (At least, so goes the party line.) The first syllogism is invalid—counterexamples are easy to imagine. For example, a prediction from the hypothesis "Unicorns run around at night in Golden Gate Park" (U) is that animal droppings will be found in the park (D). That leads to a syllogism of the same form as the first one. In symbols: If U, then D. D. Therefore, U.

Although animal droppings can be found, that does not prove that unicorns roam the park. A key feature that distinguishes science from other endeavors is that scientific hypotheses and theories can be tested. Yet the invalid confirmatory syllogism form is the basis of virtually all scientific research and reasoning—and much of everyday reasoning. And your friend's generous offer is of the invalid form:

> If low doses of cyanide are healthy, then rats with cyanocobalamin-supplemented diets will live longer than rats without supplementation.

> Rats with cyanocobalamin supplemented diets do live longer than rats without supplementation.

> Therefore, low doses of cyanide are healthy.

If the preceding seems too abstract, following is a real example in which a correct prediction provides minimal support for a hypothesis. Frogs fertilize their eggs externally. The male grabs the female from above and releases sperm as she lays eggs. In some species, females then collect the eggs in their mouths until the eggs are ready to hatch. Sapolsky theorized that many women are aware of how frogs reproduce and believe that they can also become pregnant by taking things in their mouths.[166] They should therefore, according to him, become compulsive eaters if they wish to get pregnant and anorexic if they wish not to. They should also be more likely than others to interpret ambiguous ink blots (the Rorschach test) as animals like frogs. So Sapolsky predicted that women who saw a frog on the Rorschach Inkblot Test were more likely than frog nonresponders to have an eating disorder. He tested thirty-one frog responders and thirty-one controls and found a significant difference between them: nineteen in the first group, only five in the second, had eating disorders.

Some years afterward, Lykken asked twenty of his colleagues who had not read the study to estimate the extent to which they believed Sapolsky's theory.[167] Then they were given a summary of the findings and asked to reassess their beliefs. Lykken reported that, before reading, they thought it was a ridiculous idea. Afterwards? They thought it was a ridiculous idea.

Some philosophers, notably Quine, take the position that empirical data take precedence over logic, because the principles of reasoning come from experience.[168] Once again compare the two argument forms:

1. If T, then O. Not O. Therefore, not T.

---

166. Sapolsky, A. (1964) An effort at studying Rorschach content symbolism: The frog response. *J Consulting & Clinical Psych*, 28: 469-72.

167. Lykken, D. (1968) Statistical significance in psychological research. *Psych Bull*, 70: 151-9.

168. Quine, W. (1953) *From a Logical Point of View*. Cambridge, MA: Harvard U Press.

2. If T, then O. O. Therefore, T.

Why do logicians say that (1) is valid and (2) invalid? They substitute meaningful terms for T and O and try to think of counterexamples. Succeed and they call the argument valid, fail and they call it invalid. But a more powerful mind might draw different conclusions. Thus, according to Quine, the rules of logic are empirical and fallible and do not deserve special status among truth seekers. In fact, logical arguments bear a close resemblance to psychologists' descriptions of classical conditioning. When Russian physiologist Ivan Pavlov first rang a bell, his hungry dogs didn't respond. But after he had repeatedly rung the bell and always presented food immediately afterwards, the dogs began salivating at the sound of the bell. They had learned the following:

If B (bell), then F (food).
B.
Therefore, F.

A different kind of learning is called operant conditioning. Whenever an animal makes a response such as pressing a bar, it receives a reward such as food. The animal learns:

If B (bar press), then F (food).
B.
Therefore, F.

To dogs, rats, and logicians, the sequence B, then F may seem invariable and even universal. But some galactic experimenter may be having fun.

Chapter 12

SCIENCE EXCEPT
FOR QUANTUM MECHANICS

Our ancestors lived in a world of unpredictable famine, flood, plague, and saber-toothed tiger. To explain such events, the more imaginative among them constructed rich cosmologies of gods, demons, and other supernatural forces. Later in our history, a few large-brained individuals noticed that some phenomena occur in recurring patterns. These primitive scientists measured, experimented, theorized, and began to make the world comprehensible. Their intellectual descendants made science the preferred method for advancing knowledge. Shakespeare, Dosteovsky, Freud, and others may have probed deeper into the human condition, but science has dramatically changed how people live. The scientific method is the most powerful ever developed for studying the properties of the world. Science is the antidote to wild philosophizing. It is direct exploration of reality—empiricism in its most sophisticated form. But Nobel Prize winner Max Planck argued that science is limited in a crucial way. He wrote, "Science cannot solve the ultimate mystery of nature. And that is, because, in the last analysis, we ourselves are part of nature and therefore part of the mystery we are trying to solve."

There are other reasons to be wary about reports from scientific studies. Deception is a big problem. Both eminent and mediocre scientists have perpetrated frauds.

Scientists May Unconsciously Bias Results or Commit Deliberate Fraud

Editors and reviewers of scientific journals virtually never see the raw data that provide the foundation for articles; in an unknown but probably substantial number of instances, the data or computations on them are inaccurate. When psychologist Keith Wolins requested data from thirty-seven authors of published studies, only seven complied and three of the data sets had substantial errors.[169] Jelte Wicherts and colleagues asked the authors of 141 papers for their data.[170] Seventy-three percent didn't reply or said they were not willing or able to share the data, even though the journals that published the studies stipulated that they should. Wicherts and colleagues recalculated statistics from the published articles and found that authors who did not comply had, on average, weaker evidence and more errors than compliers in the reporting of statistical results.

Some scientists focus only on data that support their claims. For example, Spiro described a study on a drug for peptic ulcers: At the end of two weeks, the ulcer crater had healed in more than half the patients given the active drug and in only a third of patients taking placebos; that one observation point encouraged the researchers to claim that the drug speeded the healing of peptic ulcer. But at every other period of assessment, the drug and the placebo were equally effective.[171]

In the 1930s and 1940s, Nobel Prize winner Robert Millikan was the most famous U.S. scientist. Millikan's own notebooks

---

169. Wolins, K. (1962) Responsibility for raw data. *American Psychologist*, 17: 657-8.

170. Wicherts, J. et al. (2011) Willingness to share research data is related to the strength of the evidence and the quality of reporting of statistical results. *PLoS ONE* 6(11): e26828. doi:10.1371/journal.pone.0026828.

171. Spiro, H. (1997) Clinical reflections on the placebo phenomenon. In Harrington, A. (Ed.), *The Placebo Effect: An Interdisciplinary Exploration*. Cambridge, Harvard U Press.

reveal that he discarded data that didn't fit his hypotheses. Cyril Burt became famous in the 1920s for his research on the inheritance of intelligence. He became influential on educational matters and helped set up a system for segregating British students based on their IQ scores. After Burt's death in 1971, psychologist Leon Kamin scrutinized his data and became suspicious.[172] Burt had reported correlations between IQ scores of sets of twins who had been separated shortly after birth, and three different sets gave results identical to the third decimal point. The reported correlations of twins reared together were also identical in three separate studies. Such results are extremely implausible.[173] A reporter for London's *Sunday Times* failed to locate two people named in Burt's articles as his collaborators and who had signed several reviews praising him (in the *British Journal of Statistical Psychology*, which Burt edited). Burt's housekeeper acknowledged that he frequently used pseudonyms, and the reporter concluded that the "collaborators" had never existed.

Prior to Bruno Bettelheim's suicide in 1990, he had developed an international reputation for restoring severely disturbed children, especially autistic ones, to normal lives. He blamed autism on bad mothering. In his best-selling 1967 book *The Empty Fortress*, Bettelheim wrote that "the precipitating factor in infantile autism is the parent's wish that his child should not exist." He compared parents of autistic children to devouring witches, infanticidal kings, and SS guards in concentration camps. The accusations, which caused thousands of parents tremendous guilt and anguish, had no evidentiary support. Richard Pollak, on the basis of documents and interviews with people who had known, worked with,

---

172. Kamin, L. (1974). The science and politics of I.Q. *Social Research*, 41: 387–425.

173. If a fair coin is flipped 1,000 times, we'd expect to end up with about fifty percent heads. But it would be surprising if we got exactly 500 heads. And if we repeated the 1,000 tosses a few more times and got 500 heads each time, we'd have good reason to suspect chicanery. Burt's reported results are even more implausible.

and been patients of Bettelheim, wrote a damning biography.[174] He revealed Bettelheim's lies about the extent of his university training (no connection with the Vienna Psychoanalytic Institute), awards (no Summa cum Laude), and authorship of books. Bettelheim claimed to have cared for an autistic girl in his Vienna home, so Pollak interviewed her. She had lived in his house but was not autistic and had received care exclusively from his wife. Bettelheim claimed an eighty-five percent cure rate for his autistic children. That too was false. Moreover, most of the children had been neither severely disturbed nor autistic. Many of them reported that they had been subjected to physical brutality and sexual abuse.

The problem of scientific fraud is not restricted to a few rogues. In their book *Betrayers of the Truth*, reporters William Broad and Nicholas Wade documented many cases of fraud and then suggested that three factors influence its frequency of occurrence: the potential rewards, the personal ethics of scientists, and the perceived chances of getting caught.[175] The rewards, in many cases, are substantial. Several people who conduct clinical tests of drugs are paid by the drug manufacturers and gross more than one million dollars a year. Scientists' ethics, they argued, are probably similar overall to those of other members of society. Because access to laboratories and data is restricted, the only people close enough to suspect misconduct are likely to be friends of or collaborators with the perpetrator, with no power or inclination to investigate. So, the chance of getting caught is minuscule. Most frauds have been uncovered by accident. Broad and Wade speculated that for each case of major fraud uncovered (substantially more than one per year for the last fifty years), about 100,000 major and minor ones go undetected.

Fanelli meta-analyzed surveys of researchers on various ques-

174. Pollak, R. (1997) *The Creation of Dr. B: A Biography of Bruno Bettelheim*. NY: Simon & Schuster.

175. Broad, W. & Wade, N. (1982) *Betrayers of the Truth*. NY: Simon & Schuster.

tionable behaviors and reported that about two percent of respondents *admitted* to either making up or altering data to improve the outcome of a study at least once.[176] Even with anonymous surveys people are reluctant to admit that they've committed a wrongdoing, so the two percent figure is probably very conservative. About thirty-four percent admitted to failing to present data that contradicted their previous research or dropping data points from analyses based on a gut feeling that they were inaccurate. Fourteen percent said they knew someone who had fabricated, falsified, or altered data, and seventy-two percent said they knew someone who had taken part in other questionable research practices. Fanelli's data suggest that thousands of scientists get away with misconduct each year.

Wikipedia lists known examples of fraud in virtually every scientific discipline even though most cases probably go unreported—whistleblowers don't usually fare well. American scientists can go to the Office of Research Integrity to report misconduct, but whistleblowers in Europe have to go to their employer, who has a vested interest in covering up cases of misconduct.

In 1976, there were fewer than ten fraud retractions for every million published scientific studies. In 2007, there were 96 per million. The journal *Nature* reported in 2011 that, while the number of articles had increased forty-four percent over the past decade, retractions had increased tenfold. Brainard and Jia wrote that the number of retractions had risen from fewer than 100 annually before the year 2000 to nearly 1000 in 2014.[177] Ferric Fang and colleagues attributed the increase to both pressure to succeed in science and an increase in deception in overall society that science

---

176. Fanelli D (2009) How many scientists fabricate and falsify research? A systematic review and meta-analysis of survey data. *PLoS ONE* 4(5): e5738. https://pubmed.ncbi.nlm.nih.gov/19478950/

177. Brainard, J. & Jia, Y. (2018) What a massive database of retracted papers reveals about science publishing's 'death penalty.' https://www.sciencemag.org/news/2018/10/what-massive-database-retracted-papers-reveals-about-science-publishing-s-death-penalty

may be mirroring.[178] They found that only 21.3% of retractions were attributable to error; 67.4% were due to misconduct, including fraud or suspected fraud. The *people who committed the most fraud were professors* (not graduate students or postdocs).

RetractionWatch catalogues papers that have been withdrawn from the scientific literature. In 2015, more than 800,000 scientific articles were published and 684 retracted. If Fanelli's conservative estimate of two percent fraudsters is used, that leaves more than 16,000 that go undetected annually. As of January 2020, the Retraction Watch Database contained 21,792 items.

John Budd and colleagues have conducted several analyses of retractions and their aftermaths.[179] Their 1999 study found that 235 articles retracted during 1966–96 received more than 2,000 post-retraction citations. Fewer than eight percent of the citations acknowledged the retraction, and many treated the retracted papers as valid. More recently, Budd and colleagues reported that, of 2,491 articles retracted from the years 2010 through 2014, 64.8% were due to misconduct or presumed misconduct. They also looked at 265 retracted papers from the years 2001 through 2005. They found approximately 6,400 citations to those papers, and roughly ninety-six percent were positive in some way.

Uri Simonsohn exposed two serious cases of fraud in 2012. He believes that as much as five percent of all published research contains fraudulent data. "There are probably several very famous papers that have fake data, and very famous people who have done it."[180]

---

178. Casadevall, A. et al. (2012) Misconduct accounts for the majority of retracted scientific publications. *Proc Natl Acad Sci.*,109:17028-33. doi: 10.1073/pnas.1212247109. Epub 2012 Oct 1. Erratum in: Proc *Natl Acad Sci.*, 2013, 110:1137.

179. http://www.ala.org/acrl/sites/ala.org.acrl/files/content/conferences/ confsandpreconfs/national/2011/papers/retracted_publicatio.pdf; Budd, J. et al. (2016) An investigation of retracted articles in the biomedical literature. https://doi.org/10.1002/pra2.2016.14505301055

180. Buranyi, S. (2017) The hi-tech war on science fraud. https://www. theguardian.com/science/2017/feb/01/high-tech-war-on-science

Another common problem under the umbrella of misconduct is that of image manipulation or duplication.[181] Bik and colleagues scanned 20,000 biomedical papers containing photos and found duplicated or manipulated photos in about 800 (four percent) papers.[182] Even unmanipulated images can be presented in such a way that they are misleading or, less charitably but more accurately, fraudulent. Below is an example:

A temperature anomaly is the temperature difference between a particular year and an averaged reference period. Figure 11 seems to show that temperature anomalies have always been about the same, which undermines concerns about climate change. But the graph covers only the years 2002 – 2013. Figure 12 gives a more complete picture, from 1951 to 2016, and shows that there is considerable reason for concern.[183]

---

181. Of course, scientists are not the only ones who doctor photos. To take one example: On June 12, 2020, *Fox News'* site featured a photo of a man with a military-style rifle standing in front of what appears to be a smashed retail storefront. The photo was "actually a mashup of photos from different days, taken by different photographers – it was done by splicing a photo of an armed man, who had been at the protest zone June 10, with other images from May 30 of smashed windows in downtown Seattle." https://www.msn.com/en-us/news/politics/photojournalist-experts-criticize-fox-news-for-altering-images-of-protests-in-seattle/ar-BB15rtrC?ocid=spartanntp

182. Bik, E, et al. (2016) The prevalence of inappropriate image duplication in biomedical research publications. *mBio,* 7 (3) e00809-16; DOI: 10.1128/mBio.00809-16.

183. https://towardsdatascience.com/misleading-with-data-statistics-c6d506bdb9cf

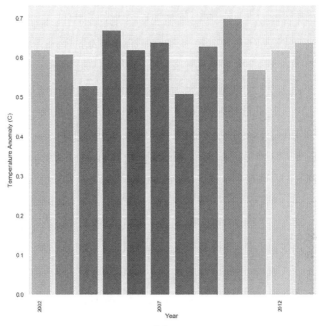

Figure 11: Temperature
Anomaly 2002–2013 (Source: NASA).

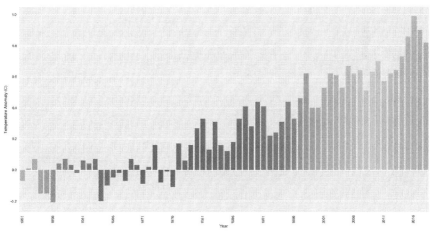

Figure 12: Temperature Anomaly Complete (Source: NASA).

Fang noted that newly graduated Ph.D.s must seek jobs in an increasingly competitive market. In 1973, most biologists had a tenure-track job within six years of getting a Ph.D. In 2006 the figure was fifteen percent. Yet lab directors, eager to generate research, continue to take on graduate students. For them, publishing in a prestigious journal often means the difference between a career in science and the need to seek new employment. Fang said that administrators count papers, look at the prestige of journals, and see how many grant dollars scientists garner. If they don't have funding, they don't get promoted. "It's not about the quality of the research." The scramble never ends. Everyone feels nervous even when they're successful, and the pressure drives many scientists to submit papers for publication before fully checking for errors and possible alternative explanations of their data. Delay might allow someone else to publish the same results.

The publish or perish mentality has led to the founding of about 10,000 journals that charge fees to publish non peer-reviewed work. By 2015, they had published about half-a-million dubious papers. Pisanski and her colleagues selected 360 journals, 120 each from two legitimate directories of science journals and 120 from a compendium of suspect journals.[184] All 360 got a letter from "Dr. Szust" seeking a position on their editorial board. The letter included a resume that listed phony degrees and invented book chapters.

Of the 240 legitimate journals, eight made a job offer. Of the other 120, forty offered her an editorial spot and four offered her the top slot—editor in chief. The journals made their motivations clear. In some cases, they asked for a direct payment, such as a subscription fee of $750. Some wrote that any money Szust generated by attracting scientists who would pay to publish would be split with the journal. One wrote, "If you want to start a new journal... you will get thirty percent of the revenue earned thru you." Clearly, the articles published in such journals cannot be trusted.

Personal biases influence experimental outcomes, as can be inferred from inspecting scientists' collected works. In areas of controversy,

---

184. Sorokowski, P. et al. (2017) Predatory journals recruit fake editor. *Nature*, 543: 481–3.

unbiased researchers might be expected to find both confirmatory and disconfirmatory evidence for a particular position. More typically, the most productive scientists report results exclusively on one side of the controversy. Pastore reported an almost perfect relationship between scientists' advocacy of conservative philosophies and research that emphasized hereditary influences on behavior; and liberal philosophies and emphasis on environmental factors. He wrote, "This inner relationship suggests that it would be as reasonable to classify the nature-nurture controversy as sociological in nature as to classify it as scientific in nature."[185] Similarly, biographical data of psychologists accurately predicted how the psychologists had interpreted studies on racial differences in IQ scores.[186]

Gould documented many instances of both unintentional (possibly) and clearly intentional bias perpetrated by leading psychologists in the intelligence testing field.[187] Lewis and colleagues published an article thirty years later in which they concluded that almost every detail of Gould's analysis is wrong.[188]

Bero and colleagues examined 192 published results of trials comparing one cholesterol-lowering statin drug to another or to a nonstatin drug. The reported results favored the funding company's drug about twenty times more often than the comparison company's drug. The interpretation of results favored the funding company's drug about thirty-five times more often than the comparison company's drug.[189]

---

185. Pastore, N. (1949) *The Nature-Nurture Controversy*. NY: King's Crown Press.

186. Sherwood, J. & Nataupsky, M. (1968) Predicting the conclusions of Negro-White intelligence research from biographical characteristics of the investigator. *J Personality Social Psych*, 8: 53-8.

187. Gould, S. (1981) *The Mismeasure of Man*. NY: W.W. Norton.

188. Lewis, J. et al. (2011) The mismeasure of science: Stephen J. Gould versus Samuel George Morton on skulls and bias. *PLoS Biol*, 9:e1001071+, doi:10.1371/journal.pbio.1001071, PMC 3110184.

189. Bero, L. (2007) Factors associated with findings of published trials

New drugs are protected by patent, so drug companies prefer having them turn out superior to older ones. In studies comparing new with old drugs, forty-three percent funded by a drug company and only thirteen percent funded from other sources favored the new. Furthermore, "In no case was a therapeutic agent manufactured by the sponsoring company found to be inferior to an alternative product manufactured by another company."[190]

Schrag wrote[191] that many of the most prolific drug researchers are also paid consultants to drug firms. Many work for the *National Institute of Mental Health* (NIMH) and the Food and Drug Administration (FDA), which licenses the drugs. They review each other's grant proposals, sit on committees together, and write for each other's journals. NIMH employees should act independently, but they often collaborate with drug-company consultants in mental health research and appear before FDA review committees on behalf of drug companies. Most medical journals are heavily supported by drug-company advertising, and editors of the journals serve on "impartial" FDA committees that review the safety and efficacy of drugs produced by their advertisers.

Reutlinger documented three types of sponsorship bias.[192] He gave one example of many possible for each type.

- Choice of experimental design. Bisphenol A is used in the manufacture of plastic materials contained in many common items including food and beverage cans. Ninety percent of publicly funded studies on exposure to Bisphenol

---

of drug-drug comparisons: Why some statins appear more efficacious than others. https://www.ncbi.nlm.nih.gov/pmc/articles/PMC1885451/.

190. Davidson, R. (1986) Source of funding and outcome of clinical trials. *J General & Internal Medicine*, 1: 155-8.

191. Schrag, P. (1978) *Mind Control*. NY: Pantheon

192. Reutlinger, A. What is epistemically wrong with research affected by sponsorship bias? the evidential account. http://philsci-archive.pitt.edu/16934/

A reported increased cancers in rats exposed to low doses; none of the industry-funded studies reported such effects. But the industry-funded studies used rats known to be insensitive to low-doses of substances similar to Bisphenol A. Publicly funded studies relied on sensitive animals.

- Selection and representation of the data obtained in a study. Celebrex, used to treat arthritis, was the subject of a year-long study sponsored by its maker. The study purported to show that Celebrex causes fewer side effects than six older arthritis drugs. It later turned out that the encouraging results were based on the first six months of the study. When the whole study was considered, Celebrex held no advantage over older and cheaper drugs.

- Choice of the scientific concepts used to interpret the results of a study. Reutlinger used tobacco to illustrate the problem. The choice of concept concerns the notion of causation. Tobacco companies hired scientists to undermine medical research supporting the claim that smoking cigarettes causes lung cancer. They noted that the data were only correlational. In addition, they used biased counter-studies that used inadequate statistics, ad hoc adjustments, and inconsistent data fitting along with incorrect empirical statements. Data were often manipulated or deliberately ignored.

All ten senior editors of the journal *Nutrients* resigned, alleging that the publisher pressured them to accept manuscripts of mediocre quality and importance.[193] Authors pay fees to *Nutrients* for their published articles, so the publisher has an incentive to publish as many as possible.

In 2006, the Union of Concerned Scientists and Public Employees for Environmental Responsibility distributed a 38-question

---

193. De Vrieze, J. (2018) Open-access journal editors resign after alleged pressure to publish mediocre papers. https://www.sciencemag.org/news/2018/09/open-access...

survey to 5,918 U.S. Food and Drug Administration (FDA) scientists in order to examine the state of science at the FDA.[194] The results are chilling.

- Eighteen percent answered "yes" to the statement "I have been asked, for non-scientific reasons, to inappropriately exclude or alter technical information or my conclusions in an FDA scientific document."

- Sixty-one percent knew of cases in which "Department of Health and Human Services or FDA political appointees have inappropriately injected themselves into FDA determinations or actions."

- Sixty percent knew of cases "where commercial interests have inappropriately induced or attempted to induce the reversal, withdrawal or modification of FDA determinations or actions."

- Twenty percent said they "have been asked explicitly by FDA decision makers to provide incomplete, inaccurate or misleading information to the public, regulated industry, media, or elected/senior government officials."

- Twenty-six percent feel that FDA decision makers implicitly expect them to "provide incomplete, inaccurate, or misleading information."

- Forty percent said they could not publicly express "concerns about public health without fear of retaliation."

- Thirty-six percent did not feel they could do so even inside the confines of the agency.

- Forty-seven percent think that the "FDA routinely provides complete and accurate information to the public."

Arturo Casadevall, editor in chief of the journal *mBio*, said that there are "perverse incentives that lead scientists to cut corners

---

194. (2008) https://www.ucsusa.org/resources/survey-fda-scientists

and, in some cases, commit acts of misconduct."[195]

Statcheck is a software package designed to detect statistical errors in peer-reviewed psychology articles by searching them for statistical results, redoing the calculations described in each paper, and comparing the two values to see if they match. When statcheck scanned papers published between 1985 and 2013, it found serious errors in about twelve percent.[196]

Honest Science

Even the most scrupulously honest scientists use methods that many of their colleagues disparage; and their inferences never come remotely close to exhausting the possibilities. Physics is the most sophisticated and powerful of all the sciences. Although the two main theories of modern physics, quantum theory and relativity, have both been tested to a degree of accuracy that would have astounded physicists of a century ago, they are incompatible with one another. For additional problems, read on.

The Basic Observations May Be Wrong

Scientists, no less than laypeople, are vulnerable to distorting effects of observations. They are subject to perceptual and other illusions.

Miniscule Changes in Initial Conditions May Produce Huge Changes in Ultimate Observation

"A slight variation in the axioms at the foundation of a theory can result in huge changes at the frontier."—Stanley Gudder

---

195. https://www.nytimes.com/2012/04/17/science/rise-in-scientific-journal-retractions-prompts-calls-for-reform.html

196. Stokstad, E. (2018) The truth squad. *Science*, 6408:1189-1191. DOI: 10.1126/science.361.6408.1189.

Determinism is the belief that all events are inevitable consequences of antecedent causes. Scientists work on the assumption that the world is deterministic, that the same initial conditions always produce the same results. Nobel Prize winner Max Planck wrote, "The assumption of an absolute determinism is the essential foundation of every scientific enquiry." Isaac Newton said that if he could know the position and motion of every particle in the universe at any one moment, he could predict the future of the universe into the infinite future.

The belief in determinism has served scientists well. Think about the amazing precision needed to send a manned rocket ship to the moon and back, and see below for discussion of the accuracy of quantum physics. Although Newton's vision can of course never be realized, other scientists worked on the assumption that they could make accurate long-term predictions of any physical system if they knew the starting conditions well enough. But more than a century ago, mathematician Henri Poincaré suggested that long-range accuracy will probably never be achieved in many fields. Poincaré analyzed a problem known as the n-body problem to predict the motion of a group of celestial objects. He found that even slight imprecisions such as rounding off a planet's mass soon became greatly magnified. He concluded that accurate prediction of outcomes was impossible. Poincaré was a forerunner of chaos theory. In a 1903 essay, he wrote, "...it may happen that small differences in the initial conditions produce very great ones in the final phenomena. A small error in the former will produce an enormous error in the latter."[197] He was correct, even for systems that are fully determined with no random elements involved.

Back then and until relatively recently, scientists thought that small initial differences in procedures, purity of materials, or composition of subjects had at most a trivial effect on outcomes. They hoped to shrink the uncertainty in the final prediction by

---

197. Poincaré, H. *The Foundations of Science*, NY: Science Press.

measuring the initial conditions to greater and greater accuracy. But minuscule variations in initial conditions are unavoidable and can lead to extremely discrepant long-term outcomes. Reasons for initial differences include such factors as background noise and less than infinitely precise instrumentation. Borwein and Rose suggested that readers think of a game of billiards. "No matter how consistent you are with the first shot (the break), the smallest of differences in the speed and angle with which you strike the white ball will cause the pack of billiards to scatter in wildly different directions every time."[198] The uncertainty principle of quantum mechanics (see p. 204) prohibits perfect accuracy, so conditions at any one moment can never be perfectly known.

In 1961, meteorologist Edward Lorenz set up a computer with several equations for modeling air currents.[199] One day he wanted to see a particular sequence again and, to save time, started in the middle of the sequence instead of the beginning. He entered the number off his printout and let it run. To his great surprise, the second run produced a much different sequence than the original. He eventually realized that, although the computer's memory stored the numbers to six decimal places, he had printed out only three decimal places. He had truncated the number .506127 to .506. A difference of one part in a thousand had led to a very different final result.

Lorenz's work became known as the butterfly effect, because the difference in the starting points of his two sequences is comparable to the change in atmosphere produced by a butterfly flapping its wings. The picturesque inference is that, whether or not a butterfly flaps its wings on one side of the world can determine whether or not a storm arises one year later on the other side. Chaos theory can be applied to the growth of populations, weather systems, behavior of water boiling on a stove, migratory patterns of birds, and

198. Borwein, J. & Rose, M. (2012) Explainer: What is chaos theory? https://www.sbs.com.au/news/explainer-what-is-chaos-theory.

199. Lorenz, E. (1963) Deterministic nonperiodic flow. *J Atmospheric Sciences*, 20: 130–41.

the spread of vegetation across a continent. Chaos is everywhere. Following are some examples.

Physicist Mitchell Feigenbaum and biologist Robert May developed a mathematical example of chaos as applied to the growth of a population.[200] They developed an equation that predicted population growth from the following factors:

P: The current year's population. P = 1 represents the maximum possible population and P = 0 represents extinction.

R: The rate at which the population would grow if there were no deaths.

PN: The next year's population.

It might seem that, as R increases, so too should PN. And that's just what happens—but not always. At low values of R, the population stabilizes at a single number. R = 2.0 is the replacement rate. (If two parents produce two children, the overall population won't grow or shrink. So, for R = 2.0 the population stabilizes at .5. For R = 1 the population goes extinct. For R = 2.8, the population stabilizes at .64. The initial population is irrelevant.

Then, for R = 3.2, a strange thing happens: the population oscillates between .5 and .8—one value for one year, another value the next, with a forever repeating cycle. Raising R to 3.5 causes P to oscillate between four different values, and raising it slightly more causes an oscillation between eight values. And then the really bizarre—raising R to 3.57 causes P to vary unpredictably from year to year, with even miniscule changes in the starting population leading to radical changes in PN. Continuing to raise R gives islands of stability in PN amid the chaos. The key point is that accurate predictions become impossible.

Douglas Wahlsten and colleagues tried to standardize various tests used to measure mouse behaviors.[201] In Portland, Albany,

---

200. http://www.andrewclem.com/Chaos.html

201. Wahlsten, D. et al. (2003) Different data from different labs: Lessons

and Edmonton, Canada, they tested animals of exactly the same age (to the day) on the same date at the same local time. The animals had been weaned at the same age, and all their mothers had been weighed at the same time. The mice were all kept in the same kind of cage, with the same brand and thickness of sawdust bedding, which was changed on the same day of the week. All were handled at the same time by human hands sheathed in the same kind of surgical glove. They were fed the same food, kept under the same kind of lighting, all at the same temperature. Their tails were marked for identification only with a Sharpie pen. Then the scientists tested eight different strains of mice with six standardized behavioral tests. (A strain is a population of mice that has been maintained by successive brother to sister matings over many generations.)

For some of the tests, the results were quite similar within strains and laboratories, which indicates that the researchers were careful and competent. But for some tests, the same strain performed radically differently from laboratory to laboratory. One test measures the effects of cocaine on a mouse's activity level. In the Portland lab, cocaine-treated mice increased their activity by an average of 667 centimeters of movement per fifteen minutes. In Albany, the average increase was 701 centimeters. In Edmonton, the same strain increased by an average of more than 5,000 centimeters. Sapolsky wrote, "Imagine, for comparison, that a set of identical triplet boys were all training for the Olympics. On a given day, the three brothers compete together; all have the same night's rest, all have the same breakfast, all feel fine. The first brother clears eighteen feet on the pole vault; the second clears eighteen feet, one inch; and the third brother launches himself 140 feet into the air."[202]

Two prominent characters in the 2005 movie *Crash* are a police detective played by actor Don Cheadle and his street criminal

---

from study of gene-environment interaction. *J Neurobiol*, 54: 283-311.

202. Sapolsky, R. (2000) Genetic hyping. *The Sciences*, 40: March/April.

brother, played by Larenz Tate. Several other films contrast sibling pairs, making such contrasts almost a Hollywood cliché. They show that small variations in genetics or early environment may produce enormous differences in final character.

Mark Oliver gave 10 examples of butterfly effects that changed the world. Three of his examples are described below:

1. Elián González was a five-year-old Cuban boy whose mother drowned in 1999 while attempting to leave Cuba with him. His rescue by two fishermen set off a bitter custody battle. His father, still in Cuba, wanted Elián returned to him. President Bill Clinton sided with the father. Elián's Miami relatives wanted him to stay with them, and Vice President Al Gore initially sided with them. But then he changed and supported Clinton's position. The Florida Cuban-American community was incensed about the Democrats' handling of the custody battle. Analysts have estimated that, in the ensuing presidential election between Gore and George Bush, as many as 50,000 Cuban-Americans in Florida who would have otherwise stayed home or voted Democratic voted Republican. Bush won Florida by only 537 votes, and Florida won him the election. If Elián Gonzalez had not gotten on that boat to America, Al Gore would have become President and the Iraq War almost certainly would not have happened.

2. Actress Jeri Ryan was married to Jack Ryan, a candidate in the 2004 U.S. Senate race in Illinois. During the election, the Ryans' divorce papers got out to the press, revealing that Jack Ryan had tried to take his wife to some less-than-wholesome clubs. Jack, she said, "wanted me to have sex with him there, with another couple watching. I refused." In the ensuing scandal, Ryan dropped out of the election, and Barack Obama, who would have had a tough fight, won handily. With his spot as Senator, he started moving toward becoming the first black President—all because Jeri Ryan

refused to go to a sex club.

3. Lionel Logue was the speech therapist who helped King George VI overcome his stammer. Before that, he helped aspiring reporter Keith Murdoch overcome a heavy stutter. Thanks to him, Murdoch went on to a successful career as a journalist and newspaper magnate. Upon Murdoch's death, his son Rupert took over the company and eventually created Fox News. Fox has changed the way Americans think. According to one study, up to eight percent of people who have seen Fox News switched from Democrat to Republican because of it. It has been called the "single most important player" in American elections. Without it, the Tea Party movement never would have happened.

For other examples, see https://listverse.com/2017/05/15/top-10-butterfly-effects-that-completely-changed-the-world/.

Clearly, seemingly unrelated events separated by both time and place can have profound effects on long range, complex human behaviors. Don Cheadle and his brother could have easily switched roles.

New Unpredictable Phenomena May Emerge

Chaos theory shows that even tiny differences in starting point can lead to huge differences in results. Emergent phenomena pose a different but also probably insurmountable problem for knowledge seekers. Before the remarkable discoveries of quantum mechanics, most scientists believed that the properties of all objects could be reduced to their constituent atoms. They were reductionists. Reductionism implies that a system is nothing but the sum of its parts. For example, the behaviorist school of psychology assumes that all complex behaviors can be reduced to a series of stimulus-response chains; and many neuroscientists believe that all human emotion and cognition will someday be fully explained by brain chemistry.

But not all phenomena can be accurately predicted from their constituent parts. Sometimes entirely new properties and behaviors emerge, so the behavior of the whole is unpredictable even with knowledge of the nature of its parts. Salt, for example, looks nothing like either of the two elements, sodium and chlorine, of which it is comprised. Here are a few more examples of complex behaviors that arise spontaneously from relatively simple elements:

- A single human neuron isn't very smart, but put billions into a brain, have them connect with each other, and you may get an Einstein or Leonardo.

- A single ant is also not very smart, but thousands of simple individuals emerge as an ant colony. The colony acts en masse to explore and exploit its surroundings. It reacts appropriately to food sources, floods, enemies, and other phenomena.

- Living cells consist mostly of carbon, hydrogen, and oxygen. The three elements individually give no hint of life. But combine them properly and a living organism emerges.

- Flocking of birds emerges from simple rules followed by each bird: stay aligned with your nearest neighbors and avoid predators. Flocking is not predictable from knowing all there is to know about any single bird.

- Social networks started out as a way for people with common interests to meet. They have emerged as political weapons. In 2016, Russian cyber hackers used social media to suppress voting in Democratic precincts, enhance turnout in Republican precincts, and control the topics of news networks. Their efforts helped elect Donald Trump.

The Data May Not Be Replicable

The next few criticisms apply primarily to medical and behavioral research. The reason is that living organisms are variable, so chance factors can play an important role. As the previous section showed, identical procedures may not give identical results.

Biomedical

Although obesity often leads to diabetes, and cigarette smokers have shorter life expectancies than nonsmokers, not all obese people become diabetic and some smokers are centenarians. The average man is taller than the average woman, but many women tower over many men. This variability has consequences, especially for biomedical scientists. It makes replication crucial for inspiring confidence that reported phenomena are real rather than artifacts of unusual properties of the original subjects or experimental procedures. Hersen and Barlow called replication "the heart of any science."[203] Without replication, a chance positive finding may be accepted by the scientific community for a long time. But there's a problem: Replication research is discouraged by reviewers and editors. They want to publish original material.

Hubbard and Vetter analyzed eighteen business journals covering the years 1970-1991.[204] Replications constituted less than ten percent of empirical work in the accounting, economics, and finance areas, and five percent or less in management and marketing areas. When such work was undertaken, the results *usually* conflicted with existing findings. The true percentage of conflicting studies is probably substantially higher, since many disconfirming studies are not published. (There is a bias against publishing negative results. See below.)

Evanschitzky and Armstrong found that, in the two major forecasting journals, 35.3% of the replications provided full support for the findings of the initial study, 45.1% provided partial support, and 19.6% provided no support.[205] C. Glenn Begley was head

---

203. Hersen, M. & Barlow, D. (1976) *Single Case Experimental Designs: Strategies for Studying Behavior Change*. NY: Pergamon.

204. Hubbard, R. & Vetter, D. (1996) An empirical comparison of published replication research in accounting, economics, finance, management, and marketing. *J Business Research*, 35: 153-64.

205. Evanschitzky, H. & Armstrong, J. (2010) Replications of forecasting

of global cancer research at Amgen, and he and Lee Ellis identified fifty-three important publications in top journals from reputable labs. Hoping to build on them for drug development, they had their team try to reproduce the findings. They were unable to replicate forty-seven of them.[206]

Prinz and colleagues also tried to validate several exciting published articles.[207] They wrote that their studies "... have often resulted in disillusionment when key data could not be reproduced. Talking to scientists, both in academia and in industry, there seems to be a general impression that many results that are published are hard to reproduce." They queried scientists who had worked within their company during the previous four years on projects in oncology, women's health, and cardiovascular diseases. Of sixty-seven separate projects, the findings of their scientists were completely in line with the relevant published data in only twenty to twenty-five percent of the cases. In almost two-thirds of the projects, there were inconsistencies between published data and in-house data that either considerably prolonged the duration of the target validation process or, in most cases, resulted in termination of the projects.

Mobley and colleagues surveyed the faculty and trainees at MD Anderson Cancer Center with an anonymous questionnaire. About fifty percent of respondents reported having failed at least once to reproduce published data.[208]

Nosek organized a 4-year study with the goal of replicating 100 prominent psychology papers. Only thirty-nine percent could be

research. *International J Forecasting.* 26: 4-8.

206. Begley, G. & Ellis, L. (2012) Drug development: Raise standards for preclinical cancer research. *Nature,* 483: 531-3.

207. Prinz, F. et al. (2011) Believe it or not: How much can we rely on published data on potential drug targets? *Nature Reviews Drug Discovery,* 10: 712. https://www.nature.com/articles/nrd3439-c1

208. Mobley, A. et al. (2013) A survey on data reproducibility in cancer research provides insights into our limited ability to translate findings from the laboratory to the clinic. *PLoS One.* 8(5): e63221.

replicated unambiguously.[209] A more recent project attempted to replicate all twenty-one experimental social science papers published in *Science* and *Nature* between 2010 and 2015. Thirty-eight percent of the studies did not replicate successfully.[210]

John Ioannidis and colleagues have used a variety of methods to evaluate the trustworthiness of biomedical data. In a 2005 paper, Ioannidis reported that one out of every three highly cited studies published in influential medical journals is either refuted or seriously weakened by subsequent research. Of forty-nine of the most widely-cited studies published between 1990 and 2003 in several of the world's most prestigious medical journals, later research contradicted sixteen percent and considerably weakened an additional sixteen percent. In a follow-up article, Ioannidis argued that the vast majority of published research claims are incorrect.[211] The studies are too small and have too much flexibility in designs and definitions. Financial interests influence reported results; and intense competition to publish first on hot topics skews research priorities. More recently, Ioannidis's team found thirty-seven clinical trials that had been reanalyzed, and they compared the reanalyses with the originals. In thirteen cases (thirty-five percent), the conclusions were at odds with those of the original authors. Tom Jefferson, a researcher who reviews studies for the nonprofit Cochrane Collaboration, said, "The process [of analyzing clinical trials] is so subjective, you can twist it any way you want."[212]

---

209. Bohannon, J. (2015) Many psychology papers fail replication test. *Science*, 349: 910-11.

210. Servick, K. (2018) Social science studies get a 'generous' test, *Science*, 361: 836.

211. Ioannidis, J. (2005) Why most published research findings are false. *PLoS Medicine*, 2: e124; Ioannidis J. (2005) Contradicted and initially stronger effects in highly cited clinical research. *JAMA*, 294: 218-28. doi:10.1001/jama.294.2.218.

212. https://www.washingtonpost.com/news/morning-mix/wp/2014/09/10/why-medical-clinical-trials-are-so-wrong-so-often/

Medical reversals occur when new clinical trials, superior to their predecessors because they used better controls or a better study design or a larger sample size, show that current medical practices do not work or do more harm than good. The reversals may occur for both medications and surgical procedures. A recent meta-analysis of 3,000 studies published in three prestigious medical journals over the last fifteen years identified 396 cases of medical reversals.[213]

The Data May Have Been Analyzed Incorrectly

Another major problem is data analysis. Reviewers of manuscripts submitted for publication often do not evaluate either arithmetic computations or statistical procedures. Yet McGuigan found statistical errors in forty percent of articles in the *British Journal of Psychiatry*, and Welch and Gabbe reported a nineteen percent error rate in use of statistics in the *American Journal of Obstetrics and Gynecology*.[214] In the official journal of the *American Heart Association*, Glantz wrote: Approximately half the articles published in medical journals that use statistical methods use them incorrectly.[215]

Eklund and colleagues found that certain widely used statistical methods in fMRI research inflate statistical significance.[216] This calls

---

213. Herrera-Perez, D. et al. Meta-research: A comprehensive review of randomized clinical trials in three medical journals reveals 396 medical reversals. https://elifesciences.org/articles/45183 accessed on 6/11/2019

214. Welch, G. & Gabbe, S. (2002) Statistics usage in the *American Journal of Obstetrics and Gynecology*: Has anything changed? *Am J Obstet Gynecol*, 18: 584-6.

215. Glantz, S. (1980) Biostatistics: how to detect, correct and prevent errors in the medical literature. *Circulation*, 61:1-7.

216. Eklund, A. et al. (2016) Cluster failure: Why fMRI inferences for spatial extent have inflated false-positive rates. *Proc Natl Acad Sci*, 113: 7900–05.

into question the validity of a great many published fMRI studies.

Whereas a competent chemist can mix hydrogen and oxygen in the proper proportions and synthesize water every time, the most that a pharmacologist testing a new drug or a clinical psychologist evaluating a new type of therapy can generally hope for is that the treated and untreated groups differ on average. They typically evaluate the differences with statistics. The standard statistical procedure is called null hypothesis significance testing. The null hypothesis is that the two groups don't differ, i.e., the treatment did not have an effect. The researcher's goal is to show that the null hypothesis is incorrect. Many eminent scientists disapprove of the strategy, asserting that it is so misguided as to produce uninterpretable data.

As indicated above, cheating in science is not rare. One reason is that professional advancement depends on publishing, and statistically significant results make publication much easier. Suppose a scientist predicts that a coin will be biased toward heads. If he flips the coin 1,000 times, 527 hits is a statistically significant result (the probability that the results occurred by chance alone is only 4.6%, i.e., $p = .046$), but 526 heads is not ($p = .053$, and the standard cut-off point is $p < .05$). If publication depended on showing statistical significance, he would be sorely tempted in the second case to mis-score one flip. A picture posted by Peter Ubel strongly suggests that many scientists have given in to temptation.[217] If research were conducted honestly, a roughly equal number of results should be just above the magic 0.05 level as just below. As Figure 14 shows, such is not the case. Larry Wasserman created the graph from 3,627 p-values collected from reputable journals. The far too many p-values just a little bit less than 0.05 (to the left of the red line) compared to the number just greater than 0.05 suggest that something fishy is going on.

---

217. https://www.peterubel.com/a-picture-of-scientific-publication-bias/

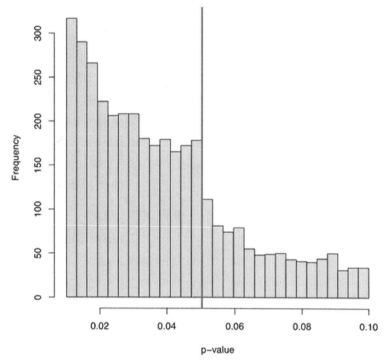

Figure 13: p-values below and above .05.

Null hypotheses are nearly always false. Treatment A is virtually never *exactly* as effective as treatment B. Not to fifty decimal places. Given enough data, some difference is almost certain to show up. Although tossing a fair coin should result in an approximately equal number of heads and tails, a slight nick or smudge might create a tiny advantage for one side over the other. If such a coin is tossed a billion times, the result is likely to be statistically significant but absolutely unimportant.

In a typical brain analysis using functional magnetic resonance imaging (fMRI), about 130,000 voxels are investigated. (A voxel is the smallest unit of three-dimensional space in a computer image.) Some voxel clusters will almost surely be statistically significant just by chance. (If enough people toss a fair coin ten times, someone will get ten heads.) Bennett and colleagues showed the absurdity of the approach of many neuroscientists by using an fMRI scanning session with a dead salmon.[218] They exposed it to a social perspective-taking task. There were statistically significant active voxel clusters in the salmon's brain cavity and spinal column.

Suppose that treatment A is compared with placebo and the results are statistically significant. Then treatment B is compared with placebo and the results are not statistically significant. That would not justify concluding that A differs significantly from B. Maybe A versus placebo just reached significance and B versus placebo just missed. Then A and B might be virtually identical. The proper way to test whether A and B are significantly different is to compare them directly. Nieuwenhuis and colleagues reviewed behavioral, systems, and cognitive neuroscience articles in five top-ranking journals and found that seventy-eight used the correct procedure and seventy-nine the incorrect one.[219]

Observations Reported in Scientific Publications May Differ Considerably from Equally Careful Observations over the Same Material that Go Unpublished

Research requires financing, and granting agencies award money to applicants with goals compatible with their own. Funders of medical research want to show that their products are safe and effective. Therefore, much more money is available for research on drugs than on non-patentable vitamins; and much more is available to show the benefits rather than adverse effects of drugs. A well-documented reason for non-publication is that the funding company's product was ineffective or harmful. Walton surveyed studies of aspartame (Nutrasweet®) to see if funding source was

---

218. Bennett, C. et al. (2009) Neural correlates of interspecies perspective taking in the post-mortem Atlantic salmon: an argument for proper multiple comparisons correction. *J Serendipitous Unexpected Results*, 1: 1-5.

219. Nieuwenhuis S. et al. (2011) Erroneous analyses of interactions in neuroscience: A problem of significance. *Nature Neuroscience*, 14: 1105 – 07.

related to study outcome.[220] The Nutrasweet® industry had funded seventy-four studies, and 100% of them attested to aspartame's safety; of the ninety-two independently funded studies, ninety-two percent identified a health problem. A bibliography supplied by the Nutrasweet® Company included many studies of questionable validity and relevance, with multiple instances of the same study being cited up to six times.

There is a more insidious problem. Imagine a researcher who claims to know magic words that enable people to fly. If he succeeds, magazines and scientific journals will fight to publish his results. If he fails, nobody will be interested. It's sensible to publish and publicize positive results and pay less attention to negative ones. But a consequence is that if a treatment is ineffectual, most researchers who test it won't see an effect and may not submit their results for publication; if they do submit, reviewers and editors may not be interested. Dickersin estimated that about half of the 60,000 clinical trials ongoing in the United States will never be published in a scientific journal. So, few people will learn about the failures, and other researchers might try the same study. Someone might get positive results purely by chance. (If enough people flip a coin ten times, someone will get ten heads.) So, while the negative results remain unknown, the chance positive results will be published and add to the misinformation that already fills our heads. Following are three examples:[221]

- In the 1980s, sixteen published studies indicated that a combination of two drugs increased survival time in certain cancer patients. John Simes tracked down the unpublished studies on the drugs (possible because the National Cancer Institute had records of all the research the NCI had

---

220. Walton, R. Survey of aspartame studies: correlation of outcome and funding sources. https://www.lightenyourtoxicload.com/wp-content/uploads/2014/07/dr-walton-survey-of-aspartame-studies.pdf

221. (2005) Clinical trials registration: Overdue yet elusive. https://www.jhsph.edu/news/stories/2005/dickersin.html

funded). When he combined the results from all methodologically sound studies, the apparent advantage of the drug combination disappeared.

- In the 1980s and early 1990s, anti-arrhythmic drugs were used extensively in heart patients with arrhythmias. But then an unpublished study was discovered that proved that the drugs harm cardiac patients. Doctors stopped prescribing them for cardiac patients, but not before an estimated 50,000 to 70,000 patients in the U.S. had died each year from the drugs.

- In the 1990s, twenty-seven published studies suggested that hormone therapy for menopausal women might cause heart trouble. But the results were not statistically significant, so they were largely ignored. Then seven unpublished studies were found that pointed to the same result. Taken together, the thirty-four studies revealed the dangers of hormone therapy. Women were not warned of the problem until six years later.

Turner and colleagues examined seventy-four FDA-registered studies of antidepressants.[222] Of the thirty-eight positive studies, thirty-seven were published as positive. Studies viewed by the FDA as having negative or questionable results were, with three exceptions, either not published (twenty-two studies) or published in a way that conveyed a positive outcome (eleven studies). According to the published literature, it appeared that ninety-four percent of the trials conducted were positive. By contrast, the FDA analysis showed that fifty-one percent were positive. .

The bias against publishing negative results has another consequence. Null hypothesis significance testing permits only dichotomous decisions (results either are or are not statistically significant). So, if two scientists get almost identical results but one set

222. Turner, E. et al. (2008) Selective publication of antidepressant trials and its influence on apparent efficacy. *New England J Medicine*, 358:252–60.

of data just reaches statistical significance and the other just misses, the second researcher may be tempted to cheat. Sometimes, falsifying the score of even a single subject is sufficient. As discussed above, the spate of recent scandals makes clear that many scientists have succumbed to temptation.

As a result of the problems noted above, many beliefs that endured in science for a long time were eventually shown to be wrong. Samuel Arbesman applied the concept of half-life, the time required for half the atoms of a given amount of a radioactive substance to disintegrate, to the dissolution of facts.[223] He cited a study on the decay in the truth of clinical knowledge about cirrhosis and hepatitis. The researchers gave a pile of fifty-year-old articles to a panel of experts and asked them which were still regarded as true and which had been refuted or were no longer considered interesting. They found that the half-life of truth was forty-five years. That is, half of what physicians thought they knew about liver diseases was wrong or obsolete forty-five years later. Some medical schools tell students that, within a few years, half of what they've been taught will be wrong—they just don't know which half. Appendix 6 gives a few examples. For many more, just Google "science overturned facts."

The Media Distorts the Public's Views of Scientific Findings

Most people get their science news from the mass media, and the media want to make the news exciting. That means no qualifiers, no mention of risks or side effects, no "maybe this will be useful in a few years," "this worked fairly well with rats but hasn't been tried with people yet." The first paper to present sensational news seizes the readership, so science writers report incomplete works. They often write about studies presented at scientific conventions; these

---

223. Arbesman, S. (2013) *The Half-Life of Facts: Why Everything We Know Has an Expiration Date*. NY: Penguin.

have frequently not been reviewed for methodological soundness, and they may never be published. But science writers report about them as though they are well established. Reporters and editors, concerned about readability, may omit or compromise crucial information. Many are trained in journalism, not science. In any case, science has become tremendously specialized, yet many newspapers have only a single reporter to cover all the sciences.

Hard Sciences

To serious skeptics, variability of subjects, conflicts of interest, fraud, and methodological errors are almost irrelevant. They would distrust scientific knowledge even if all scientists were highly competent and scrupulously honest. For, no matter how flawlessly a research project is conducted, speculations concerning its meaning are always tentative and probably wrong. New theories constantly replace old ones and inviolable laws are superseded.

Chapter 13

INFERENCES

Data, once collected, must still be interpreted. Imagine a study in which people receive a treatment and experience an improvement in their condition. Many lay people would conclude that the treatment was the cause of the change. But there would be several plausible alternatives. Three obvious ones are that (1) the condition treated would have changed naturally with the passage of time—think of the common cold; (2) the treatment had no specific effects and acted only by modifying the recipient's expectations; and (3) the posttreatment change occurred by chance. Scientific researchers in medicine and related fields maximize the probability that their interpretation is correct by eliminating as many plausible alternatives as possible. So they typically use many subjects and randomly assign some to a control group. They treat experimental and control subjects exactly the same except for the treatment itself. Then, subsequent differences between the groups can reasonably be attributed to the treatment. To prevent bias, researchers do not let subjects know which group they are in; nor do they themselves know until after the data have been collected. The procedure, called the double-blind randomized controlled trial (RCT), is the most rigorous design available to researchers in many scientific fields. It is the evidentiary gold standard. But the RCT does not yield unambiguous results. In fact, there are often powerful plausible alternatives to the interpretation of an RCT.

As indicated above, the lure of money, fame, and job security has persuaded many scientists to distort their findings. Some do studies that are double blind in name only. Both researchers and subjects can observe clinical improvement and side effects and thus correctly guess which group the subjects are in. Furthermore, when Schulz quizzed 400 researchers after promising them anonymity, more than half admitted opening unsealed envelopes containing the group assignments, or cracking codes meant to hide the identity of the groups, or searching for a master list of codes, or holding sealed envelopes up to the light.[224]

The conclusions drawn from many types of research designs can be reduced to syllogisms of the following form:

Theory T predicts that, under carefully specified conditions, outcome O will occur.

A researcher arranges for the conditions, and the predicted outcome O does occur.

Therefore, theory T is correct.

As discussed on p. 155, such syllogisms are invalid. That is, even if they have true premises, their conclusions may be false.

Try solving the problems of Problem set 2. See page 264 for the answers.

Problem Set 2
Ridiculous Problems

1. Fill in the blanks. 1 2 ? ? ?
2. Now try. 1 2 3 4 5 ? ? ?
3. A car has crashed into a tree. Explain what happened.
4. A car has crashed into a tree. There is an oil slick on the road

---

224. Schulz, K. (1995) Empirical evidence of bias. Dimensions of methodological quality associated with estimates of treatment effects in controlled trials. *JAMA*, 273: 408-12.

and skid marks from the car. Explain what happened.

Back in high school, my fellow physics students and I dropped rocks from different heights and measured their times to hit the ground. Our teacher then showed that the equation $T = \sqrt{D}/16$ (Time in seconds = the square root of distance in feet divided by 16) fit the data—not perfectly, because some error is unavoidable—but quite closely. He assigned us to drop additional rocks from new distances to see if the equation generated correct answers. We did and it did. Even without the equation, a bright lay observer could have made fairly accurate predictions. More than 150 years ago, Thomas Huxley noted that, "The method of scientific investigation is nothing but the expression of the necessary mode of working of the human mind. It is simply the mode at which all phenomena are reasoned about, rendered precise and exact."

Stripped to the bone, science is a search for relationships between variables. Scientists observe and experiment to determine how one variable changes with another. Then they try to find equations that relate the variables mathematically, and they create theories to explain the equations. For example, an industrial psychologist might vary the number of motivational lectures given to different groups of salespeople, then record their average number of sales per week. She might then record her data in a table such as Table 4. The equation $Y = X + 1$ fits the data perfectly, but using the equation reveals a devastating weakness of science and a therefore equally devastating weakness of empiricism and the normal working of the human mind: Although it fits the data, the equation is not unique. In fact an infinite number of others also fit, yielding an infinite number of mathematically correct predictions of time for distances not yet tried. The proof is too complex for me to show, but I can give two examples.

Table 4

X (number of lectures)	Y (number of sales per week)
1	2.0000
2	3.0000
3	4.0000
4	?
5	6.0000
6	7.0000

For Table 4, the obvious prediction is that the missing value is 5.0000. But two other equations that also fit the data of Table 4 are:

$$Y = \frac{X^5 - 17X^4 + 107X^3 - 307X^2 + 576X}{180}$$

and

$$Y = \frac{X^7 - 1582X^4 + 14651X^3 - 49322X^2 + 101772X}{32760}$$

When X = 4, the three equations give Y values of 5.0000, 5.0667, and 5.0974, respectively. The differences may seem trivial, and in any case show that increases in X are associated with increases in Y. So, look at Table 5.

Table 5

X	Y
1	2
2	3
3	?
4	5

Again, the obvious solution is that $Y = X + 1$ and the missing $Y = 4$. But another equation that fits the data is:

$$Y = \frac{55X^4 - 382X^3 + 749X^2 - 374X}{24}$$

Solving when $X = 3$ gives a Y value of -10. And an equation can be found to give any other Y value desired. The only reason for preferring the predictions of $Y = X + 1$ to those of any other equation is that our little brains prefer simplicity. This is not just about equations, mathematics, or science. It applies to every relationship, every event, every phenomenon of life. The more we learn, the more readily we detect flaws in initially plausible explanations for phenomena. Eventually, our minds harden and all but one of the few alternatives that we considered is discredited thoroughly. But inability to imagine other alternatives indicates only a failure of imagination—the alternatives are there—an infinite number. For any prediction or explanation about anything, there are an infinite number of conceivable alternatives.

Einstein said about his theory of relativity: "It will have to yield to another one... The process of deepening the theory has no limits." And Joseph Traub, quoted in *The End of Science*, said "We humans may believe Occam's razor—which holds that the best theories are the simplest—because these are the only theories our puny brains can comprehend."

Chapter 14

QUANTUM MECHANICS

The possible outcomes of some scientific studies, such as double-blinds to evaluate whether a treatment is effective, can be anticipated in advance. The answer will be yes or no, although critics may dispute results because of concerns about unavoidable errors, statistical aberration, incompetence, or dishonesty. Other scientists try to answer their research questions by developing and testing several hypotheses until they find one that fits and seems to explain the data. Some scientists encounter unanticipated findings that require revision of accepted doctrine. Examples are studies that overthrew the belief that neurons can produce only a single type of neurotransmitter; that new neurons cannot be created in adult mammalian brains; and that the inert gases never bond with other elements.

A fourth category of results, those from quantum mechanics (QM), calls into question the very notion of objective reality. Although discussions of the bizarre quantum world have enlivened many cocktail parties, the incredible implications are largely ignored. Yet they require reevaluation of historic events, relationships, morality, goals, the aftermath of death, and whether there are exceptions to the rule that red wine should never be drunk with fish.

Chaos theory shows that, even if the universe were completely deterministic, miniscule differences in starting positions would often lead to enormous discrepancies in final output. See p. 171. QM deals an even more severe blow to would-be prognosticators—it shows that the universe is not completely deterministic. There is an underlying, impossible to overcome, randomness.

Consider syllogism 6 from p. 81: Naive realism (the belief that the theories of science give a literally true account of the way the world is) leads to physics. Physics, if true, shows that naive realism is false. Therefore naive realism, if true, is false. Therefore it is false. The logic is unassailable; but how exactly should someone deal with the conclusion that naïve realism is false and objective reality a myth? The author of the syllogism, Bertrand Russell, had early twentieth century developments in physics in mind. Of all the sciences, physics has had the greatest success. Many and probably most physicists are reductionists—they believe that the features of the world we see can ultimately be explained by (reduced to) the movements and interactions of elementary particles such as electrons and photons. For example, botanist Robert Brown looked through a microscope at a drop of water that contained tiny pollen grains, and he noticed that the grains moved continuously in a seemingly random way. Almost eighty years later, Albert Einstein explained the puzzling Brownian motion by assuming that the pollen grains were continuously colliding with the water molecules. Einstein claimed that it was possible to calculate the average deflection of the particles and, from that, the sizes of molecules and atoms. Three years later, experimental results confirmed Einstein's theory.

Einstein's theorizing helped provide the foundation for quantum mechanics, which has achieved unparalleled success in experimental tests. It has accounted in a quantitative way for atomic phenomena with numerical precision never before achieved in any field of science. For example, the theoretical prediction for a quantity known as Dirac's number is 1.00115965246; the value obtained by experiment is 1.00115965221. Such accuracy holds for an extremely wide range of phenomena. The results of quantum physics are reliable, easily demonstrated in laboratories, and underlie much modern technology. About thirty-five percent of the U.S. gross national product is based on inventions made possible by quantum mechanics; these include semiconductors in computer chips, lasers in compact-disc players, magnetic resonance imaging in hospitals, and much more. Nobel Prize winner Murray Gell-Mann wrote, "All of modern physics is governed by that magnificent and thoroughly confusing discipline called quantum mechanics....It has survived all tests and there is no reason to believe that there is any flaw in it." In fact, not a single prediction from quantum mechanics has been contradicted by experiments. Nobel Prize winner Richard Feynman wrote, "If your model contradicts quantum mechanics, abandon it!"

As noted above, reductionism implies that results found at any level are relevant to all other levels. Thus, the results of QM are relevant to understanding the macroscopic world. And the results of QM call much "knowledge" into question. More than that, they undermine the notion of objective reality. I am not a physicist, and my summaries of a few QM phenomena come from several popular accounts. They are included because of the reasonable assumption that the world we experience is comprised of the smaller elements of the quantum world. That quantum world is bizarre beyond most people's imaginations. Readers who find some of the following difficult should take heart from quotes by Nobel Prize winning physicists.

> "Those who are not shocked when they first come across quantum theory cannot possibly have understood it."—Niels Bohr

> "I think I can safely say that nobody understands quantum mechanics."—Richard Feynman

> "...the system of delusions of an exceedingly intelligent paranoic."—Albert Einstein

Unstable Elements and Watched Pots

Radioactive elements are unstable, which means that individual nuclei within a sample of the element occasionally shoot off an elementary particle. The process is called radioactive decay. The particle is inside the nucleus at one instant and outside an instant later. According to quantum theory, no physical process connects the two states of being and there is no intermediate state. A second feature is that quantum theory predicts only the probability of a certain result. In a given time interval a certain fraction will decay, and calculations can tell precisely what that fraction will be. But QM cannot predict which particular nuclei will decay. The decay is completely random. Even though one nucleus decays and another does not, they were previously in an identical state.

Einstein did not accept the randomness and famously said that God does not play dice. He believed that the nuclei were not initially in an identical state. Instead, he postulated that some other property—presently unknown, but existing nonetheless—is different for the two nuclei. This type of unknown property is termed a hidden variable. See below for John Bell's idea for testing for hidden variable theories. Spoiler alert: There are no hidden variables.

In the quantum world, the phrase "A watched pot never boils" has real meaning. An unstable nucleus that is continuously watched does not decay.[225] Atoms can be placed in unstable high energy states. Left alone, they quickly jump down to a more stable lower energy state. But if there's an observer in the room, they stay put.

The Single – and Double-Slit Experiment

Nobelist Richard Feynman called the double-slit experiment the central mystery of quantum mechanics. Imagine a thick concrete wall with a small vertical slit drilled through it and a large target directly behind. Shoot a few thousand bullets at the wall. Most will be stopped, and the small percentage that get through the slit will cluster within a small area on the target. Drill a second slit near the first and shoot a few thousand more bullets. The result

---

225. http://rickbradford.co.uk/QM12QuantumZenoEffect.pdf

will be two clusters. When any type of macroparticle, whether bullets, rocks, or spitballs, is aimed at the slits, the ones that get through will cluster within two small areas.

Next, project a beam of light onto a wall with a small slit in the center and a screen of photographic film behind it. The intensity of the light on the screen will be greatest directly behind the slit and, just like the pattern for bullets, will drop off with increasing distance from the slit.

Now I'll describe several experiments that can be done with microparticles like electrons and photons and ask readers to guess the outcomes.

1. Make a second slit near the first and repeat the experiment with the light beam. What will show on the screen?

   The screen will initially show piles of individual tiny hits, just as with bullets or other particles. But some areas on the screen that photons hit regularly when one slit is open are never touched in the two slit set-up. And when enough light has hit the screen, something startling will emerge. Instead of two clusters of light, there will be bands of alternating light and dark regions. This interference pattern is characteristic of waves like ripples of water on the surface of a pond. Bright stripes on the screen show where crests from the waves overlap; dark stripes show where a crest and a trough cancel each other. The inescapable conclusions are that the photons interact with each other and that light can be a particle or a wave. But it's puzzling, since particles and waves are quite different. A second mystery is how the photon "knows" whether one or two slits are open.

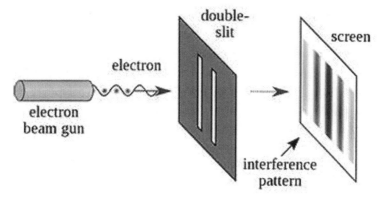

Figure 14: The double-slit experiment.

2. Okay, make the light intensity so weak that only a single photon goes through at a time. This will prevent the photons from interfering with each other. What will you see?

   An interference pattern will develop. If one slit is always open and the other opened and closed at random, the photon will go through as either a wave or a particle depending on the configuration at its moment of choice.

3. Place a photon detector by one or both slits so that you will know which slit the photon has gone through. What will you see?

   Every photon will act like a particle and pass through one slit or the other. There will be two clumps on the screen and no interference pattern. Somehow, observing the photons changes their nature.

4. Trick those frisky photons. Mount a detector but turn it off before the photon reaches the slits. What will you see?

   An interference pattern. Somehow the photon "knows" that it's no longer being watched.

5. Turn the detector on after the photon has gone through the slit(s) but before it reaches the screen. What will you see?[226]

---

226. Alberto, P. et al. (2012) A delayed choice experiment. *Science*, 338:634-7.

No interference pattern. Think about that. Since the detector wasn't on when the photon reached the slit(s), it must have gone through both of them in preparation for producing an interference pattern. But something about the detector has caused the past to be rewritten. It has taken the photon backwards in time to determine its physical reality (wave or particle). Wait, it gets weirder.

6. Kwiat and colleagues set up a two-slit experiment with polarizing filters in front of each slit for their detection device. Photons going through one slit were polarized in one way and photons going through the other slit in a different way. So, the researchers could tell through which slit each photon had passed. Was there an interference pattern?[227]

   No. No matter how the photons are detected, detection does not allow an interference pattern.

7. Then Chaio and Garrison placed a third filter between the slits and the screen. The new filter erased the information about which photon had gone through which slit.[228] Same question.

   The interference pattern appeared; the photons had somehow undone the past and changed their nature.[229]

John Wheeler was a colleague of Albert Einstein and worked with Niels Bohr on early groundbreaking experiments in quantum mechanics. He introduced the concept of wormholes and coined the term "black hole." He made important contributions to the understanding of nuclear structure and the mechanisms of fission and fusion and was the principal contributor to the growth

---

227. Kwiat, P. et al. (2004) Three proposed "quantum erasers." *Physical Review*, 49: 61-8.

228. Chiao, R. & Garrison, J. (2014) *Quantum Optics*. NY: Oxford U. Press.

229. The May, 2007 issue of *Scientific American* magazine describes, using readily available equipment, how to carry out a home experiment that shows the quantum eraser effect.

of gravitation physics. Wheeler pointed out that the findings described above could be applied to a device of interstellar dimensions. Wheeler imagined a large galaxy situated between Earth and a very bright star. A photon from the star heading towards Earth would have to "decide" whether to go by one way around the galaxy, traveling as a particle, or both ways around by traveling as a wave. He believed that, if telescopes on Earth were placed to detect light on both sides of the galaxy, they would act like photon detectors. The light would show the particle pattern. But if a device were set up so that the light from both sides reached it simultaneously, the precise source of the light would not be known, i.e., the side the light came from could not be detected. Then, a photographic film would show the interference pattern. So, by deciding which method of measurement to use today, the researcher would control which route the light had already taken to reach Earth. Today's observations would decide the path the photons took billions of years ago.[230]

8. Several researchers have made a start to testing Wheeler's idea. Vedovato and colleagues sent laser light to a device called a beam splitter, which created pairs of photons.[231] They were sent on two different paths of unequal length. The two paths merged before heading to a satellite about 2,200 miles away, with one photon lagging behind the other. From there they were bounced back to Earth, where a random number generator determined whether a device would do either nothing, so the photons would arrive at a detector at different times, or hold up the lead photon so the pair would arrive simultaneously. The random decision was made well after the photons had started on their journeys.

---

230. A photon is going through airport security. The TSA agent asks if it has any luggage. The photon says, "No, I'm traveling light."

231. Vedovato, F. et al. (2017) Extending Wheeler's delayed-choice experiment to space. *Science Advances*. Vol. 3, no. 10, e1701180. DOI: 10.1126/sciadv.1701180

So, did the researchers measure waves or particles?

When the photons that took the longer path arrived after the others, the researchers could tell which path each took. So, they saw particles. When the photons arrived at the same time, the detectors could not tell which path each took. They saw the interference pattern.

9. Kim and colleagues used a laser to generate photons and pass them through a double-slit apparatus.[232] A prism then split them into entangled pairs. (Quantum particles are called entangled if the measurement of one particle's quantum state determines the quantum states of the other particle. See below for further discussion.) One of each pair was sent to a detector, called $D0$. The researchers did not know whether those photons had gone through the top or bottom slit, and under such circumstances an interference pattern is typically produced.

Special mirrors were used to direct the other photons along one path if the original photons had come from the bottom slit, and a different path if they had come from the top slit. These entangled photons had an equal chance of ending up at any of four detectors, depending on the paths they took. So,

- a photon detected at $D1$ or $D2$ could have come from either the top or the bottom slit.
- a photon detected at $D3$ must have come from the bottom slit.
- a photon detected at $D4$ must have come from the top slit.

The paths from the slits to $D1$, $D2$, $D3$, and $D4$ were longer than the path from the slits to $D0$. What pattern was shown at $D0$ when the partner reached $D1$ or $D2$? When the partner reached $D3$, or $D4$?

The photons at D0 whose entangled partners were detected at D1 or D2 showed interference patterns. The photons at

---

232. *Kim, Y. et al. (2000) A delayed "choice" quantum eraser. Physical Review Letters, 84: 1–5*

D0 whose entangled partners were detected at D3 or D4, did not. What makes these results astonishing is that the "choice" of which path to take by the second photons was not made until after the first photons had already been measured at D0. The photons at D1 and D2 must have sent information into the past to tell their entangled partners at D0 to become a wave. The photons at D3 and D4 must have sent information into the past to tell their entangled partners at D0 to become a particle.

Many physicists have interpreted this result to mean that the delayed choice to observe or not observe the path of the photon changes the outcome of something that happened in the past. This brings ideas of time and causal sequence into question. An alternative explanation is that the first photon somehow compels the second to take a particular path. That would be equally bizarre.

Interpretations

Nobel Prize winner Werner Heisenberg is best known for his uncertainty principle—the idea that certain properties of a system cannot be known simultaneously with unlimited precision. The more precisely one property is measured, the more error there is in the measurement of a complementary property.[233] Heisenberg initially believed that measurement difficulties accounted for the inability to simultaneously determine complementary properties such as position and momentum. According to this interpretation, measuring the position of an electron changes its momentum and measuring momentum changes its position. Nobelist Neils Bohr had a different interpretation, and he eventually converted Heisenberg. Whereas virtually everybody probably believes that baseballs and flowers exist independently of whether

---

233. Heisenberg was speeding down the highway. A highway patrolman pulled him over and said, "Do you have any idea how fast you were going back there?" Heisenberg answered, "No, but I knew where I was."

anyone observes them, Bohr believed that quantum particles do not have definite properties until those properties are measured. They don't exist in a single state but in all their possible states at once. He called this superposition. Only when we observe its state does a quantum particle choose, and that's the state we observe. Wave functions—mathematic equations that describe the state of a system—are what pass through the slits in the double-slit experiments. When a wave function interacts with a photographic plate, it "collapses" into a definite state.

Max Born wrote, "At every instant a grain of sand has a definite position and velocity. This is not the case with an electron." According to Bohr, matter starts to exist only at the moment the observer learns about its existence.

Bohr's interpretation (called the Copenhagen interpretation, or CI) undermined certain basic assumptions of science, for example, that the same causes lead to the same effects. Kant had written, "Causality is the basis of all scientific work. Causality is the condition that renders science possible." But Heisenberg eventually concluded, "The law of causality is no longer applied in quantum theory." And, "In the Copenhagen interpretation of quantum mechanics, the objective reality has evaporated, and quantum mechanics does not represent particles, but rather, our knowledge, our observations, or our consciousness of particles." Davies and Gribbin stated that "This fundamental limitation represents a breakdown of determinism in nature. It means that identical electrons in identical experiments may do different things."[234] Richard Feynman wrote, "A philosopher once said, 'It is necessary for the very existence of science that the same conditions always produce the same results.' Well, they don't!"[235]

---

234. Davies, P. & Gribbin, J. (2007) *The Matter Myth: Dramatic Discoveries that Challenge Our Understanding of Physical Reality.* NY: Simon & Schuster

235. https://www.informationphilosopher.com/solutions/scientists/feynman/probability_and_uncertainty.html

Locality is the principle that an event that happens at one place can't instantaneously affect an event someplace else. Nonlocality means that far away objects can influence one another instantaneously, or at least much faster than the speed of light. Virtually all scientists, and everybody else, accept the principle of locality. Einstein called the alternative "spooky action at a distance." He wrote, "If this axiom were to be completely abolished... the postulation of laws which can be checked in the accepted sense would become impossible."

Whereas Einstein believed that electrons have spin, location, and other real properties even when they are not being measured, Bohr postulated that electrons and other elementary particles are in superpositions of possible states until measurements are made. Bohr also believed that either position or momentum but not both, and spin about only one axis, can be measured with great accuracy. Einstein argued that QM's inability to simultaneously measure position and momentum shows that the Copenhagen interpretation is incomplete. His friend, physicist Abraham Pais, related a conversation: "We often discussed his notions on objective reality. I recall that during one walk Einstein suddenly stopped, turned to me and asked whether I really believed that the moon exists only when I look at it." In Einstein's view, if the Copenhagen interpretation proved correct, the answer to his question would be "No."

Einstein and Bohr had a famous series of debates during which Einstein presented several challenges to CI in the form of thought experiments. Bohr answered all of them. In 1935, with the help of colleagues Boris Podolsky and Nathan Rosen, Einstein proposed what he thought would be a conclusive demonstration that one of two things is true:

1. Measuring one part A of a quantum system allows instantaneous predictions about a property of another part, B, no matter how great the distance between A and B

or

2. QM is incomplete in the sense that it cannot account for some real property of B.

Their thought experiment, called EPR, took advantage of a phenomenon in which two particles emerge from a common location with properties that are always tightly related. The particles are called entangled. For example, a neutral pion will (if unwatched) eventually decay into two photons that speed off in opposite directions with opposite spin. If photon 1 is found to have spin up along the x-axis, then photon 2 is *always* found to have spin down along the x-axis. EPR went roughly as follows. Wait for the pion to decay, or shoot off two other similarly entangled particles. Then (thought Einstein, Podolsky, and Rosen), a detector that measured the position of particle A would know the position of particle B without measuring particle B. But QM denies that B has properties before those properties are measured, so such an outcome would indicate that QM is incomplete. Also, the position of particle A could be measured with one detector and the momentum of particle B measured with a second detector. Thus, the experimenter would know both the position and momentum of particle B—knowledge specifically forbidden by QM.

Bohr thought there would be a different outcome: A would somehow communicate with B after A, but before B, was measured. EPR denied the possibility, because it would violate the principle of locality. Bohr responded that, regardless of distance, the measurement of A's position would instantaneously force B into a state of ill-defined momentum. That was a bizarre and astounding speculation: Something done at point A would *instantaneously* affect something at point B, no matter how far apart the two points were.

The Most Profound Discovery in the History of Science

EPR was only a thought experiment for many years. But in 1964, John Bell published a paper that suggested a strategy for testing it. He derived a proof showing that different probabilities would arise if reality was local rather than nonlocal.[236] See Box 1 for a simplified version. He proved that non-locality is a necessary condition to arrive at the statistical predictions of quantum mechanics. Since 1981 Bell's ideas have been tested many times with different sources and types of elementary particles. The results have always shown the same thing: Knowing what happened at measurement *A* somehow changes the probability of the result at measurement *B*. Entangled particles remain in instantaneous touch with each other no matter how wide the gap between them. Experiments suggest that, even if they were light years apart, two entangled particles would link to each other instantaneously. The experiments support CI. Einstein was wrong.

Box 1

In essence, Bell's theorem says that entangled quantum states are more highly correlated than what is allowed by the classical laws of physics. Since the 1980s there have been many Bell-type experiments and they invariably support the CI interpretation rather than Einstein's. Following is a description of one, based on an excellent article by Gary Felder.[237]

Imagine the following experimental set-up. A gun shoots out a steady stream of rubber balls, two at a time, in opposite directions. The balls may be red or blue, but the color of both members of each pair is always the same. Each ball lands at detector *A* or *B*. If the ball is red, the detector buzzes. If blue, it remains silent.

The detectors each have three buttons, numbered 1, 2, 3. If the same numbered button is pushed on both *A* and *B*, either both detectors buzz or neither buzzes when a ball reaches them. If different buttons are pushed on each detector, the detectors will

236. Bell, J. (1964) On the Einstein-Podolsky-Rosen paradox. *Physics*, 1: 195-200.

237. http://www.felderbooks.com/papers/bell Spooky action at a distance: An explanation of Bell's theorem.

sometimes but not always give the same response.

If the two detectors are far enough apart, and the measurements are done at almost exactly the same time, locality says that nothing which happens at one of the measurements can affect the result of the other one.

Suppose the buttons on the two detectors are pushed independently and randomly. Some balls might cause a detector to buzz no matter which button is pushed, and others might never cause a detector to buzz. Since both balls in a given pair are always the same color, the two detectors for those pairs will *always* give the same result. Some balls might cause zero, one, or two detectors to buzz, depending on the button pushed. The key question is, "Overall, how often will the two detectors give the same result?"

Let $A1B1$ mean that button 1 was pushed on both detectors; $A2B3$ means that button 2 was pushed on detector A and button 3 on detector B; and so on. Consider a ball that causes a buzz when buttons 1 or 2 have been pushed but no buzz when button 3 has been pushed. There are 3 x 3 = 9 possible combinations for the two detectors:

$A1B1$ = the two detectors would agree; $A1B2$ = agree; $A1B3$ = disagree; $A2B1$ = agree; $A2B2$ = agree; $A2B3$ = disagree; $A3B1$ = disagree; $A3B2$ = disagree; $A3B3$ = agree

So, the detectors agree in five cases and disagree in four, which works out to 55.5% agreement. The same reasoning leads to 55.5% agreement for the other possibilities except for those pairs that always or never cause a detector to buzz. For them, the detectors agree 100% of the time. So, the total agreement between detectors is at least 55.5%.

If only a few trials were run with the set-up as described, it's possible that by chance alone the detectors would agree less than 55.5% of the time. If thousands of trials were run, there would almost certainly be at least 55.5% agreement. But that is with relatively large items like rubber balls. The outcome in quantumland is different. When quantum particles, say electrons, are measured instead of macroscopic ones, the detectors agree only fifty percent of the time. How can the difference between the two outcomes be explained?

Einstein believed that the only explanation for such results was local realism coordinated by hidden (unknown) variables. Local means that events cannot affect each other instantly at a distance; and realism means that particles have definite values for all of their properties at all times, even when they're not observed. Hidden variable explanations presuppose that the particles involved are in definite states.

But Bell-type experiments show that any hidden variable theory would require giving up locality; or permitting locality but having hidden variables that travel faster than the speed of light (expressly forbidden by the theory of relativity).

The CI explanation is that the measurement of one particle immediately changes the properties of the other. Why the change occurs is not explained.

Graduates of Evelyn Woods speed reading course might find the above discussion interesting and move on. But a little reflection raises deep philosophical questions. Eminent physicist Henry Stapp called Bell's theorem the most profound discovery in the history of science.[238]

Physicists Abner Shimony and John Clauser wrote, "The conclusions from Bell's theorem are philosophically startling; either one must totally abandon the realistic philosophy of most working scientists or dramatically revise our concept of spacetime."[239]

Physicist Bernard d'Espagnat wrote, "The world we perceive is merely a shadow of the ultimate reality and some of our most engrained notions about space and causality should be reconsidered." And again, "The outcome confirmed that entanglement-at-a-distance does physically exist, in the sense that it has

---

238. Stapp, H (1975) Bell's theorem and world process. *Nuovo Cimento, 29B:* 270–6.

239. Shimony, A. & Clauser, J. (1978) Bell's theorem: experimental tests and implications. *Rep. Prog. Phys,* 41: 1881-1927.

physically verifiable (and verified) consequences."[240]

Nicolas Gisin and colleagues provided a dramatic demonstration. They sent pairs of photons in opposite directions to villages in Geneva that are nearly 7 miles apart. At the ends of their paths, the photons had to make random choices between alternative, equally possible routes. The independent decisions by the paired photons always matched, even though no signal of any kind was transmitted between them.[241]

Many Worlds

CI and Einstein's realism are not the only approaches to quantum phenomena. At least ten interpretations have been proposed by respected scientists. Physicist David Mermin once quipped, "New interpretations appear every year. None ever disappear." I'll mention only one other, because many eminent physicists subscribe to it. Hugh Everett III proposed that whenever a measurement forces a particle to make a choice, the entire universe splits into two separate universes; the particle goes one way in one universe and the other way in the other.[242] Proponent David Deutsch wrote that "...our universe is only a tiny facet of a larger multiverse, a highly structured continuum containing many universes." He added, "Everything in our universe — including you and me, every atom and every galaxy—has counterparts in these other universes."[243] A 1991 poll of seventy-two quantum cosmologists and other quantum

240. D'Espagnat, B. (2009) Quantum weirdness: What we call 'reality' is just a state of mind. https://www.theguardian.com/science/blog/2009/mar/17/templeton-quantum-entanglement.

241. Tittel, W. et al. (1998) Violation of Bell inequalities by photons more than 10 km apart. *Physical Review Letters*, 81:3563.

242. Byrne, P. (2007) The many worlds of Hugh Everett. *Scientific American*, December.

243. Deutsch, D. (1998) *The Fabric of Reality; The Science of Parallel Universes—and Its Implications*. NY: Viking Press.

field theorists showed fifty-eight percent agreement with "Yes, I think the many worlds hypothesis is true."[244] The agreers include such luminaries as Murray Gell-Mann, Stephen Hawking, and Steven Weinberg. Hawking, shortly before his death, submitted a paper describing how scientists might detect parallel universes.[245] I don't believe the many worlds hypothesis. (Fools rush in...)[246]

Beyond Quantum Mechanics

Several developments in science outside of QM are also unsettling for any commonsense view of reality. When Einstein proposed that space and time were unified into a single four dimensional structure called space-time, he startled the scientific community. Less well known is that in 1921 physicist Theodor Kaluza postulated a fifth dimension that unifies gravity and electromagnetism. A modern version of his theory postulates eleven dimensions, and physicists called string theorists have proposed a universe of twenty-six dimensions—although most string theorists are willing to

---

244. Tipler, F. (1994). *The Physics of Immortality*. NY: Penguin

245. (2018) https://www.telegraph.co.uk/science/2018/03/18/stephen-hawking-leaves-behind-breathtaking-final-multiverse/

246. The proliferation of universes would be vastly greater than proponents imply, since each choice point gives rise to not two but an infinite number of alternatives. A coin is not restricted to landing heads or tails; it might end up balanced on its edge, rolling down a sewer, snapped up in midair by a bird, etc. Furthermore, we make dozens (thousands?) of choices every day, from deciding whether to get out of bed immediately or stay in for another ten minutes. Then, still half asleep: Which socks? Eggs or cereal? Do I start on the front page or turn right to the sports section? Every decision has the potential to be consequential and so would result in a splitting of universes. That's just on day one. Each split would create two worlds full of choices, and the number of splits would then grow beyond any of Cantor's infinities. Finally, unless solipsism is a feature of the many worlds hypothesis, alternative universes are constantly created for every living person and maybe even every living creature.

make do with a mere ten.

Many modern physicists believe that only about four percent of the universe is made of the kind of matter that our senses can detect even with the most powerful equipment. The other ninety-six percent does not consist of atoms or the particles from which atoms are made, that is, the constituents of "normal matter." This "dark matter" does not interact with electricity or magnetism. Space also has "dark energy," which is far more abundant than all the rest of the energy in the universe. Dark energy drives things apart, including space itself. As a consequence, the universe is expanding at an ever-accelerating rate.

Chapter 15

REASON AND SCIENCE IN ALMOST ONE VOICE

Philosophers like Bertrand Russell who analyze the foundations of knowledge have been drawn to the belief that only the self exists and is real, a position called solipsism. (Russell rejected solipsism but only on esthetic grounds.) Many of the leading interpreters of quantum mechanics hold views not far different. They believe that the process of measurement creates reality (elementary particles have no properties until measured), and a conscious observer is required for measurement to occur. In syllogistic form:

> Measurement creates reality.
> <u>A conscious observer is required for measurement to occur.</u>
> Therefore, there is no reality independent of a conscious observer.

Theoretical physicist John Wheeler, whose delayed choice thought experiment was discussed above, called reality a participatory phenomenon. He described a game of 20 questions which he had played. In the standard version, one player leaves the room while the rest of the group selects a person, place, or thing. The player is then called back to try to guess the chosen object by asking no more than twenty questions that can be answered only by yes or no. When it was Wheeler's turn, the other participants secretly changed the rules. "There had been a plot *not* to agree on an object to be guessed, but that each person, when asked, must give a truthful answer concerning some real object that was in his mind, and which was consistent with all the answers that had gone before." With only one question left, Wheeler[247] guessed: "Is it a cloud?" The answer was "Yes!"

The important point is this: Had the questions been asked in a different order, the answer would almost surely have been different. The answer "cloud" was brought into existence only by the last question. Wheeler believes there is a parallel in QM in that an electron's properties are unreal until somebody observes it. "Not until you start asking a question, do you get something," he said. Wheeler asserted that, if the prediction from his thought experiment were confirmed, it would indicate that method of measurement can change history. As noted above, several experimental tests have confirmed the prediction and suggest that similar results occur on a cosmic scale.

> "Observations not only disturb what has to be measured, they produce it... We compel the electron to assume a definite position... We ourselves produce the result of the experiment."
> —Pascual Jordan

Of course, if there is no reality prior to the observer, then the observer's beliefs must create that reality. It seems as though faith gets put back into the equation.

---

247. Gribbin, J. & Gribbin, M. (1998) *In Search of Schrodinger's Cat.* London: Black Swan.

Chapter 16

RECAPITULATION

- In the past, you have sometimes believed erroneously. Some of your current beliefs—maybe all of them—may be incorrect. You have no criteria for distinguishing between currently correct and erroneous beliefs.

- Babies enter the world prepackaged with bits of knowledge, but the knowledge is not necessarily correct.

- Religious faith is hope masquerading as knowledge—an insane hope that the ancient past, the present, and the post-death worlds have been accurately portrayed in a book (one of more than 1,000 such books, all with different portrayals) written more than 2,000 years ago by a primitive people and subsequently interpreted by a slew of money – and power-grabbing demagogues.

- Reason cannot be relied on to provide useful information about the world:

  o Although an argument such as 2 elephants + 2 elephants = 4 elephants is valid, it says nothing about whether elephants exist. Equally valid arguments are that 2 unicorns + 2 unicorns = 4 unicorns; and 2 BRDX:&G# + 2 BRDX:&G# = 4 BRDX:&G#. Syllogisms allow for the rearrangement of information but don't provide new knowledge.

  o Logical arguments begin with premises—statements assumed to be true—and skeptics demand proof of their truth.

o Skeptics also demand proof that the premises have been properly combined to yield the conclusion.

o Push back far enough and all logical "proofs" reduce to matters of faith. Finding an unequivocally sound argument would be more surprising than finding a unicorn.

Our senses may give an accurate picture of the world. They may not. We'll never know.

Scientific exploration represents empiricism at its best. Although there is no single scientific method, most investigations begin with one or more observations. But as discussed on p. 91-94, observations may be distorted—by some aspect of nature or by deliberate deception. Distortion is also introduced by selective publication of research findings. Scientists and nonscientists alike often make invalid inferences from their observations. A scientist may predict, "If my hypothesis is true, then if I arrange conditions just so, I should observe result X." But even if X is observed, there will always be not one but an infinite number of alternative possibilities. So, scientific hypotheses and theories can never be proven.

Many and probably the vast majority of scientists believe that the universe is deterministic (at least for inanimate objects) and all events have causes. They accept the principle of locality. (If two measurements are far enough apart in space, one cannot influence the other.) They conceive of their job as learning about, understanding, and explaining objective reality; and they probably all agree that we are much closer to that goal than our forefathers of 1,000 years ago. The results from several scientific disciplines and especially quantum mechanics challenge those beliefs.

Scientists' answers, although often surprising, usually fall within a limited range of possibilities and fit into existing knowledge frameworks. For example, when trying to understand where memories are stored, neuroscientists are likely to explore various areas of the brain. They might find that other body organs contribute to memory storage, but they go no farther afield than the individual body. However, if the findings from memory research had characteristics similar to those of quantum mechanics, the seat of memory would just as likely be found in a cookie jar in a basement apartment in downtown Minneapolis.

Although all of the methods of knowing are problematic, a distinction (of questionable importance) might be made between them. Reason and empiricism may not lead to genuine knowledge, but they are the best we can do. Religious faith, on the other hand, is often held in opposition to reason and empiricism. As long as wishing that X is true is not equivalent to X being true, religious faith should be dismissed as even a potential way of knowing.

Another Way of Looking at It

The previous chapters showed that the various ways of (seemingly) acquiring knowledge cannot be trusted. The problem of knowledge acquisition can be approached from a different perspective, but the conclusion will be the same—radical skepticism is correct.

The Future: Nobody knows the future. Nobody has ever been there.

Except for highly efficient people about to commit suicide, the future is uncertain. No place on earth has banished unexpected catastrophe, whether in the form of accident, plague, homicide, earthquake, or flood. Lightning may strike at any time. We may be trapped in an elevator with an insurance salesman.

David Hume wrote convincingly that there is no logical justification for expecting the future to resemble the past or from making any generalizations from the known to the unknown. In fact, it is certain (hey author, you said there were no certainties) that at some distant time the future will not resemble the past. The sun won't rise forever. Furthermore, inductive inferences are not straightforward. Predicting that the next emerald you see will be green is no more justified than predicting that it will be grue. See p. 73.

Among other problems in trying to predict:

- The Heisenberg uncertainty principle ensures that there will always be a certain amount of randomness.

- Chaos theory shows that even slightly different starting points can lead to vastly different end points.
- Even if the component parts of a phenomenon are understood, the phenomenon might show emergent properties at any time.

Appendix 1 and the study described on p. 72 show that so-called pundits do a very poor job of predicting. So do brides and grooms. They promise to love "till death do they part," yet the lifelong probability of a marriage ending in divorce is forty to fifty percent in the U.S.

> Amy: My grandpa knew the future—the exact time, day, and year he was going to die!
>
> Bob: What an evolved soul? How'd he know?
>
> Amy: The judge told him.
>
> The Past: Russian proverb: The past is unpredictable.

Nobody can be sure about the past. Our memories are not perfect replicas of events we've experienced and are not played back the way tape players play back recordings. Each recalled memory is actually a reconstruction, with details often added or changed. Long-term memories are very susceptible to change, and false memories are easily implanted. Furthermore, when we try to remember things that we've only read or otherwise been told about, we can never be sure that our sources have been accurate or truthful.

> Patient: "Doctor, I have a serious memory problem. I can't remember anything!"
>
> Doctor: "Since when did you have this problem?"
>
> Patient: "What problem?"

The Present:
At least three factors prevent us from knowing about the present. First, we are vulnerable to illusions and have no way of estimating their frequency. Several illusions have been identified but

there may be others that have a huge effect that we will never know. Second, much of our thinking about the present relies on memory which, as just discussed, cannot be trusted.

The third and by far biggest factor is that some person(s) or other worldly being(s) or substance(s) in the environment are, deliberately or not, deceiving us on a massive scale. We can't know how likely that is, but a few comments are in order:

1. Deception is everywhere: between spouses, lovers, best friends, slight acquaintances, business people, buyers and sellers, politicians, and everyone not mentioned.

2. Many deceptions have been successful—so successful that the deceived never suspected anything.

3. Neurophysiologists and chemists have developed powerful tools for changing people's perceptual worlds.

4. Physicists, including several Nobel Prize winners, have put forth theories to explain the bizarre world of quantum mechanics. The theories show that ultimate reality is almost certainly very different from the common sense view.

5. Given the vastness of the universe and our limited intellectual capabilities, we should be very humble about declaring that we understand how the world works; it follows that we can't know anything for sure.

Although people may accept that absolutely certainty is impossible, they may readily believe that some things are more likely than others. But without some underlying certainty, there is no basis for estimating probability. And, always, the specter of deception looms large.

I leave the final word to Albert Einstein. "Once you can accept the universe as being something expanding into an infinite nothing which is something, wearing stripes with plaid is easy."

Chapter 17

CERTAINTY, LIKELIHOOD, AND PROBABILITY

"Doubt is not a pleasant condition, but certainty is absurd."—Voltaire

"Inquiry is fatal to certainty."—Will Durant

Science fiction writer/chemist Isaac Asimov offered a rebuttal of radical skepticism.[248] He argued that right and wrong are not absolute, that some things are more right than others. He gave an example of two grade school students asked to spell "sugar." According to Asimov, "shuger" would be more right than "pqzzf." He noted that Newton's theories of motion and gravitation were very close to right; they would have been absolutely right if the speed of light were infinite, that is, if light took zero seconds rather than 0.0000000033 seconds to travel a meter. Einstein's theory corrects for the speed of light, so it replaced Newton's. Newton's theory was wrong as all scientific theories are ultimately wrong, but only minutely. And when Einstein's theory is inevitably overthrown, the correction will be even smaller.

Asimov conceded that scientists can never be absolutely certain. Still, he claimed that routine accuracy of more than ninety-nine percent is achieved in many disciplines; and that, although specific predictions may turn out false, we can be certain about many

---

248. Asimov, I. (1989) The relativity of wrong. *The Skeptical Inquirer*, 14: 35–44.

broad classes of events. For example, the air we breathe is comprised of about twenty percent oxygen. Molecules move randomly, so all the oxygen molecules in a room could conceivably migrate to the ceiling and leave the occupants in a suffocating atmosphere. But it's highly improbable that even a single living creature in the entire history of our planet ever suffocated in that manner.

Many people consider themselves highly skeptical. They distrust politicians, television commercials, and claims of innocence from athletes accused of using steroids. Popular use of the term "skeptical" connotes worldliness and lack of gullibility. If we weren't at least moderately skeptical, we'd have closets overflowing with shampoos, laundry detergents, and lite beer, each superior to the rest. Still, most "skeptics" should be sued for misappropriating the term. They aren't skeptical in the philosophical sense, in the sense that Asimov was criticizing, because they don't take their (non)belief to its logical extreme. Some open-minded readers may be unconvinced by Asimov's position and willing to acknowledge the possibility that the world is very different from how it appears. Having acknowledged, they recite the cliché "Nothing is certain but death and taxes" and blithely move on. My goal is to end blitheness.

Although the above cliché refers only to future events—people must pay taxes and inevitably die—lack of certainty applies equally to the past and present. The preceding chapters showed that the only certainty is that certainty is *never* justified. But if you concede the point, you're on the road to radical skepticism. Even your own origin will be in doubt. So, struggling to keep a straight face, perhaps you'll acknowledge that "The infinitesimal possibility exists that I was the sole survivor of an explosion that destroyed my home planet Krypton; that my loving father placed me in an escape rocket and sent it to the planet Earth; and when I'm mature enough (in Krypton years) to handle the responsibility, my amnesia will be reversed and my amazing though latent super powers will be revealed to me."

If you're still straight-faced, consider this. To accurately compute the probability of dangerous molecular movements, scientists assume many certainties. That is, they invoke much prior knowledge. Otherwise, probability calculations would be impossible. C.I. Lewis had much to say on the subject:[249]

- Unless something is certain, nothing else is even probable.

- The immediate premises are, very likely, themselves only probable, and perhaps in turn based upon premises only probable. Unless this backward-leading chain comes to rest finally in certainty, no probability-judgment can be valid at all.

- Statements of the form 'x is probable' only make sense if one assumes there to be a y that is certain.

- The probabilistic conception strikes me as supposing that if enough probabilities can be got to lean against one another they can all be made to stand up. I suggest that, on the contrary, unless some of them can stand up alone, they will all fall flat.

In other words, we assess probability by using evidence that itself has a probability relative to further evidence. Without some certainty to rest on, probability cannot be assessed. In calculating the probability of getting two sixes on a roll of dice, it is assumed among many other things that (a) the dice are fair; (b) the roll is fair; (c) the numbers that come up on the two die are independent of each other; (d) the probability of a six coming up on one die is 1/6; and (e) the probability of two independent events occurring simultaneously is the product of their independent probabilities. If any of the assumptions are wrong, so is the final probability.

Hans Reichenbach disagreed with Lewis.[250] He claimed that probabilities can be computed without any underlying certainty.

---

249. Lewis, C. (1952) The given element in empirical knowledge. *Philosophical Review*, 61: 168–75; Lewis, C. (1929) *Mind and the World Order: An Outline of a Theory of Knowledge*. NY: Charles Scribner's Sons

250. Reichenbach, H. (1952) Are phenomenal reports absolutely certain? *Philosophical Review*, 61: 147–59.

The two men carried on a lengthy debate, both public and private, that continued until Reichenbach's death in 1953. Neither man ever convinced the other and, even today, philosophers disagree about who was right. Nevertheless, even if Reichenbach was right and some probabilities can be computed or approximated, most cannot.

Philosophers called fallibilists (which includes most epistemologists) disagree with Lewis. Most acknowledge that certainty is impossible but say that some things are more probable than others. I'm sure they'd agree that both A and B below are possible but insist that A is vastly more likely. Do I seriously want to dispute this?

A. Sometime in the next week, at least one person in Paris will speak in French.

B. You will wake up in bed tomorrow next to a large bullfrog wearing a tutu.

I do dispute that A is more likely. But before sending people in white coats after me, imagine the following hypothetical discussion:

> Logician: The probability of ever finding a bald-headed man with hair is zero.
>
> You (in training to be a lawyer): Here comes a bald-headed man. He's got hair on his face, chest, arms, legs, genitals, and even coming out of his nose and ears.
>
> Logician: True, but when I said hair I meant specifically and exclusively hair on the head.
>
> You, undeterred: Okay, but when I look at his scalp through a powerful magnifying glass, I see several tiny hairs.
>
> Logician: I'll define my terms more carefully. Totally baldheaded men have no hair at all on their heads. Partially baldheaded men have microscopic hairs. I restrict the discussion to totally bald-headed men.

You, creatively: Here's a totally bald-headed man. I'll give him a toupee.

Logician: More refinement is needed. The probability of ever finding a totally bald-headed man with his own hair (not reattached from an earlier, more hair-prosperous time) is zero.

You: Okay, I agree. But who cares?

Call a totally bald-headed, nontoupeed man Case 1. If we accept the conventional laws of reasoning, Case 1 is a logical impossibility. It is self-contradictory. The probability of ever finding such a man is zero. Now consider two more cases.

Case 2: What is the probability of tossing a fair coin two times and having it come up heads twice?

Case 3: What is the probability of tossing a fair coin 1,000 times and having it come up heads each time?

Although the likelihood of occurrence of Case 3 is (seems to be) vanishingly small, the likelihood is not zero. Thus, it is more like Case 2 than Case 1. Exact probabilities can be computed for both (although, as just discussed, they can't be trusted; there is no underlying certainty). Now one final case:

Case 4: What is the probability that you were the sole survivor of an explosion that destroyed your home planet Krypton? How likely is it that your loving father placed you in an escape rocket and sent it to the planet Earth; and that, when you're mature enough (in Krypton years) to handle the responsibility, your amnesia will be reversed and your amazing though latent super powers will be revealed to you.

Case 4 differs from Cases 2 and 3 in that its probability can't be computed. Nevertheless, it has more in common with them than with the logically impossible (probability of zero) Case 1. The probability of Case 4 might be infinitesimally small—or it might not be—but it is not zero. Any logically possible event has a greater than zero chance of occurring. How much greater? There is no formula for computing. Not even Pat Robertson or the Pope knows.

On pages 143-144 I conclude with an alternative account to the traditional one about the fate of President John Kennedy. You may consider it entirely frivolous. Even if you are a conspiracy theorist who believes there was more than one assassin, you are probably certain that Kennedy was assassinated. Although you might be willing to (grudgingly, with great reluctance) concede the (extremely remote) possibility that he's alive and well, in fact you have no idea what the odds are.

What is the probability that your next-door neighbor or close friend, the one you've had over for dinner, who has babysat your children, who was maid of honor/best man at your wedding, is a serial killer? Al Qaeda fighter? Participant in a witness protection program? Of the other gender from what you think? CIA spy? Polygamist? Embezzler? You may say zero, but people just like you have been stunned to find out otherwise. The best spies do not look like Sean Connery in his prime, bench press 500 pounds, and drink double martinis, shaken, not stirred. Their friends would swear they couldn't do anything requiring brains or skill or guts. Then, even if they get caught, allowances are made.

But ossifer, I dint know this here place wuz jes fer soldiers. I thot it might be mighty fine fer huntin. Hope I dint inconvenience no-one.

Following are a few statistics and other matters of note:

Since 1982, fifty-four percent of mass shootings in the U.S. were committed by white men, many of whom had been abused as children. Most shared several other characteristics: They enjoyed setting fires and hurting animals, were fascinated by guns, had a sadistic streak, and lacked compassion. Mike Aamodt explored a database that, as of September 4, 2016, contained information on 4,743 serial killers.[251] The typical psychological profile was similar to that of the mass shooters. But many of both groups did not fit

---

251. http://maamodt.asp.radford.edu/Serial%20Killer%20Information%20Center/Project%20Description.htm

the profile; and many who fit have led seemingly normal lives. Homicide archivist Thomas Hargrove estimated that two thousand serial killers are at large in the U.S.[252] Psychologists cannot accurately predict who will go on to become a mass murderer—and that includes you and your next door neighbor. Following are four descriptions of men who were mass murderers:[253]

Harold Shipman was a successful professional (a general practitioner working for the National Health Service). He was considered a pillar of the local community, won a professional award for a children's asthma clinic, and was interviewed by Granada *Television's World in Action*. Dennis Nilsen was an ex-soldier turned civil servant and trade unionist who had no previous criminal record when arrested. Vlado Taneski was a career journalist. Russell Williams was a successful and respected career Royal Canadian Air Force Colonel. Before they were exposed, it's likely that their neighbors would have said, "I grant the possibility that he's a serial killer but the probability is infinitesimally low."

Gene Abel estimated that between one percent and five percent of our population molest children.[254] Charles Montaldo wrote that pedophiles can be anyone—old or young, rich or poor, educated or uneducated, non-professional or professional, and of any race. Most are neighbors, teachers, coaches, members of the clergy, music instructors, babysitters, and family members.[255] Ernie Allen said, "There are 400,000 registered sex offenders in the United States, and an estimated 80,000 to 100,000 of them are missing. They're supposed to be registered, but we don't know where they're living."[256]

---

252. https://www.newyorker.com/magazine/2017/11/27/the-serial-killer-detector

253. https://en.wikipedia.org/wiki/Serial_killer.

254. Abel, G. (2012) CNN *Specials* Transcript #454-Thieves of Childhood.

255. Montaldo, C. https://www.thoughtco.com/profile-of-pedophile-and-common-characteristics-973203

256. Allen, E. https://www.cbsnews.com/news/jessicas-law-eyes-sex-offenders/

The Espionage Database Project tabulates data on all American citizens who are known, from publicly available sources, to have betrayed their country. The project identified 150 cases of citizens who committed espionage against the United States since the beginning of the Cold War in the late 1940s. Most were men, married, white, heterosexual, and born in the U.S. Nothing about them seemed extraordinary.[257]

Marquet International, Ltd. studied more than 2,000 major embezzlement cases over a recent five year period. Most embezzlers were trusted employees who had worked for the organization for years. Two-thirds were women, and only four percent had a criminal history.[258]

Given the preceding, what makes you immune from the possibility that your colleague/classmate/best friend/cousin has committed or is about to commit some dastardly crime? What gives you the right to say that JFK, beyond a shadow of a doubt, is not alive and well? More to the point, what gives you the right to say that there is only a shadow of a doubt that he is alive and well? To be certain that something is true, we must be equally certain that other things—in fact, an infinite number of other things—are false. If Kennedy was assassinated, then he didn't cut a deal with Oswald or anyone else. Martians didn't abduct him or inhabit his body. He didn't have a sex change operation or develop the ability to make himself invisible.

So, as earlier chapters showed, certainty is beyond our grasp. Then, so too is probability. You might even accept the skeptical argument in its strongest form: EVERYTHING we think we know is probably false, since our assumptions are selected from an infinite pool of alternatives.

One more takeaway: Stay away from Kryptonite.

There are other reasons to reject the fallibist position. Nobel

---

257. https://www.wrc.noaa.gov/wrso/security_guide/numbers.htm.

258. https://www.inc.com/courtney-rubin/who-is-most-likely-to-embezzle.html

Prize winning physicist Murray Gell-Mann proclaimed what has become a mantra in quantum physics: "Everything not forbidden is compulsory."[259] He was referring to quantum phenomena, but his proclamation can be extended to include large, tutu-wearing bullfrogs.

Many eminent physicists have tried to develop a theory of everything: an all-encompassing framework that fully explains and links together all physical aspects of the universe. Although they are far smarter than me, as a card-carrying radical skeptic I am convinced that they are doomed to failure. Imagine a person examining a drop of ocean water and declaring to have developed a theory of everything about water. Or formulating universal laws after inspecting a grain of sand or speck of dust. Ridiculous.

Nobelist Richard Feynman had two relevant comments:

"Nature's imagination is so much greater than man's, she's never going to let us relax."

"Philosophers say a great deal about what is absolutely necessary for science, and it is always, so far as one can see, rather naive, and probably wrong."

In John Wheeler's later years, he incorporated ideas from quantum theory to suggest that human observations contribute to the creation of physical reality. He argued that the universe exists in a state of undefined quantum potential until the conscious observer collapses reality down into a single state. To Wheeler we are not simply bystanders on a cosmic stage; we are shapers and creators living in a participatory universe. Nobelist Ilya Prigone agreed. He wrote, "Whatever we call reality, it is revealed to us only through an active construction in which we participate."[260] Physicist Andrei Linde also agreed. He wrote, "The universe and the observer exist as a pair. I cannot imagine a consistent theory of the universe that

---

259 Gell-Mann, M. (1956). The interpretation of the new particles as displaced charge multiplets. *Nuovo Cimento.* 4: 848.

260 Prigogine, I. & Stengers, I. (1984) *Order Out of Chaos: Man's New Dialogue with Nature.* NY: Bantam Books.

ignores consciousness."[261] And from Nobelist Werner Heisenberg: "The idea of an objective real world whose smallest parts exist objectively in the same sense as stones or trees exist, independently of whether or not we observe them ... is impossible."[262]

261. Linde, A. (1998) Universe, life, consciousness. https://static1.squarespace.com/static/54d103efe4b0f90e6ca101cd/t/54f9cb08e-4b0a50e0977f4d8/1425656584247/universe-life-consciousness.pdf

262. Heisenberg, W. (1958) *Physics and Philosophy*. NY: Harper and Row.

Chapter 18

REASONS FOR RESISTANCE

This chapter presents several reasons, primarily psychological, for clinging to the belief that we know a great deal about the world—and responses in italics to those reasons. Next come summaries of some Herculean attempts to salvage the belief.

1. Radical skepticism is a preposterous affront to common sense. No wonder the commonsense view toward it is one of disdain. Sensible people conclude that the reasoning process leading to skepticism must be flawed. Flaws can be subtle, and time and intellectual energy are precious, so reasonable people shouldn't waste time worrying about ridiculous assertions.

    For more than 2,000 years, the greatest human intellects have sought for flaws in the skeptics' position. They have found none. So, either there are no flaws or our pride-and-joy intellects are stone-age tools. To put it differently, we must give up on the possibility of either knowledge or reason.

    Predictions of the taken-for-granted technology of today would have seemed preposterous to Plato and even to our grandparents. Descriptions of automobiles, airplanes, space travel, computers, penicillin, telephones, and refrigerators might have been dismissed as drivel. Yet the pace of technological advances quickens. The gadgetry featured on today's Star Trek episode is tomorrow's Radio Shack special. Today's 'knowledge' will illuminate tomorrow's textbooks on primitive mythology.

Here is an argument no less believable than most:

All major scientific theories have been supplanted within 200 years. (The scientific community has always eventually concluded that the theories were wrong.)

<u>*The future will resemble the past.*</u>

Therefore, all of today's theories will meet the same fate.[263]

2. Certain skeptical arguments have been refuted, such as the one that we can know nothing at all. (To know that we can know nothing is to know something.)

   Defenders of the faith have beaten up on such straw men, so that casual readers of philosophy may have the false impression that the skeptic has lost. The fundamental conclusion has not been refuted.

3. David Hume contended that humans are psychologically constructed to believe in induction. Hume could not logically justify predicting the consequences of any of his actions, but he did not eat poison or jump off a tall building, and he lived to old age.

   Granted, we are psychologically constructed to believe in induction—but that only describes, doesn't justify. We are (maybe) constructed to grow old and die, but we try to fight those fates. If the belief in induction is wrong, we should fight it too.

   "Our most important thoughts are those which contradict our emotions."—Paul Valery

4. Although the arguments for radical skepticism are intellectually powerful, they can't be too compelling even to me— I act as though much of my world is predictable. Every moment of my existence disputes them.

   See previous.

---

263. In 2014, *Epoch Times* published an article by Tara Macisaac entitled "9 Scientists Who Dispute Theory of Gravity." https://www.theepochtimes.com/9-scientists-who-dispute-the-theory-of-gravity_589863.html

5. The arguments may be simple and compelling, but they were available to the most brilliant people who ever lived (if they ever lived)—Aristotle, Einstein, Shakespeare, and Madame Curie, to name a few. None of them became radical skeptics. Why should you be the first on your block?

   See previous.

6. Religion and science, the most unlikely of bedfellows, unite in opposition.

   Religious leaders oppose all challenges to dogma. Scientists, as philosopher Paul Feyerabend noted, are equally dogmatic except to data, theories, and methodologies conflicting with their own. Science, no less than religion, is a matter of faith. Radical skepticism challenges both religion and science; not surprisingly, it is opposed by both.

7. Almost all scientists except those strange quantum physicists assume that a deep reality underlies appearances; universal laws await discovery; and the universe is deterministic. Lay persons implicitly assume the same beliefs, which skeptics disavow. People resist changing toothpastes and breakfast cereals, let alone religions. Belief in a real, nonrandom universe is most fundamental of all—and seems critical for continued existence.

   Obsessive-compulsive psychotics believe that their bizarre rituals are critical for continued existence. They resist treatment. Paranoid schizophrenics, notoriously treatment-resistant, constantly defend against a myriad of (their psychiatrists assume) imaginary dangers. So-called normal people outnumber obsessive-compulsives and paranoids, but reality isn't decided by majority vote.

8. Taking skepticism seriously forces confrontation with meaninglessness and danger. If knowledge is illusion, all courses of action are equally justified. The skeptic should eat cyanide as eagerly as bread. All values, expectations, everything that gives life meaning, are on a par.

The implications of adopting skepticism are profound and far-reaching. If nothing is certain, then nothing is certainly denied. Whereas knowledge claimants insist on the correctness of one particular world view and deny alternatives, skeptics are receptive to extraordinary worlds of possibility. The feelings of meaninglessness may be temporary, caused by eliminating comforting but false gods. Refusal to confront dangers head on rarely eliminates danger; consider the fates of cattle in slaughter houses and Jews in Nazi Germany.

9. True disbelievers are unsure about the existence of other minds. In fact, they are unsure about all external reality. Their imagination might create all. So they should find better things to do than try to convince nonexistent others of the validity of their beliefs. If solipsism is the correct philosophical position, and there is no external world, I'm writing to myself. I'm a unicorn testifying to the nonexistence of unicorns.

Bergen Evans wrote that, to the naïve, skepticism often seems malicious perversity. Then he quoted Edward Topsell: "Only some secret enemy in the inward degenerate nature of man could lead anyone to doubt the existence of the unicorn."[264]

The skeptic is agnostic about most things. That is, s/he doesn't categorically deny the existence of an external world—but does insist that there is no convincing evidence for it, and our beliefs are contaminated by conditioning and wishful thinking. Dreams on occasion seem incredibly real, and the imagination that generates dreams may be just as active during so-called waking. The entire universe may be a product of that same vivid imagination.

Given the possibility of an external world, the skeptic need not feel hypocritical about addressing arguments to others. On the other hand, if there is only one mind, then that belongs to the reader. You. Even if you don't remember doing so (you've forgotten some vivid dreams, too), you're the one who refused to sit in the back of the bus, breathed life to War and Peace, and oversaw a death camp.

---

264. Evans, B. (1946) *The Natural History of Nonsense.* NY: Alfred A. Knopf.

Chapter 19

RESISTANCE IS FUTILE

Given the many and varied reasons for resisting radical skepticism, it's not surprising that philosophers have waged a many-centuries assault against it. Rene Descartes was a seventeenth century assailant. First he constructed many powerful arguments for skepticism such as the "evil demon" scenario discussed on p. 103. He also wrote that, to gain knowledge through experience, people would have to know they weren't dreaming when they had the experience. But we can't distinguish dreaming from wakefulness. Any evidence for believing we were not dreaming could itself be the result of a dream. He concluded that we can never be sure about sensory experiences because they might be the result of dreaming and thus might be false.

Then he tried to show that some knowledge is possible. He deduced his own existence with the famous "*Cogito ergo sum*" (I think, therefore I am). But the proof is unsatisfactory, because the conclusion (I am) is contained in the premise (I think). He could just as easily have said "I wink (stink, own a skating rink), therefore I am." In any case, it doesn't bode well for knowledge seekers that the best that a brilliant believer could come up with is that he exists.

Descartes' other proofs are also unconvincing. The essence of his argument for the existence of God is that God, by definition, is the sum of all perfections. Existence is itself a perfection, so God must exist. That's pathetic, and I doubt that Descartes really believed his defective proof. I once asked an attorney friend if, trying to make the best of a bad case, he had ever knowingly resorted to flawed arguments. He confided that on several desperate occasions he had. He added that they had frequently succeeded. His strategy was to obfuscate, to be lengthy and convoluted. In the thirteenth century, theologian/philosopher St. Augustine, another intellectual genius, presented five arguments to demonstrate the existence of God. One valid one would have sufficed. St. Augustine was probably aware of the inadequacy of each, so he played desperate lawyer and tried to overwhelm with numbers. The lesson to be learned is that success or failure of arguments may have little to do with their validity.

Descartes died in 1650. In the ensuing years, people have walked on the moon, plumbed the depths of the ocean, sequenced the human genome, and studied individual nerve cells in intact organisms. If Descartes were transported to the 21st century, he would be dazzled by those achievements. He'd marvel at cars, airplanes, TV sets, computers, and myriad other appurtenances of daily life. But he'd probably be unimpressed by modern attempts to refute skepticism.

Arguments for skepticism have an analog in Kurt Gödel's incompleteness theorems. In 1931, mathematician and logician Gödel proved that all complex formal systems are either inconsistent (contain errors) or incomplete. Incompleteness means that clear-cut statements within it cannot be proved or disproved. A proof might be constructed by developing new rules and axioms, but that would create a larger system with new unprovable statements. In every sufficiently complex system, consistency and completeness are mutually exclusive. They all have at least one proposition that says, in effect, "This proposition is unprovable." If true, the system contains a proposition that it cannot prove—it is incomplete. If false, then the proposition is provable and the system is inconsistent. Moreover, there is no method for figuring out which statements are unprovable or incorrect.

Gödel's proofs show that logic is a flawed tool for guiding abstract reasoning, and they set fundamental limits not just on mathematical, but on all logical systems. The proofs strengthen the arguments for radical skepticism (though the arguments are strong enough without ever invoking Gödel).

John Watkins categorized and exposed flaws in the various modern refutation attempts. He noted that several philosophers wrote vigorous anti-skeptical treatises and then, on the last few pages of their books, undid their arguments by acknowledging that rejection of skepticism is unwarranted. Watkin's book is brilliant until it reaches his own flawed refutation. Much of the next section owes to him.[265]

A Priorists

Immanuel Kant claimed that Hume's writings aroused him from a dogmatic slumber. A major product of his arousal, the dense, slumber-inducing *Critique of Pure Reason,* has become a landmark in western thought. Schopenhauer wrote that all men are children until they understand Kant; and Durant suggested that, to be a philosopher, one must first be a Kantian.

Hume had challenged the concept of causality. He wrote that, although one event regularly precedes another, it's possible that the first does not cause the second. Even invariant co-occurrences of events do not establish a causal link. Kant tried to refute Hume's conclusion but succeeded only in undermining the view of John Locke. Locke had claimed that minds at birth are like blank slates, to be "written" on by experiences. Kant insisted that the slate has properties, which is why experiences affect different people differently. One universal property is the readiness to impute causes to events. Human minds, according to Kant, have the notion of causality prior to experience. They have other prior knowledge as well.

The existence of a priori knowledge does not refute Hume. Existence and correctness are separate issues. Kant did not

---

265. Watkins, J. (1984) *Science and Skepticism.* Princeton, NJ: Princeton Press.

establish the correctness of a priori knowledge. See Chapter 5 for further discussion.

Non-Deductivists

Hume wrote that inductive reasoning cannot be justified. He explained that, although people have frequently experienced objects falling to the ground, they have never experienced that objects will always fall. They might say that objects fall because of the law of gravitation, but they have never experienced such a law. They have experienced only that things fall. Non-deductivists "refute" Hume by asserting that some inductions are forced upon us by nature and are thus conclusive. The meaning of "forced upon us" is that we can't choose any other path. Strawson conceded that there is no valid reason for believing in induction, but he added, "Is an 'arbitrary choice' then really open to me? Is it? (Just try to make it.)" According to Strawson, forced-upon beliefs cannot be logically invalid—they are valid by definition.[266]

> *Situations can be designed so that everyone in a particular environment has a particular false belief. Watkins sarcastically wrote that non-deductivists counter skepticism by insisting that valid inductive inferences exist but have a nature that cannot be divulged.*

Pragmatists

Pragmatists assert that the pretense of knowledge enhances life. Conceding that skepticism is irrefutable, they argue that belief systems should be evaluated for utility more than accuracy.

> *The pragmatist strategy requires that they know how to achieve various ends and how to measure utilities—that they know a lot. Many different belief systems would be possible.*

---

266. Strawson, P. (1958) On justifying induction. *Philosophical Studies*, 9: 20-1.

Still, because they concede that skepticism is irrefutable, I consider pragmatists partial (although unwilling) allies.

Transcendentalists

The transcendental refutation of skepticism takes the following form: Knowledge of the future is possible only if the principle of induction is true. Knowledge of the future is possible. So the principle of induction is true.

Can you sense the desperation of knowledge-claimants? Skeptics demand proof that non-illusory knowledge of the future is possible. They don't accept it as a given; without acceptance, the transcendental argument collapses.

Vindicationists

Vindicationists claim that induction is the best way to attempt to gain knowledge of the future. Reichenbach wrote, "The man who makes inductive inferences may be compared to a fisherman who casts a net into an unknown part of the ocean—he does not know whether he will catch fish, but he knows that if he wants to catch fish he has to cast his net. Every inductive prediction is like casting a net into the ocean of the happenings of nature; we do not know whether we shall have a good catch, but we try, at least, and try by the help of the best means available."[267] Clendinnen wrote, "Induction is to be justified by establishing that it may succeed while any alternative method is an irrational way of trying to make correct predictions."[268]

The assertion that other methods are irrational does not prove or even give the slightest bit of evidence for the validity of induction.

---

267. Reichenbach, H. (1951) *The Rise of Scientific Philosophy*. Berkeley, CA: UC Press.

268. Clendinnen, F. (1982) Rational expectation and simplicity. In McGlaughlin, R. (Ed) *What? Where? When? Why?* Holland: Reidel.

Conjecturalists

Karl Popper urged scientists to submit their conjectures (hypotheses) to severe experimental hurdles and to evaluate them by number of hurdles passed without refutation.[269] At the same time, he emphasized that the record of past performance provides no guide to future happenings. For that, inductive reasoning is required. In his words, "The observations we have made so far provide us with information about past and present facts, not about future facts. The conclusions of valid deductive arguments have no content not present in their premises. If observation and deduction are our only resources, we cannot draw any conclusions—even probabilistic ones—about the future."

But scientists try to pick the best conjectures. Watkins wrote, "It would be rational for him to choose the better corroborated one, the one which has withstood the most severe criticism, since he has nothing else to go on." Salmon disagreed, arguing that a coin flip would be just as rational; for without the principle of induction, previous corroboration has no bearing on future performance.[270] Watkins was persuaded by Salmon's rebuttal. He courageously wrote (p. 341), "Game, set and match to Salmon." Then, bloodied but unvanquished, Watkins started a new game. Suppose that, over a course of 1,000 trials, conjecture 1 has been corroborated 1,000 times while conjecture 2 has led to consistently incorrect predictions. Suppose that results are now collected from an additional 2,000 trials. Unless outcomes change dramatically, the total number of successes over the entire 3,000 trials will be greater for conjecture 1 than conjecture 2. Watkins argued that predicting a large change in outcomes makes a stronger claim about the future than predicting no change. It requires stronger assumptions. The rational person should "commit

---

269. Popper, K. (1963) *Conjectures and Refutations*. NY: Basic Books.

270. Salmon, W. (1988) Rational prediction. In Grunbaum, A. & Salmon, W. (Eds) *The Limits of Deductivism*. Berkeley, CA: UC Press.

a lesser hostage to fortune" by choosing the conjecture with the weaker assumptions.

> *Unless he accepts the principle of induction, Watkins has no reason for claiming that a large change is less likely than a small one, that one assumption is weaker than another, or that weak assumptions are preferable.*

Chapter 20

CONCLUSIONS

From the moment of birth we learn methods of coping with and making sense of the world. The methods that work are retained and built upon, and the less effective are discarded. Countless experiences let us tame the world and make it less threatening than it otherwise would be. If anarchy reigned we would, like the biblical ass between two bales of hay, starve, paralyzed by indecision. And we'd have not two, but an infinite number of options. So, we are justified in eating bread rather than cyanide—not because of any meaningful evidence that one is more likely than the other to promote health—but because we must choose between them. To eat the cyanide, or nothing, or to alternate between them, would be to commit to a different worldview, also without merit. Our worldview is shaped not by concern for the truth, but from the need to convince ourselves that we have answers.

Solipsism

Solipsism is the belief that one mind created the entire universe. Mine. (Read 'my' and 'I' in what follows as referring to you, reader.) My every waking moment is filled with sensations and perceptions of an apparent external world, but the sensations and perceptions are generated only within me. There is no external world. If solipsism is the correct philosophy, I am Einstein, Aristotle, Shakespeare, Babe

Ruth, Hitler, Queen Victoria, RinTinTin, and a pastrami sandwich.

Although radical skepticism is not synonymous with solipsism, the two are no less than cousins. Teachers of scientific methodology prescribe Occam's razor, a principle attributed to English logician William of Ockham: Phenomena should be explained with as few assumptions as possible, eliminating those that do not change the observable predictions from the explanation. Now, consider the following: We know about the world because neural impulses travel from our sensory systems to our brain. Neuroscientists, by using PET scans, fMRIs, and other modern investigative tools, have correlated activity at different brain sites with feelings of happiness, depression, anger, love, lust, and so forth. In other words, all our thoughts, emotions, sensations, and perceptions are determined by specific brain states. So, choose between A and B below.

A. You live in an infinitely large, varied, and timeless universe that includes more than 100 elements, hundreds of elementary particles, at least eight million species of animals, quadrillions of stars, and more than seven billion other brains very much like yours. Each different glimpse of that universe is associated with a different brain state.

B. There is no external universe. Your mind (not your brain—you don't have a physical brain) generates everything.

If you choose A, think about old William of O. B seems so much more in keeping with proper scientific methodology.

A staple of many introductory philosophy courses and textbooks is the brain-in-a-vat scenario. Students are told to imagine that they are actually disembodied brains suspended in vats of life-sustaining liquid hooked up to supercomputers that perfectly simulate experiences of the outside world. Such brains would give and receive identical impulses to brains in a skull. So, you cannot know whether your brain is in a skull or a vat. The crucial feature of the brain-in-a-vat scenario is that perceptions and feelings due entirely to activity within the brain are attributed to features of the external environment.

Optogenetics is a technique in which genes for light-sensitive proteins are introduced into brain cells in order to monitor and control their activity with light signals. Neuroscientist Dima Rinberg and colleagues used optogenetics to activate nerve cells in six spots in mice's olfactory bulbs, which is where clusters of nerve endings called glomeruli organize the smell signals picked up in the nose.[271] In response to a real odor, the glomeruli become active in a specific sequence. So, the researchers activated the nerve cells the way a real odor might do, in a specific order. Although there was no real odor, the mice behaved as though they smelled one. They learned to signal its presence by licking one of two spouts and reliably licked the correct spout.

> *"What I call remembering yesterday's pain is nothing more than having a certain distinctive type of experience now, an experience that I surely could have even if there had been no such pain yesterday."*—B. Mates[272]

There are precedents for such misattributions. Psychologically normal people who have had a limb amputated often experience the sensation that the limb is still attached to the body and is moving appropriately with other body parts. Approximately sixty to ninety percent of individuals with an amputation experience phantom sensations in their amputated limb. So, rejection of the vat scenario is on esthetic grounds only. Moreover, recent collaborative research from computer scientists and cognitive neuroscientists increases the brain-in-a-vat plausibility.[273]

The field of neuroscience has progressed with staggering rapidity during the past fifty years. Scientists can stimulate as well as record from appropriate brain areas, which can evoke thinking

---

271. Chong, E. et al. (2020) Manipulating synthetic optogenetic odors reveals the coding logic of olfactory perception. *Science*, 368: 1329. doi: 10.1126/science.aba2357.

272. Mates, B. (1981) *Skeptical Essays*. Chicago: U Chicago Press.

273. Shinkareva, S. et al. (2008) Using fMRI brain activation to identify cognitive states associated with perception of tools and dwellings. *PLoS One*, 3(1): e1394.

about specific objects. They can stimulate to simulate other experiences. Maybe you were an early subject. Don't worry, they probably provisioned your vat well.

Solipsism is unappealing both emotionally (obviously) and intellectually. The intellectual problems are manifold. First, as creator of the universe I might be expected to have some awareness of my abilities. Why have I deceived myself all this time into thinking there is an external world? Why was it necessary to endow that nonexistent world with so much detail? And why do I have total amnesia for all I've done? Second, why do I feel that my creation operates independently of me and my wishes? If I'm responsible for everything from kangaroos to distant galaxies, why do my powers seem so limited? Why can't I dunk a basketball? Finally, why have I experienced so much anger, anxiety, sadness, and unfulfilled dreams? If I am the creator, maybe I should conjure up a good therapist.

Free Will—Maybe

Radical skepticism permits some conclusions. Free will is the doctrine that our choices are ultimately up to ourselves rather than fixed conclusively by outside factors. People who deny the possibility of free will argue that heredity and environment interact to produce all behavior; and, of course, we choose neither our parents nor the initial environment that determines everything that follows. Immortal souls, if they exist, also lack free will. They make their earthly debuts at birth (that is, they too are inherited) in specific environments.

Although my hand moves when I want it to, my liver acts of its own accord. Hand movements require prior intentions, liver activity does not. But the intentions, no less than everything else, are determined by heredity and environment. Consider a man doing a swan dive. The controlling forces are obviously different if he is a trained athlete competing in a meet, a teenager trying to impress his girlfriend, or a terrified hostage forced to jump at gunpoint. Once in midair, he clearly has no choice about the speed of fall. These situations represent points on a continuum that seem to extend from free choice to total compulsion. Nevertheless, each behavior has a cause.

Contrary children can sometimes be tricked into doing something simply by forbidding them to do it. Reverse psychology can also work on adults and may lead to the illusion that they acted freely. Suppose I predict aloud that you are about to raise your right hand. You might disconfirm my prediction for any of several reasons:

- You might be too tired.
- Your hand might hurt.
- You might think me nervy to ask.
- You might believe that I'm trying to trick you.
- You might not want to accept orders from me.
- You might not hear me.
- Someone else may have just asked you to keep your hand lowered.

Or you might confirm my prediction for any other variety of reasons. The important point is that there are always reasons, always causes of behavior. And where there is cause, there is no free will.

Recent experiments support the view that there is no free will. For example, volunteers had sensors placed on their scalps and were asked to move their hands whenever they felt like it. At the same time they watched a dot moving around the face of a clock, and they had to tell exactly where the dot was when they decided to move. The fascinating finding was that their brains showed telltale electrical activity in specific regions *before* they said they consciously decided to move.[274]

Soon and colleagues used a brain scanner to investigate what happens just before a decision is made.[275] Participants decided if

---

274. Libet, B. (1985) Unconscious cerebral initiative and the role of conscious will in voluntary action. *Behavioral & Brain Sciences*, 8: 529-66.

275. Soon, C. et al. (2008) *Nature Neurosci*, 11: 543–45.

they wanted to press a button with their left or right hand while a computer program recorded brain activity patterns preceding each choice. After cumulating the data, the computer was able to accurately predict subsequent choices from patterns of activity in the frontopolar cortex—7 seconds *before* participants knew which option they were going to choose—that is, before they were aware that they had made their decision.

John-Dylan Haynes and colleagues put people into a brain scanner and asked them to decide whether to add or subtract two numbers from a series being presented on a screen. There were recognizable brain changes up to four seconds before the subjects were conscious of deciding.[276]

Itzhak Fried and colleagues recorded EEG signals from six patients engaged in a computer-based driving simulator. Patients decided whether to turn left or right and subsequently reported the time of the decision. Changes in EEG preceded the reported time of decision by up to 5.5 sec and allowed predictions of decisions with accuracy up to 82.4%.[277]

For yet another argument against free will, reread the materials starting on p. 112. Evidence was presented that animals, including humans, can be manipulated into behaving against their best interests. If a woman infected with *Toxoplasma gondii* has an affair or an infected man becomes super-aggressive, can they really be acting freely? Case closed, no free will.

But the case is not closed. As discussed on p. 198, quantum physics shows that the behavior of subatomic particles is inherently random and unpredictable. Thus, physical forces like gravity and electromagnetism can't completely dictate the future. The ongoing variability in neural signaling of our brains may be due to quantum processes. Bengson and colleagues speculated that this ongoing background noise "... inserts a random effect that allows

---

276. Smith, K. (2011) Neuroscience vs philosophy: Taking aim at free will. *Nature*, 477: 23–5. https://doi.org/10.1038/477023a.

277. Fried, I. et al. (2011) *Neuron*, 69: 548–62.

us to be freed from simple cause and effect and allows some freedom of will."[278]

Deniers of free will claim more than that all our choices are predetermined. They typically add that a being with complete knowledge of the state of the universe and the laws of nature could predict our future actions perfectly. The claim is meaningless, since there never will be such a being.

Purpose—Avoid

Many people who seek a purpose in life haven't properly analyzed their quest. The purpose of a bridge is to provide passage across an obstacle, the purpose of an adding machine is to do arithmetic calculations. The purpose of both is to satisfy a human need. The purpose of anything is to serve the creator's ends, whether the product is bridges, balloons, or flavorful chickens. So why should anyone devote her life to finding the best way to serve another, even if the other goes by the name of God? An answer comes to mind—our creator knows best—but that's meaningful only if he cares about our happiness. What if he has an ironic sense of humor and enjoys watching endless generations of "servants of God" embark on holy quests to slaughter in his name? Or he's an outright sadist. On the other hand, if he intended to instill reverence for life in a race of sentient beings, he has serious limitations. Less charitably, he's a monumental screw up.

But There is No God—Maybe

There is no God. The same limitations that prevent you from having certain knowledge, without which there can be only limited power, prevent anybody else from doing better. (The news from the mythical godfront isn't all bad. As a consolation, rest assured that

---

278. Bengson, J. et al. (2014) Spontaneous neural fluctuations predict decisions to attend. *J Cognitive Neuroscience*, 26: 2578-84.

there's no omnipotent devil.) Further proof against his existence is the obvious observation that no omnipotent and all-loving being would have created such a cruel world. Theologians have constructed many patently absurd arguments to explain how an all-loving creator could allow disease, hatred, war, death of a child, suffering, humiliation, torture, and condemnation to eternal torment of most people who ever lived merely because they were raised in an environment where his bible was unknown. It makes no sense.

"There can be no Creator, simply because his grief at the fate of his creation would be inconceivable and unendurable."
—Elias Canetti

The concept of God is so vague that mystics say "God is within each of us, He is in everything," and their followers don't even blink. But if he is in everything, then he was in Hitler, the Ku Klux Klan, Papa Doc, Osama bin Laden, and Saddam Hussein. He can't be all good. On the other hand, if he's not in you and me, then he can't be all-knowing. How could he know our every thought? Christians and Jews know what God looks like, since He created them in His image. That would create yet another problem. Throughout the animal and plant kingdoms, biological structures have functions. What would be the function of God's mouth? Digestive tract? Urogenital system? It seems reasonable to assume that his would be subject to the same problems as that of every human man. Given his age, his prostate gland would have enlarged to at least the size of Texas. He wouldn't be able to watch a movie without getting up at least twice to use the bathroom. If true, we would at least have an explanation for his grumpiness.

Although there's no omnipotent god, some being(s) with superhuman but not total powers may exist. They may be using us for their own purposes. We might be subjects in an experiment. They might regard us as pets or harvest some byproduct of human life. Maybe they compete to shape us to specific beliefs. Each year, U.S. college students bring their trained rats or pigeons to a common venue for the animal Olympics—the winners are the ones who've shaped their animals to do the most complex tricks. The rats and pigeons, presumably, are unaware of their roles. Maybe we're in the *Homo sapiens* Olympics. The Zeus shapers once dominated but currently fare badly against the Jesus and Muhammad entries. Maybe the shapers will someday make their presence known. We might not be pleased. If any of those wild conjectures is true, nothing can be done. We might as well accept our fates. The fly can't win against the little boy who pulls off its wings.

To be fair, my disproof of God's existence must come with a disclaimer. It is based on logical analysis, and we all know by now that logic cannot be trusted.

> "*How can I believe in God when just last week I got my tongue caught in the roller of an electric typewriter?*"—Woody Allen

Afterlife—Maybe

Nobody who talks about life after death has experienced it. Okay, maybe Shirley MacLaine.

What happens when we die? Are we thrust into oblivion? Reincarnated? Assigned to heaven, hell, or limbo? If so, do we have bodies? In what state? Do we revert to the time in our lives when we experienced maximum vigor, or are we as we were at the moment before death? Surveys show that most Americans believe in an afterlife, but probably few have considered any specifics beyond the expectation of reuniting with departed loved ones. My friends who look forward to an afterlife in heaven don't expect to see my sad face there. Truth is, I have little incentive to go. Among the minor concerns is that my wife and I often disagree about the most comfortable thermostat setting for our house, yet the heavenly climate control person would have to please not just us but also Eskimos and Saudi Arabians. I suppose that He could issue comfortable thermal underwear for everyone to insulate themselves as needed or, alternatively, Saint Peter could restrict entrance to southern Baptists.

A minor concern is that I have no ear for music. Harp-playing is out of the question and, unless death improves my voice exponentially, no self-respecting heavenly choir would allow me within a hundred cubits.

"It is impossible to experience one's death objectively and still carry a tune."—Woody Allen

"Go to Heaven for the climate, Hell for the company."
—Mark Twain

"In heaven, all the interesting people are missing."
—Friedrich Nietzsche

Although terrifyingly easy to think of an eternity of unrelieved torment, imagining how continuous pleasure would be provided is much harder. Will time pass? Will there be discrete experiences throughout alternating days and nights or an eternity of identical bliss? If never-changing, even heaven might eventually lose its luster. Singing in a choir or floating under a halo—24-7 for eternity—is not my idea of ecstasy. On the other hand, if heaven changes constantly, perpetual bliss is improbable. Our greatest rewards in the current life occur during activities such as eating, which requires that we're first hungry; and experiencing orgasm, which requires buildup of tension.

"Of the delights of this world man cares most for sexual intercourse, yet he has left it out of his heaven."—Mark Twain

"I do not believe in an afterlife, although I am bringing a change of underwear."—Woody Allen

Every atheist I know (assuming that solipsism is not the case and atheists exist) believes that death is the end—they don't anticipate an afterlife, probably because religious people attribute dual roles to God: Creator of the universe and CEO of heaven and hell. But, hypothetically, a godless universe could be populated with immortal souls. Atheists have reasons for their beliefs. They know that brain activity correlates with thoughts, feelings, and overt behavior. Neuroscientists have used a variety of sophisticated techniques to show that different brain areas become active when a person does math problems, watches a sad, funny, or scary movie, is happy, angry, or depressed, and so forth. Diminished consciousness is a common symptom of neurological impairment due to Alzheimer's disease or following certain strokes or brain tumors. None of those examples is a great revelation. Philosopher Alexander Bain wrote in 1873, "For every act of memory, every exercise of bodily aptitude, every habit, recollection, train of ideas, there is a specific neural grouping, or co-ordination, of sensations and movement, by virtue of specific growths in cell junctions."[279] Similarly, Nobel Prize winner Francis Crick argued that we are "nothing but a pack of neurons."[280]

In 1971, Finland became the first nation to adopt brain death, defined as a complete and irreversible cessation of brain activity, as the definition of legal death. Many other countries have followed suit on the presumption that a permanent cessation of electrical activity indicates the end of consciousness. It would seem to follow that permanent cessation indicates oblivion. But the relationship between brain activity and cognitive processes is less obvious than it might seem, which has implications for inferences about a possible afterlife. For example, deep anesthesia stops brain electrical activity nearly completely—patients have a flat EEG—yet some anesthetized surgical patients recall their surroundings and events related to the surgery. Awareness during general anesthesia is rare and usually occurs just before the anesthetic completely takes effect or as the patient emerges from anesthesia. But it occasionally occurs during deep anesthesia.[281]

---

279. Bain, A. (1873) *Mind and Body: The Theories of Their Relation*. London. Henry S. King.

280. https://quotefancy.com/quote/1149793/Francis-Crick-You-re-nothing-but-a-pack-of-neurons

281. https://www.aana.com/patients/all-about-anesthesia/anesthetic-awareness/anesthetic-awareness-fact-sheet

*"Aristotle taught that the brain exists merely to cool the blood
and is not involved in the process of thinking. This is true only of
certain persons."*—Will Cuppy

The average brain weight in adult males is 1,345 grams and in adult females, 1,222 grams. In humans, there is a small positive correlation between brain weight and intellectual capacity,[282] but one highly gifted person had a brain weight around 1,017 grams and a severely retarded person had one of the highest recorded human brain weights, about 2,850 grams. Intellectual French writer Anatole France had a brain just two-thirds the normal size.

Hydrocephaly is an abnormal buildup of cerebrospinal fluid in the ventricles of the brain. The fluid, under considerable pressure, may compress and damage the brain. Survivors are usually seriously handicapped, but not all of them. Neurologist John Lorber worked with hydrocephalics and reported that, although most were severely retarded, several had above normal intelligence. One young man with virtually no brain—less than 1 millimeter of cerebral tissue covering the top of his spinal column—was an honors student in mathematics at Sheffield University in England. Lorber described others with such small cerebral hemispheres that they had 'no detectable brain.' Yet some scored higher than 120 on IQ tests. Roger Lewin published an article in the prestigious journal *Science* about Lorber's studies that he (undoubtedly tongue-in-cheek) entitled "Is your brain really necessary?."[283]

The word "birdbrain" is a pejorative, implying that somebody has limited intellectual capacity. Birds' brains are tiny. But parrots, despite having brains about the size of a walnut and about one thousandth the size of a whale's, display considerable cognitive

---

282. Maybe we should be worried. Kathleen McAuliffe, writing in the January 20, 2011 issue of *Discover Magazine*, reported that the brains of humans have shrunk over the last 30,000 years. The volume of the average human male brain has decreased from 1500 cubic centimeters to 1350 cc and that of the female brain by about the same proportion.

283. Lewin, R. (1980) Is your brain really necessary? *Science*, 210: 1232.

capabilities. Parrots can learn words and use them to communicate with humans. Pigeons, with even smaller brains, can discriminate cubist from impressionistic styles of painting; crows can make tools and pass their skills on to their offspring. Some bird species can understand each other's intentions, use tools more efficiently than chimpanzees, and have an understanding of cause and effect comparable to that of a three-year-old child.

Bees have brains the size of a grass seed, with less than 1 million neurons. Yet foraging bees visit flowers at multiple locations and typically find a route that keeps flying to a minimum. That is, bees solve a problem, finding the most efficient route for travelling to several locations within a short time period, that has intrigued mathematicians and keeps computers busy for days.

Scarlett Howard has taught honeybees to add and subtract.[284] She places a bee next to a covered box shaped like a block letter Y. The bee enters the bottom leg of the Y and sees a mathematical question, expressed in shapes and colors. Blue shapes mean "add 1" to the given number of shapes, and yellow shapes mean "subtract 1." The bee chooses from one of two possible solutions posted at the entrances to the Y's upper arms. There is either a sugar water reward in the arm associated with the correct answer; or a punishment—tonic water, which bees dislike—in the arm with the incorrect answer. They learn and, like humans, show large individual differences. The moment when an individual bee switches from doing really poorly to doing really well happens at a different stage for each bee.

Even plants may have some level of awareness. Plant roots shift direction to avoid obstacles. Some plants release chemicals that attract predators of the animals that feed on them. The plants can differentiate between members of the same species and others, altering their root growth in response to the identity of the neighboring plant. Falik and colleagues subjected pea plants to drought

---

284. Moffat, A. (2020) https://www.quantamagazine.org/what-scarlett-howard-learns-from-the-bees-she-teaches-20200122/

conditions.[285] The plants relayed information to neighboring pea plants through their roots. This caused the neighbors to close their stomata—the pores that allow their leaves to breathe—in order to keep in as much moisture as possible. This helped them withstand the drought conditions. Nearby plants with roots that had no physical contact with the drought sufferers did not shut their stomata.

Berries of the barberry plant usually contain one or two seeds. If a parasitic fly infects a berry with two seeds, the developing larva often feeds on both. If the plant aborts an infested seed, the larva in that seed will die but the second seed may be saved. Meyer and colleagues found that a fruit with two seeds aborts an infected seed in seventy-five percent of cases, whereas a fruit containing only one seed aborts the infected seed in only five percent of cases. A fruit with only one infected seed that aborted it would lose the entire fruit. The researchers suggested that this complex behavior indicates that the plant can differentiate between conditions and anticipate future risks.[286]

Plants adjust how much starch they consume to prevent starvation at night. Mechanisms in the leaf measure the plant's starch store to estimate how much they need to use until dawn arrives. If the starch store is used too fast, plants starve and stop growing during the night. If the store is used too slowly, some is wasted.[287]

Forest ecologist Suzanne Simard gave a TED talk during which she detailed research showing that mother trees recognize their kin. Simard said, "…we set about an experiment, and we grew mother trees with kin and stranger's seedlings. They do recognize their own kin. Mother trees colonize their kin with bigger mycorrhizal

285. Falik, O. et al. (2011) Rumor has it…Relay communication of stress cues in plants. PLoS One, 6(11): e23625. Epub

286. Meyer, K. et al. (2014) Adaptive and selective seed abortion reveals complex conditional decision making in plants. The American Naturalist, 183: 376-83.

287. Scialdone, A. et al. (2013) Arabidopsis plants perform arithmetic division to prevent starvation at night. eLife, 2:e00669. DOI: 10.7554/eLife.00669.

networks. They send them more carbon below ground. They even reduce their own root competition to make elbow room for their kids. When mother trees are injured or dying, they also send messages of wisdom on to the next generation of seedlings...so trees talk." Mother trees prioritize their offspring when it comes to providing them with key nutrients and other resources. Mycorrhizal networks have "nodes and links." Fungi act as links, and trees as the nodes. She calls the busiest nodes mother trees. Mother trees can sometimes be connected to hundreds of trees, and the carbon they pass to those trees is said to increase seedling survival by four times.

In any case, if solipsism is correct or we are victims of intentional deception or unintentional misperceiving, the apparent relationship between brain activity and cognitive processes is meaningless. Otherwise, the relationship must be explained. The relationship is the famous mind–body problem, and it has stumped philosophers for centuries. How do conscious experiences arise out of a lump of gray matter? How does a person's desire cause specific neurons to fire and muscles to contract in exactly the right manner? How do thoughts cause actions and unconscious fantasies cause psychosomatic illnesses such as asthma and ulcers? There are several clever explanations. None are satisfactory.

Dualists argue that reality consists of two fundamentally different parts, whereas monists claim that all reality is of one kind. Idealistic monists argue that everything is mental, and materialistic monists argue that everything is physical. Epiphenomenalists state that mental events are caused by physical events in the brain but do not affect physical events. Interactionists accept that interaction between physical and mental events occurs, but they cannot explain how. None of the philosophical positions explains how the brain transforms tiny packets of chemicals into the entire panoply of human emotions and experience.

Given that some of the greatest minds (again, assuming they exist and not including parrots) have been unable to resolve the mind-body problem, how can anyone state with confidence what happens after brain death? On that issue, agnosticism is the only honest position. We won't know until we're dead. Furthermore, it is very likely that nobody has even imagined the correct answer. After all, the possibilities are infinite.

Theoretical physicist Henry Stapp worked with some of the founding fathers of quantum mechanics. Stapp accepts the Copenhagen interpretation, and he argued that belief in the soul—a personality independent of the brain that can survive beyond death—is not unscientific. He wrote: "Strong doubts about personality survival based solely on the belief that postmortem survival is incompatible with the laws of physics are unfounded."[288]

On the Positive Side

Baby elephants in India are tied to a wooden pole that they try to but cannot break. Soon, conditioned into believing they can't break it, they stop trying. Thus, mature, powerful elephants remain shackled to small, easily breakable poles. People who accept the arguments of this book can begin testing and possibly throwing off their shackles.

Questions You'll Probably Never Be Able to Answer

Are things pretty much what they seem?

Maybe, but there is no basis for knowing. We can never be certain—or even mildly confident—about almost everything. Keep the results of quantum mechanics in mind. Pop psychologists and New Agers have embraced QM, because it is mysterious with no simple explanations. So they've twisted it to pretend that it supports their far-fetched ideas. I won't do that, but it's worth noting that of the many different interpretations of QM, all but the version called naïve realism agree that ultimate reality is very different

---

288. Stapp, H. (2017) Compatibility of contemporary physical theory with personality survival. https://www-physics.lbl.gov/~stapp/Compatibility.pdf

from how most of us think it is—probably inconceivably different. Most of the leading figures in QM discount naïve realism and claim that there is no objective reality. So, if things are pretty much what they seem, we can trust the results of QM. And QM shows that things are not at all like what they seem.

Worldviews of Prominent Physicists and Philosophers

According to the Common Sense Science website, most leading modern physicists believe in the first option below.[289] They deny the existence of objective reality. But worldviews differ considerably. Every one of the possibilities below is endorsed by at least one eminent physicist:

- There is no deep reality.
- Reality is created by observation.
- Reality is an undivided wholeness.
- Reality consists of a steadily increasing number of parallel universes.
- The world obeys a non-human kind of reasoning.
- The world is made of ordinary objects.
- Consciousness creates reality.
- The world is twofold, consisting of potentials and actualities.

Call everything that comprises your present reality point A. Let your imagination run wild to conceive of a radically different reality, one that can include time machines, chit chats with creatures from distant worlds, and every kind of superpower imaginable. Call it point B. Could a Shakespeare and an Einstein collaborate on a convincing travelogue to get you thinking that B is possible?

---

289. Schlosshauer, M. et al. (2013) A snapshot of foundational attitudes toward quantum mechanics. *Studies in History and Philosophy of Modern Physics*, 44: 222-30.

I believe so—and therefore take seriously the distinct possibility that B is in my future.

How should I conduct my life?

When trying to think of precepts for living, a different form of skepticism applies. I can't even imagine a single, preeminent principle. Honest seekers would test their most cherished principles by carrying them to their logical extremes. That's a sure path to insanity.

1. Pick a principle, e.g., "honesty is the most important policy;" or "love thy neighbor."

2. Create a scenario whereby you are willing to give up the principle. (If you can't, take an enema daily for twelve years.)

3. Whatever the original principle, you could do more to achieve a universe enhanced with respect to it. You don't, because you have other interests. Each candidate for overarching principle is in conflict with others; depending on the specific circumstances, any of several principles may take precedence.

Keep on Trucking

Despite what philosophers say, philosophy books do not make good instruction manuals on how to live. This book is no exception. But it does provide a few take-home messages.

- You should gain a better understanding of the boundaries of knowledge. They are roughly this broad: ()

- If anyone claims to have colloquies with God or tells you what will happen when you die, dismiss the person as delusional, a liar, or a figment of your imagination.

- Appreciate that zero knowledge equals infinite possibilities. If nothing is known, nothing is barred. Every story you've ever read might be true.

- Explore the implications. The question isn't whether my reasoning is correct—the question is what to do next. For want of better options, keep doing what you've been doing—but take chances. Beliefs go a long way. Think of the elephant chained to its flimsy wooden stake.

EPILOGUE

Readers who have reached this point are probably willing to accept that the world is far more mysterious and unknowable than they had previously realized. They may not be card carrying radical skeptics but are convinced that histories and current events are often distorted to suit the chronicler's agenda, religions are for-profit and for-power (of a few) enterprises, science is far from infallible, there are no universally accepted standards for proper reasoning, and even if there were, pure reason does not inform about the world. Although the state of affairs may depress glass half-emptyers, half-fullers can view things differently. They live in a world of infinite possibility.

> *"Every man takes the limits of his own field of vision for the limits of the world."*—Arthur Schopenhauer

> *"Why shouldn't truth be stranger than fiction? Fiction, after all, has to make sense."*—Mark Twain

> *"...the future will be vastly more surprising than anything I can imagine. ... the Universe is not only queerer than we suppose, but queerer than we can suppose."*—Biologist J.B.S. Haldane

ANSWERS TO PROBLEM SET 1

1. Large numbers of highly select university students at Princeton, MIT, and Harvard answered ten cents. Wrong! The correct answer is five cents.

2. Many respondents divided 48 by 2, which leads to an incorrect answer of twenty-four days. The correct answer is forty-seven days.

3. A wrong answer that seems plausible may never be challenged. I've given the following problem to hundreds of students. Very few got it right, though many were sure they had done so. They would see thirteen trains. Suppose a train leaves A at 5:00 a.m. and arrives at B at 11:00 a.m. Passengers will see all the trains that left B between 5:00 a.m. and 11:00 a.m. That's 7. They will also see the six trains that left B from 11:00 p.m. to 4:00 a.m.

4. The problem was presented in *Parade* magazine, along with the correct answer that the contestant should switch. Approximately 10,000 readers, including nearly 1,000 with PhDs, wrote to the magazine with ninety-two percent arguing that the answer was wrong. Here's how to look at it. Initially, the contestant has a one in three chance of picking the right door. If she picks door one and does not switch, her chance of success remains one in three. The chance that the car is behind one of the other two doors is two in three. If the car is behind door three, the host always opens door two. That means that the door the host does not open has a two in three chance of hiding the car.

5. More than eighty percent of people tested chose C. The correct answer is A. Anne may be either married or unmarried. If she is married, the answer is A; she would be a married person

looking at an unmarried person (George). If she is not married, the answer is still A; Jack would be a married person looking at Anne, who is unmarried.

6. Only one. All the others are on the road away from St. Ives.

ANSWERS TO PROBLEM SET 2

Ridiculous problems

1. The obvious answer is not the only one possible. Here are some others:

> 4 8 16 (double each preceding number)
>
> 3 5 8 (add the two preceding numbers)
>
> 3 6 12 (add all the preceding numbers)
>
> 1 2 1 (repeating sequence)
>
> 3 2 1 (symmetry)
>
> 1 8 8 (12188 is the zip code of Waterford, NY)
>
> Joe Willie Namath (Hall of Fame quarterback's uniform number)
>
> Buckle my shoe (start of nursery rhyme)

2. Again there is an obvious answer: 6 7 8. Appropriate alternatives are harder to find but, just as in the previous problem, there are an infinite number.

3. The limited data cannot support any definite conclusions. There are an infinite number of possibilities.

4. The additional information would seemingly eliminate many initially plausible explanations. But if nothing can be known with certainty, nothing can be eliminated with certainty. In any case, eliminating implausible explanations would get no closer to the correct one. The number of remaining alternatives would still be infinite—even if the additional information included a newly fallen boulder on the road; an open bottle of alcohol on the floor; a suicide note at the driver's home; a blown out tire; another car crashed only a few feet away; bullet holes in the body...

Appendix 1

PREDICTIONS BY EXPERTS

- In 1903, the president of Michigan Savings Bank warned Henry Ford's lawyer to protect his money. "The horse is here to stay but the automobile is only a novelty—a fad," he advised.

- H.M. Warner, founder of Warner Brothers Studios: Who the hell wants to hear actors talk.

- In 1977, Digital Equipment Corp. president Ken Olson said, "There is no reason anyone would want a computer in their home."

- *Business Week*, 1968: "With over fifteen types of foreign cars already on sale here, the Japanese auto industry isn't likely to carve out a big share of the market for itself."

- "It will be gone by June." Variety Magazine, predicting the demise of rock-and-roll in 1955.

- In 1913, a U.S. District Attorney prosecuted inventor Lee DeForest for fraudulently selling stock for his Radio Telephone Company. The prosecutor said, "Lee DeForest has said that it would be possible to transmit the human voice across the Atlantic before many years. Based on these absurd and deliberately misleading statements, the misguided public ... has been persuaded to purchase stock in his company ..."

- Lord Kelvin, British mathematician and physicist, president of the British Royal Society, in 1895.

- "Heavier-than-air flying machines are impossible."

- "X-rays will prove to be a hoax."

- "There is nothing new to be discovered in physics."

- "There is not the slightest indication that nuclear energy will ever be obtainable. It would mean that the atom would have to be shattered at will." Albert Einstein, 1932.

- "The cinema is little more than a fad. It's canned drama. What audiences really want to see is flesh and blood on the stage." -- Charlie Chaplin, actor, producer, director, and studio founder, 1916.

- "The world potential market for copying machines is 5,000 at most." IBM, to the eventual founders of Xerox, 1959.

- Napoleon Bonaparte, when told of Robert Fulton's steamboat: "How, sir, would you make a ship sail against the wind and currents by lighting a bonfire under her deck? I have not the time to listen to such nonsense."

- NY Times, 1936: A rocket will never be able to leave the Earth's atmosphere."

- Darryl Zanuck, movie producer, 20th Century Fox, 1946: "Television won't be able to hold on to any market it captures after the first six months. People will soon get tired of staring at a plywood box every night."

- Oxford professor Erasmus Wilson "When the Paris Exhibition [of 1878] closes, electric light will close with it and no more will be heard of it."

Appendix 2

UNETHICAL EXPERIMENTS
ON HUMANS

Terrible things have been done to people in the name of research. The most infamous examples occurred during World War II, when Nazi scientists conducted experiments such as measuring survival times of concentration camp prisoners forced to ingest poisons or sit in ice water. But research conducted in the United States by respected scientists and often with government backing does not seem strikingly different. Below is a very partial listing of additional examples. For references and many more examples, see https://en.m.wikipedia.org/wiki/Unethical_human_experimentation_in_the_United_States; and Moreno, J. (1999) *Undue Risk: Secret State Experiments on Humans*. NY: W. H. Freeman. Moreno also surveys the awful history of human experimentation in several other countries, including the Soviet Union, Nazi Germany, Japan, South Africa, and Iraq.

- From 1950 to 1960, children with cerebral palsy were taken to Sonoma State Hospital in northern California, where doctors performed unnecessary spinal taps and experiments with radiation on them. A *60 Minutes* investigation uncovered over 1,400 deaths of children due to the experimentation.

- In 1955, the CIA released whooping cough bacteria just

outside of Tampa Bay, Florida. The experiment killed twelve people.

• Starting in the 1930s and continuing until 1972, 399 African American men with syphilis were led to believe they were being given excellent medical treatment when in fact they were deliberately not treated. Penicillin, effective against syphilis, was withheld so scientists could study the course of the disease. By the end of the study, only seventy-four of the men were alive, forty of their wives had been infected, and nineteen of their children were born with congenital syphilis. The U.S.-led Guatemala syphilis experiment is a lesser-known version of the same.

• From 1944 to 1946, Dr. Alf Alving at the University of Chicago Medical School infected psychiatric patients at the Illinois State Hospital with malaria so that he could test experimental treatments on them.

• The father of modern gynecology, J. Marion Sims, gained much of his fame by doing experimental surgeries, without anesthesia, on slave women.

• In 1908, researchers infected dozens of children with tuberculin at the St. Vincent's House orphanage in Philadelphia, causing permanent blindness in some of the children and painful lesions and inflammation of the eyes in many of the others.

• In 1950, in order to conduct a simulation of a biological warfare attack, the U.S. Navy sprayed dangerous bacteria over San Francisco. Many citizens contracted pneumonia-like illnesses, and at least one person died as a result. The tests were continued until at least 1969.

• Between 1949 and 1969, the U.S. Army conducted over 200 "field tests" as part of its biological warfare research program, releasing infectious bacterial agents in cities across the U.S. without informing residents of the exposed areas.

- In 1950, Dr. Joseph Stokes of the University of Pennsylvania infected 200 female prisoners with viral hepatitis.

- In 1952, at Sloan-Kettering Institute, 300 healthy women were injected with live cancer cells without being told. The doctors stated that they knew at the time that it might cause cancer.

- From 1963 to 1969, the U.S. Army sprayed several U.S. ships with various biological and chemical warfare agents while thousands of U.S. military personnel were aboard the ships. The personnel were not notified of the tests.

- In 1966, the U.S. Army released *Bacillus globigii* into the tunnels of the New York City subway system to test the vulnerability of subway passengers to covert attack with biological agents. The Chicago subway system was subject to a similar experiment.

- In 1949, the U.S. Atomic Energy Commission released iodine-131 and xenon-133 into the atmosphere in Washington, which contaminated a 500,000-acre area containing three small towns.

- In 1946, six employees of a Chicago metallurgical lab were given water contaminated with plutonium-239 so that researchers could study how plutonium is absorbed into the digestive tract. In the 1960s, over 100 Alaskan citizens were continually exposed to radioactive iodine.

- In 1961 and 1962, ten Utah State Prison inmates had blood samples taken which were mixed with radioactive chemicals and reinjected back into their bodies.

- Between 1960 and 1971, the Department of Defense funded non-consensual whole body radiation experiments on mostly poor and black cancer patients, who were not told what was being done to them. Patients were told that they were receiving a treatment that might cure their cancer, but the Pentagon was trying to determine the effects of high levels of radiation on the human body.

- From 1942 to 1944, the U.S. Chemical Warfare Service conducted experiments that exposed thousands of U.S. military personnel to mustard gas, in order to test the effectiveness of gas masks and protective clothing.

- In June 1953, seven research projects involving chemical weapons to be tested on human subjects were approved by the Secretary of the Army.

- From 1964 to 1968, the U.S. Army paid professors Albert Kligman and Herbert Copelan to perform experiments with mind-altering drugs on 320 inmates of Holmesburg Prison. The goal was to determine the minimum effective dose of each drug needed to disable fifty percent of any given population. Kligman and Copelan initially claimed that they were unaware of any long-term health effects of the drugs; however, documents later revealed that this was not the case.

- In August 2010, U.S. weapons manufacturer Raytheon announced that it had partnered with a jail in Castaic, California, in order to test prisoners for a device that "fires an invisible heat beam capable of causing unbearable pain."

- Researchers from the University of California experimented on 113 newborns ranging in age from one hour to three days. In one study, researchers inserted a catheter through the babies' umbilical arteries and into their aortas, then submerged their feet in ice water. In another study, they strapped fifty newborns to a board and turned them upside down so that all of their blood rushed into their heads.

- The CIA tested LSD and other hallucinogenic drugs on Americans, without their knowledge, in experiments on behavior modification. The program left many victims permanently mentally disabled, and at least one man committed suicide.

- During the decade of 2000–2010, artificial blood was transfused into research subjects across the United States without their consent. The artificial blood caused a significant increase in the risk of heart attacks and death.

- The U.S. Army used its soldiers to test the effects of mustard gas in tropical environments. As many as 1,200 recruits were tested for several weeks. The men were ordered to strip to the waist, then sent into a wooden chamber and doused with the chemical agent. According to one survivor, all of the men began writhing around and screaming in pain as the chemical burned through their skin. Some pounded on the walls and pleaded to be let out. The doors were locked and opened only when the time was up.

- In September 1950, a U.S. Navy ship near San Francisco sprayed tons of bacteria into a bank of fog that was drifting over the city. Thousands of people were infected and one may have died, but the human experiments kept going.

- From 1946 to 1953, the U.S. Atomic Energy Commission and the Quaker Oats Corporation cosponsored an experiment at the Walter E. Fernald State School in Massachusetts. It involved giving 73 mentally disabled children oatmeal containing radioactive calcium in order to track how nutrients are digested. The children and their parents were told that they were joining a science club.

Appendix 3

MYTHS OF HISTORY

- Slavery was confined to the south.

  It existed in all 13 British Colonies (later to become U.S. states) by the end of the 17th century. Slavery did not end in New York until 1827. Connecticut ended slavery later still.

- Christopher Columbus discovered North America.

  It had probably already been discovered by the Norseman Leif Erickson 500 years before Columbus. And Native Americans were there thousands of years earlier.

- Abraham Lincoln owned slaves.

  False.

- Hardly anyone in history seriously thought that the earth was flat. It's a modern myth that the ancients believed in a flat earth.

- George Washington, as a six-year-old boy, did not chop down his father's cherry tree. The event was invented by Washington biographer, Mason Locke Weems.

- The Island of Manhattan was not purchased for twenty-four dollars worth of beads. It was purchased from Native Americans, but there's no mention of the items involved in the trade. The Native Americans probably conceived of the cost like rent, since they believed that land, air, and waterways could not be owned as property.

- The light bulb had been around for years before Thomas Edison set out to improve it. He did not invent the light bulb. His contribution was to improve on the filament by using a sealed vacuum bulb.

- No people convicted of witchcraft were burned at the stake in Salem. About twenty people were executed, nineteen by hanging and one by pressing (in a large vise).

Appendix 4

PERFECTLY PLAUSIBLE SCENARIOS

1. OBEJAN: When I was twenty-seven I went to my doctor for a routine check-up. It turned out to be anything but routine. He ordered me to take several tests, and the next day he informed me that I had a rare bone disease and would probably not live till Christmas. It was June 18.

   My friend Richard is an anthropologist. When I told him the sad news he urged me to visit a tiny village in southern Mexico to see a healer there. He said he had become friends with the healer and had watched him perform minor miracles. Desperate people take desperate measures, so I went. But I didn't entertain even a remote hope of being cured. I just needed a diversion from self-pity.

   Obejan agreed to see me. We chatted for a bit, and then he asked, "Will you let me photograph you as you follow my directions, and will you show the photographs to your classes? Will you tell your students that you saw me not as a scientist but as a man seeking to be healed?"

   "There's no need for that," I said. "Isn't it enough that I agreed to meet your price?"

   Obejan said "You are a drug expert. What happens when a person receives a pill with no genuine medicine in it but is told that the pill contains a powerful drug?"

"The person would probably behave as though given the drug. It's the placebo effect."

"Ah, and if a person gets a powerful drug but is told it's just a sugar pill?"

"The drug effects would be weakened."

Obejan smiled. "So, you know that belief in a treatment affects the outcome, yet you disbelieve and even disdain my methods. You think my tribe is primitive, cannibals perhaps. "He grinned as I flinched involuntarily. "You live in a technological society. My tribespeople marvel at your cars, your medicines, your televisions and computers and smart homes. They have none of those, but they have always esteemed the search for knowledge and have passed down their learnings from generation to generation. Can you accept the possibility that our eons of accumulated wisdom give us answers as inaccessible to you as your iPhones are to us?"

I started to respond, but he interrupted. "What do you think would happen if you were forced to sit naked in a room at 40 degrees Fahrenheit temperature with a wet sheet around you? Suppose you were kept there for an hour?"

"I'd probably die."

"Yes, you would. But a sect of Tibetan priests seem perfectly comfortable in such a condition. They can even raise their body temperature so steam comes from the sheets." He told me to prepare for our next meeting by watching a video at https://video.search.yahoo.com/yhs/search?fr=yhs-avast-secure-browser&hsimp=yhs-securebrowser&hspart=avast&p=herbert+benson+monks+youtube+videos#id=3&vid=143820c-058c7ed4331d8f1b777ef5ae6&action=click.

I watched, and a few days later told him that I had been astounded.

"I can't do what the monks do, but I hope the video showed you that the world is much larger than the small part you inhabit. Now let's work on your recovery."

Last December I celebrated my eightieth birthday.

2. 300 IQ: My focus in psychopharmacology is on proper ways of doing drug experiments, so I'm often asked to review book manuscripts and articles written for scientific journals. Three years ago, following a major neuropharmacology conference, I got together with GE, an old friend from graduate school. He told me that a chemist friend of his had been working in a top security lab in Bethesda on a biological weaponry project. He had been attracted to it by the promise that he could use their magnificent facilities for his private research, and he'd spent the previous year working to develop a drug to increase human intelligence. GE told me the friend's name and address, and I contacted him the next day. He said he would send me a protocol of his experiments and whatever additional information I wanted, except for the molecular formula of the drug. He swore me to secrecy, a vow that I've honored until today.

His findings were astonishing. Both rats and monkeys, on a variety of tasks, learned in about one-quarter the number of trials when they received the drug instead of a placebo. I searched for methodological flaws but found none. If I had been refereeing for a scientific journal, I would have recommended that his studies be published. He promised to keep me informed but denied my request—actually, a plea—to serve as his first human subject.

I never heard from him again. I sent two letters but they were returned stamped MOVED: NO FORWARDING ADDRESS. I called GE and he tried unsuccessfully to find out. Relatives and other friends were no help. GE and I have spent hours speculating about the possibilities, and we agree on one thing— the drug works. We're convinced that he has developed an intelligence beyond the comprehension of an Einstein. We wonder about his ultimate goals and hope he thinks kindly of us.

3. THE BILLIONAIRE'S GAME: Ten of the wealthiest men in the world gathered in a seaside village in Cyprus. They all recognized each other, either because they had had direct interactions or just from reputation. The host said, "Thank you all for coming. You'll be glad you did. I've been bored lately. Used to be a big sports fan, but last time I went to a baseball game I nodded out before the third inning. My stomach's a wreck. I know every four-star restaurant maître d' in the world but these days I chew more Tums than lobsters. Sex? I pay for incredibly beautiful women, but lately it's been as boring as baseball."

Several of the men nodded empathetically.

"Competition is my lifeblood but I haven't had any serious challenges lately. I need worthy foes, so I invented a game and hope that you will enjoy playing it with me. It's a shame we'll have to play secretly, or I'd someday be ranked with James Naismith and Abner Doubleday.

"It's very simple. First, I want each of you to think of the most demeaning, idiotic, out-of-character, possibly illegal, acts that a person could do. For example, run naked onto the field during a baseball game, claim to a reporter to have been abducted by aliens, write a check for your entire bank balance and hand it to a homeless person. Describe each act on a piece of paper, and drop the paper into the hat over there.

"When you pay an entry fee of $10,000 you will get a target, a person picked at random from any of several sources. You will also each get a task picked randomly from the hat. Your goal will be to get the target to do your assigned task."

A Chinese man stood up. "So, the one to get there first is the winner and collects the pot. I would just hold a gun to the target's head and make him do it."

"Good point, but the game is more complex than that. Style counts as much as speed. Holding a gun to a target's head is unesthetic and uncreative and would receive a low score. But surreptitiously convincing him that he's the reincarnation of Ghengis Khan, and getting him to behead ten people, would be the stuff of legends."

The Frenchman rose on wobbly legs. "The great French philosopher Descartes imagined an evil genius who fooled all humanity. You are an embodiment of the genius. I salute you for letting me participate."

The game has expanded to include thirty people and is now in its twelfth year.

Appendix 5

DOCUMENTED CONSPIRACIES THAT WERE INITIALLY COVERED UP

- Shortly after the end of World War II, the U.S. government began trying to measure the effects of nuclear fallout on the human body. They needed young tissue, so they recruited agents to find recently deceased babies and children and then take body parts including entire limbs. The parents were not told.

- In March, 1968, in My Lai, Vietnam, American soldiers herded civilians into a ditch and killed hundreds of them. Official army reports proclaimed a great victory. In October, soldier Tom Glen accused several U.S. military units of routine brutality against Vietnamese civilians. U.S. Army Major Colin Powell investigated and refuted the charge. But after soldier Ron Ridenhour heard five eyewitness accounts of the massacre, he began investigating and was shocked by what he learned. In March, 1969, he sent letters to President Nixon and several members of Congress. Most ignored him, but Representative Morris Udall pushed for a full investigation. Dozens of witnesses gave testimony that established clearly that war crimes had been committed. Later investigations found that My Lai was not an isolated incident.

- Between 1926 and 1933, the federal government encouraged manufacturers of industrial alcohol to use strong poisons to discourage bootleggers from turning the alcohol into moonshine. More than 10,000 Americans died from drinking tainted booze.

- President Woodrow Wilson suffered a debilitating stroke towards the end of his presidency. He became incapable of governing, and his wife stepped in. The public didn't learn about the stroke for months, during which time his wife made most of the executive decisions.

- The FBI considered Black Panther leader Fred Hampton dangerous. His bodyguard was persuaded to give information about him in return for having felony charges dropped. The bodyguard told FBI agents of Hampton's apartment floor plan and the number of people living there, and the state attorney authorized a raid. On December 4, 1969, heavily armed police knocked down the front door, shot and killed Hampton, and fired on and wounded several others. The state attorney presented evidence that seemed to exonerate the police, but members of the Black Panther party charged that the evidence was fabricated. They pointed out many inconsistencies in the police version. Forensic evidence showed that four bullets left the Panther's apartment and approximately 200 entered.

- During the 1960s, the Dalai Lama worked for the CIA. The CIA funded the Tibetan exile movement with $1.7 million per year with the goal of disrupting China's infrastructure. During that time they paid the Dalai Lama $180,000 annually.

- Beginning in the 1950s, research showed a clear link between smoking and lung cancer. Not until the late 1990s did cigarette manufacturers acknowledge the link.

Appendix 6

ONE-TIME SCIENTIFIC BELIEFS THAT ARE NOW CONSIDERED FALSE

Most diamonds are formed from compressed coal.
Diamonds are compressed and heated ninety miles below the surface of the Earth.
Coal is found about two miles below the Earth's surface.

Dinosaurs died off because of a volcano.
Most scientists now believe that an asteroid impact killed them off.

There is a lot of genetic difference between the races.
There are larger genetic differences between Africans than there are between Africans and Eurasians.

There are only nine planets in the entire universe.
There are billions and billions of planets.

Neanderthals were not smart.
Neanderthals had advanced tools and were skilled hunters and socializers.

Neanderthals didn't exist at the same time as humans.
Archaeologists dated some old human skeletons which proved that Neanderthals and humans co-existed for thousands of years.

Neanderthals didn't have sex with humans.
>Researchers sequenced the Neanderthal genome in 2010. They determined that most humans living outside of Africa have about one to four percent Neanderthal DNA.

Complex organisms like humans have more genes than simple organisms like amoebas.
>Humans have around 19,000-20,000 genes. A tiny moss plant has around 32,000 genes.

The universe is slowing down.
>Until the late 1990s, scientists thought that gravity must be slowing down the expansion of the universe. They now believe that the universe is flying apart ever faster.

Stomach ulcers are caused by stress.
>Most stomach ulcers are caused by bacteria.

Black holes don't exist near young stars.
>The Hubble telescope found evidence of a massive black hole in the center of our own galaxy.

The tongue has specific taste zones.
>All zones of the tongue can sense all flavors.

It's important to stretch before exercise.
>Stretching actually slows you down. Stretching before a run generally results in a reduction of efficiency. There is no good scientific evidence that pre-exercise stretching reduces injury risk. See https://ebm.bmj.com/content/8/2/54.

Cholesterol in eggs is bad for the heart.
>Dozens of studies have found that dietary cholesterol does not negatively raise body cholesterol.

Dogs age at seven years per one human year.
>Dogs mature faster than humans and reach the equivalent of twenty-one years in only two. Then aging slows down to about four human years per year. To calculate your dog's human-age equivalent, subtract two from its age, multiply that

by four and add 21.

Oh yes, both radioactive material and cigarettes were once considered healthy.

Acknowledgments

I would like to thank David Ross and Kelly Huddleston for their unwavering encouragement, support, and outstanding editorial help with all phases of the writing and production.

INDEX

Made in the USA
Middletown, DE
31 August 2021